For the Republic

Political Essays by George Scialabba

For the Republic

Pressed Wafer | Brooklyn

ISBN 978-0-9831975-9-1
FIRST EDITION

Pressed Wafer, 375 Parkside Avenue, Brooklyn, New York 11226
Printed in the United States

Contents

We are never permitted to despair of the commonwealth.

THOMAS JEFFERSON

While this America settles in the mould of its vulgarity,
  heavily thickening to empire
And protest, only a bubble in the molten mass, pops and
  sighs out, and the mass hardens,
I sadly smiling remember that the flower fades to make
  fruit, the fruit rots to make earth.
Out of the mother; and through the spring exultances,
  ripeness and decadence; and home to the mother.
You making haste haste on decay: not blameworthy;
  life is good, be it stubbornly long or suddenly
A mortal splendor: meteors are not needed less than
  mountains: shine, perishing republic.

ROBINSON JEFFERS

For Chomsky, Nader, Greenwald—model citizens
—and in memory of Aaron Swartz.

Foreword

Nobody likes a pessimist—at least not in can-do America, where willed optimism is a presidential strategy and happiness a social duty. Maybe this is why our public discourse has become so flat and impoverished in recent decades. As the clamor to "say something positive" intensifies, the mere tendency to criticize or question conventional pieties can be dismissed as "negativity"—or pessimism. Failure to join the din of national self-congratulation provokes suspicion and resentment. Independent thinkers have a hard row to hoe in a country built on positive thinking.

Still, they keep resurfacing, providing intellectual oxygen to a public discourse that often seems near asphyxiation. Indeed there has been a close (one is tempted to say dialectical) relationship between the figure of the independent intellectual and the forces massed against intellectual independence in modern mass society—in either its bureaucratic statist or corporate capitalist forms. Consider Irving Howe's classic manifesto, "This Age of Conformity" (1954), which lamented the celebratory embrace of American culture by former radicals. They had forgotten, he charged, that "the most glorious vision of the intellectual life is still that which is loosely called humanist: the idea of a mind committed yet dispassionate, ready to stand alone, curious, eager, skeptical. The banner of critical independence, ragged and torn though it may be, is still the best we have." Howe warned that "all of life" was "a conspiracy against that independence of mind"—and especially the sort of comfortable, stable life increasingly offered to intellectuals by universities, mass media, and other established institutions in the prosperous post war era. Even when New York Intellectuals were supposedly still "arguing the world," the specter of lost autonomy already haunted the aspiring free-lance. Independence has never been easy.

Twenty years on, in the early 1970s, Christopher Lasch voiced a critique that echoed Howe's. Despite the misdeeds and mendacity of the national security state (revealed in the Pentagon Papers and the Church Committee Report), despite the protracted disgrace of Nixon and his minions, political options in American were as limited as ever. As Lasch observed, politics remained "blandly 'pragmatic' and public discussion feeble and banal, confusing class interests and private gain, seldom acknowledging publicly what people knew privately, concerning itself with portentous trivia." It was only a few years before the ascendancy of Ronald Reagan, who would remind his countrymen that "America is back" and who would preside over a decisive rightward shift in the fulcrum of public debate. Positions that had once seemed the exclusive property of a right-wing fringe—free-market fundamentalism, economic austerity, militarist bellicosity—soon acquired the patina of "responsible opinion."

One can only imagine the reaction of Lasch or Howe (who both died in the early 1990s) to the state of public discourse today. Popular concerns about mass joblessness and economic inequality have been eclipsed by bipartisan obsession with the national debt—which is mistakenly equated with private, household debt by everyone from President Obama to the callowest new recruit in the punditocracy. Less popular concerns about warrantless surveillance, torture, and indiscriminate drone attacks disappear from public view as Obama embraces his (apparently popular) new role as Assassin-in-Chief. Democratic victories in the realm of cultural politics allow Democratic politicians (many of them, anyway) to abandon any vestigial worries about the ravages of unregulated capitalism or the abuses of the national security state. Amid looming catastrophe, we remain inundated by inane chatter.

Fortunately we still have George Scialabba. So we do not have entirely to imagine what Howe or Lasch would say. We have on hand a vibrant representative of their Independent Left tradition—a man who has stayed outside the academy (where so much critical thinking has disappeared or been rendered unintelligible in recent decades), who has continued to think and write in the interstices of his 9 to 5 job. His métier is the reflective review essay; his output is stunning in quality and quantity. In this, his third collection, he ranges from moral philosophy to fiction to public policy, from the triumph of Ignazio Silone to the failure of Christopher Hitchens. Throughout, he reveals the same sensibility that has characterized independent Left thinking at it its best, in the work of George Orwell, say, or I.F. Stone—a humane concern for the powerless and voiceless, an intolerance for cant and euphemism, a determination to expose the hypocrisies and pretensions of the powerful: whether in regard to "the budget debate" or "the war on terror."

Still, Scialabba is always careful to remain scrupulously fair in his summation of the significance of any particular thinker's ideas—as he does, for example, in his discussion of the moral psychologist Jonathan Haidt's challenge to liberal rationalism—even as he prepares to shred that thinker's specific claims, as he does by exposing Haidt's astonishing ignorance of American political conditions. To be sure, there are times when Scialabba may bend over backwards a little too far to be fair. Despite his generous words for Stanley Fish and Thomas Friedman, he will never persuade me that Fish is anything more than a compulsively clever contrarian or Friedman any more than an airheaded huckster for the computer industry. But this is the defect of Scialabba's virtue of generosity, which he combines with an ever-sharp critical edge and a keen awareness of the contrast between "How We Live, and How We Might Live"—as William Morris put it more than a century ago.

The key to Scialabba's persistent strength is his capacity to resist or (even better) ignore the techno-utopianism that has captured so many able minds and prevented them from seeing policy matters as anything more than adjustment to inevitable, beneficent change. Indeed, he repudiates the utopians' assumptions of beneficence, recognizing (as he writes in his essay on Friedman) "that information technology might have the effect of making life, at least in some respects, less gracious, subtle, sensuous, and profound, but instead more sterile, frenetic, shallow, and routine"--and that we as citizens have a right to ask the political question: is this what we want? Politics is not about inevitabilities; it is about decisions informed by debate. This is harder than ever to remember in our sped-up, networked, 24-7 society, which poses an even greater threat to sustained independent reflection than Irving Howe's conformist society did. "Deep experiences of any kind—grappling with art or philosophy, having one's mind changed about politics, or simply possessing one's soul—require a modicum of silence, slowness, and solitude," Scialabba observes. "For most Americans, that modicum is vanishing." This is not the result of inevitable technological change but of political and economic decisions that can be challenged, changed, or reversed. Whether they will be or not is another question.

But if the forces of inevitability triumph (as their prophets claim they inevitably will), it will not be George Scialabba's fault. Through the dark decades of Reaganism and neo-liberalism, he has helped us sort through the portentous trivia and see (against all the odds) what really matters. He has done this, moreover, amid a lifelong struggle with depression, which he recounts tersely and movingly in these pages. One is reminded of William James, who (according to John Jay Chapman) always seemed as if "he had just stepped out of this sadness in order to meet you." Sometimes even everyday acts require a quiet heroism. We can only be grateful that Scialabba, like James, has continued to summon it.

Jackson Lears is a professor of history at Rutgers University and the editor of *Raritan*.

I. Theories

Afterthoughts of a Nader Voter

In December 2000, as Americans debated the Florida vote count, the eminent conservative judge and author Richard Posner pronounced the Florida election "a statistical tie." No sensible observer could disagree. Like molecular trajectories, vote counts cannot, even in principle, be measured with limitless accuracy.

Since the meaning of a tie is that neither side has won, let us leave Florida aside. In the other 49 states Al Gore received a half-million more citizens' votes and 25 more Electoral College votes than George W. Bush. That margin would have been considerably larger if not for a third-party candidate, most of whose supporters, according to exit polls, would have voted for Gore.

Nonetheless, because of the peculiar character of the American electoral system, George Bush was declared president. Since then, despite assuming office with a lower level of voter support than nearly any other in the nation's history, the Bush administration has been one of the most partisan and high-handed in our history. Its judicial nominations, policy-level appointments, and legislative proposals have been extreme and one-sided; its openness to media scrutiny and citizen participation has been minimal; its public rhetoric has been deceptive and uncivil. Evidently democracy was not well served by the presidential election of 2000.

Who's to blame? Almost unanimously, Democrats and liberals blame the third-party candidate, Ralph Nader. Nader, they say, ought to have recognized that his candidacy might well tilt the election to Bush and that such an outcome would be of far greater consequence than winning federal funds for the Green Party. Nader supporters reply that Gore cost Gore the election, and did so by not sounding more like Nader. Gore's voter support rose and fell, they point out, with his willingness to take strong populist, egalitarian, environmentalist, and good-government positions.

Both sides have a point. Though second to none in my admiration for Nader, I accept the "lesser evil" argument. A Gore administration would have been a routine misfortune: tepid, unimaginative, deferential to corporate and financial elites. The Bush administration has been a catastrophe: destructive of fiscal stability, heedless of civic solidarity, indifferent to environmental health, hostile to workers' rights, contemptuous of international law, and (as New York Times columnist Paul Krugman has demonstrated week in and week out for the last several years) brazenly and relentlessly dishonest. Nader ought to have foreseen this, acknowledged it, and either withdrawn late in the race or urged supporters in closely contested states to vote for Gore (or to trade their votes with Gore supporters in less closely contested states). On the other hand, Gore lost the election not only because of his robotic centrism but also through his pusillanimous and unsporting refusal to debate Nader. A direct appeal to Nader voters on lesser-evil grounds would, I suspect, have won over at least a few percent of them—more than enough to have elected Gore.

What is surprising, though—amazing, in fact—is how few on either side have blamed our electoral system. The American electoral system is an affront to reason. To start at the top: the Electoral College has no function except to frustrate equal political representation: i.e., to prevent each vote cast in presidential elections from counting as much as every other vote. The Framers may have envisioned the College as a deliberative body, but it has not deliberated once in 200 years and never will. Actually, the Framers were ambivalent about the Electoral College, rejecting it several times and finally approving it just before adjourning the Constitutional Convention. That was a mistake. In no less than four presidential elections, the candidate with the greatest number of popular votes was not chosen as president. Overwhelming majorities regularly tell pollsters that the Electoral College should be abolished. Seven hundred proposals to reform or abolish it have been introduced in the House, the most recent of which (in 1989) passed with an 83 percent majority. As always, the Senate blocked any action.

Why? Because the Senate is itself a deeply undemocratic institution. According to Article V of the Constitution, "no state, without its consent, shall be deprived of its equal suffrage in the Senate." That is, each state, regardless of population, was to have two senators. As a result, two centuries later half the U.S. population sends 18 senators to Washington, while the other half sends 82. Twenty senators represent 54 percent of the population; another twenty represent less than 3 percent. California gets two senators; the 20 least populous states, which combined have roughly the same number of people as California, get 40 senators. Senators elected by 11 percent of the population can kill proposed legislation with a filibuster; senators elected by as few as 5 percent of the population can block a constitutional amendment.

Besides these constitutional absurdities, there is the historical absurdity of two-party duopoly. As Michael Lind has written: "Because of our peculiar electoral law, the American government is divided between two parties. The American people are not." Nine out of ten incumbents who seek reelection to the House of Representatives win. And yet, because of low voter turnout and our "winner-take-all" electoral rules, only about a quarter of Americans are represented in Congress by someone they actually voted for.

Two-party dominance allows disproportionate influence to swing voters, single-issue constituencies, and campaign contributors; it promotes negative, contentless campaigns; it rewards grossly inequitable redistricting schemes; and it penalizes those who disagree with both parties but fear to "waste" their votes. (Which is why Nader probably lost many more voters to Gore than Gore lost to Nader.) And then there is behind-the-scenes hardball. The historian Walter Karp put it colorfully: "Challenge a local party syndicate in a mere state legislative district and you will find your ballot petitions falsely voided, your district lines redrawn, your votes miscounted, your supporters bribed, threatened, or beaten—not in some benighted backwoods but in a middle-class neighborhood in New York City in this very year of grace [1979]." Those who criticize Nader for not running in the Democratic primaries underestimate the extent to which party regulars and Gore operatives doubtless stood ready to sabotage his—or any other insurgent's—candidacy.

What should we the people do about all this? We should do what nearly every other established democracy has done: change our "first-past-the-post," "winner-take-all" system to proportional representation (PR). Under our current system, a party that gained a one-vote plurality in every electoral district would win 100 percent of the seats in the legislature. Even if the two major parties received all votes cast, this would leave 49.999 percent of voters unrepresented—hardly fair. Or a party could win half-plus-one of the electoral districts by one vote each, receive no votes whatever in all the other districts, and still control the legislature. This would leave a huge majority of voters unrepresented—even less fair. These precise results are not at all likely, of course; but some version of them, with some, perhaps significant, overrepresentation and underrepresentation, is quite likely. The Electoral College and the Senate are guaranteed to produce unequal representation—that's what they were designed to do.

In a proportional system, the number of seats each party gets corresponds to the percentage of votes it receives (as long as it reaches a specified minimum, e.g., five percent). There are several varieties of PR, including some that allow for geographical representation (the sole basis of the current U.S. system) and others more adapted to non-partisan elections like city councils. But in any form, PR is a ticket of admission for small parties and new candidates: it liberates them from the role of "spoilers," and it spells an end to the stifling dominance of the two major parties.

Defenders of the two-party system argue that multi-party PR societies are prone to gridlock, citing Italy and Israel. But it isn't so. Other PR societies, like Germany, Switzerland, Sweden, and the Netherlands, are much more efficient at enacting policy than the United States. Besides, are winner-take-all rules discredited by the fact that very imperfect democracies like Algeria, Pakistan, and India have adopted them?

America is, needless to say, the greatest country that ever was. But mightn't the rest of the world be right about *something*? According to the Center for Voting and Democracy: "Currently there are 41 well-established democracies with at least two million inhabitants and high ratings from the human rights organization Freedom House, and of these 41 nations only two—the United States and Canada—do not use a form of proportional or semi-proportional voting systems to elect one of their national legislatures." (How Canada can be enlightened enough to have a single-payer health care system and at the same time benighted enough to have a winner-take-all electoral system is something of a puzzle.) And according to Arend Lijphart (past president of the American Political Science Association) and other researchers, PR democracies generally outperform winner-take-all democracies on such measures as voter satisfaction, accountability, and macroeconomic management.

The office of the presidency being (for better or worse) indivisible, the president cannot be elected by PR. But there is another simple reform that would enhance equal representation: instant-runoff voting (IRV). Even if the Electoral College were abolished, the winner of a three-way race for the presidency might very well not be the choice of a majority of voters. To take another hypothetical case: if candidates A and B each receive 33 percent of the vote while C receives 34 percent, then even if the second choice of all A's voters is B and vice versa, C will nevertheless become president. Once again, this particular example is unlikely, though spoilers and split votes are hardly uncommon. If, however, voters are allowed to rank the candidates in order of preference, it is a simple matter for modern voting machines to calculate which candidate has the most popular support. Two years ago this system would have prevented America's becoming an international laughingstock, not to mention awarding the presidency to a man whom the majority of voters did not want to have it.

Do PR and IRV sound impractical, even utopian? A little historical perspective may be useful. Many practices that now seem patently indefensible—the divine right of kings, the union of Church and State, racial segregation, the subordination of women, child labor—once seemed perfectly natural to most people, even if to others it was plain that they could not survive indefinitely. Our electoral system is just such a dinosaur. It has nothing going for it except the inertia of the many and the interests of a few (i.e., those who own the Democratic and Republican parties). Our descendants will wonder what we were thinking of to let it go unreformed for so long.

One thing is certain: if proportional representation, instant-runoff voting, and kindred reforms had been in place in 2000, all three leading presidential candidates would be happier today. George Bush could have played golf all winter and sailed his father's boat all summer. Ralph Nader would have successfully launched the Green Party into national politics. And Al Gore would be in the White House.

Starting Over

Writing in 1843, Marx cautioned that "it is not a matter of drawing a great dividing line between past and future, but of fulfilling the aspirations of the past ... human kind begins no new work, but consciously accomplishes its old work." In other words, one way to rouse people is, rather than inviting them to spurn received values as altogether fraudulent or irrelevant, to point out that the values most of them already hold, or profess to hold, imply radical social transformation. This is the approach taken in two important recent books: *A Preface to Economic Democracy** and *A Citizen Legislature*.† Both argue from the common premises of American democratic ideology to very radical conclusions about the implications of that ideology for everyday life.

As Robert Dahl points out in *A Preface to Economic Democracy*, the American tradition has always harbored a crucial ambiguity about the relations between freedom and equality. Does "democracy" mean the freedom, restricted only by rules of procedural fairness, to amass unlimited wealth? Or does it imply a right to effective—not just nominal—individual autonomy and to an equal say in collective decisions? One of the historic blessings of American abundance is that this ambiguity has seldom ripened into a contradiction. But the contradiction is there; and prolonged economic decline will sooner or later jeopardize the fragile coexistence of capitalism and democracy.

To acknowledge this contradiction is to step outside the circle of academic orthodoxy. For the most eminent political scientist in America to take that step is something of an event.

A Preface to Economic Democracy by Robert A. Dahl. University of California Press, 1985.

†*A Citizen Legislature* by Ernest Callenbach and Michael Phillips. Banyan Tree Books, 1985.

It is admirable that Robert Dahl has seen through the mystique of propertarianism; even more so that he's gotten there not by renouncing his former intellectual commitments but by deepening them. Unlike most of his colleagues, Dahl takes democracy seriously, and so he has become a radical, albeit the most respectable of radicals. The result is a book that argues quietly, almost pedantically, for a fundamental change in the relations of production.

For nearly thirty years Dahl has been one of the most influential students and theorists of American democracy. His early work described American society as a "polyarchy": a collection of active, self-interested minorities, each lobbying intensely on a few issues of special concern rather than putting forth a public philosophy. That is, pluralism. This sort of analysis seemed to presuppose consensus and an end to ideology: everyone taking for granted the basic organization of polity and economy, while haggling over the details. Given the role of fascist and Leninist ideologies in mobilizing mass support for totalitarian regimes, a theory of democracy that did not appear to insist on mass participation or to emphasize abstractions was welcome in the 1950s; and Dahl was widely acclaimed as pluralism's leading exponent.

The theory of pluralist democracy rested on the (usually implicit) assumption that political actors compete on roughly equal terms. As Dahl came to question this assumption—to recognize that America has a ruling class—the center of gravity of his work shifted leftward. In 1976, Dahl and Charles Lindblom reissued their classic textbook *Politics, Economics, and Welfare* with a surprising new preface that assailed the "incapacities" and "perversities" of capitalist society. "Existing American political institutions will not solve the problem," they announced, and called on their social-scientific colleagues to find "new mechanisms" for realizing liberal and egalitarian values without the "harsh bias of market innovation."

A Preface to Economic Democracy is Dahl's response to his own summons. What is democracy, he asks, and when is it morally requisite? He answers that the members of an association are entitled to insist that it be governed democratically when the following conditions hold: the group must reach some decisions that are binding on all members; discussion and collective decision-making are feasible; membership is stable, i.e., those who make the decisions will be subject to the consequences; and there is a rough equality of competence, i.e., members are capable of judging their own interests and also of judging which decisions they must delegate to experts.

As a definition of political democracy, this is not especially controversial. But Dahl goes on to argue that the conditions hold for corporations no less than for political communities. Is this momentous analogy defensible? One obvious objection is that, unlike laws, management decisions are not binding—employees can quit. The answer to this objection, only a little less obvious, is that in the real world (very different from the world of perfect competitive equilibrium and smoothly clearing labor markets) the costs of renouncing employment are frequently as great as the costs of renouncing citizenship. In a way, they are even greater: one is assured of alternative citizenship merely by moving into another community, whereas no one is assured of alternative employment, especially in the face of formal and informal employer blacklists or simply of most employers' notion of proper discipline. Another possible objection is that management requires special skills, which workers may not possess; Dahl replies that workers are no less capable of hiring and supervising managers than stockholders are, indeed more so. Still another objection, based on Robert Michels' "iron law of oligarchy," holds that any sizable association tends to be dominated by those with the most aptitude and ambition; Dahl points out that the same objection applies to political democracy, which no one proposes abandoning on that account.

Apart from these logical and technical objections, there is a possible moral objection as well: aren't stockholders entitled to own and control the firms they invest in? The answer is: only if they have a moral right to the spare money they've invested.

Dahl disposes of this objection with a brief, devastating critique of entitlement theories from Locke to Nozick.

At this point the reader may ask: how, lacking any logical or moral foundation, has the separation between politics and economics become so entrenched in American democratic ideology? Dahl solves this riddle with a fine piece of historical interpretation. At its origin, the United States was an agrarian republic, with an extraordinary degree of equality (at least among white males) in economic, and therefore political, resources. Given the vast quantity of unoccupied western land (that is, occupied by nonwhites), this rough equality of resources—the ideal precondition of democracy—looked permanent. The agrarian economy generated what Dahl calls a "self- regulating egalitarian order," so the Framers and the classical American theorists from *The Federalist* through Tocqueville could afford to worry mainly about the threats that political majorities, acting through the state, might pose to minority rights. The result was an anti-majoritarian Constitution and an anti-statist popular ideology.

The rise of corporate capitalism changed the "self-regulating egalitarian order" into a drastically inegalitarian one. But in a breathtaking act of ideological piracy, apologists for the new order appropriated the individualist bias of agrarianism and transferred it to corporate capitalism. That is, they succeeded in portraying giant corporations as the moral equivalent of individual farmers vis-à-vis the state—a success crowned by a famous series of Supreme Court decisions granting corporations the political rights of individuals. The private property of yeomen had been a genuine bulwark against centralized power; it had earned its democratic prestige. The private property of corporations was another matter: it rapidly conquered or co-opted state power—indeed, compared with labor and government, business *was* centralized power in America. But the connection between property and liberty persisted in law and popular ideology. Here, Dahl argues, lie the roots of Americans' maddening imperviousness to collective thinking. This analysis offers, implicitly, the most plausible answer I have ever encountered to that perennial question: why has there been no socialism in the United States?

Having established that the economy as well as the polity ought to be democratically governed, Dahl goes on to specify what "democratically governed" implies for our actual economic arrangements. It implies, among other things, the illegitimacy of private, concentrated ownership of the core economy. Dahl's early work included a conception of "procedural democracy": a description of the requirements of fair political competition. One of these requirements was that group members have equal access to relevant information about group decisions and equal opportunity to place items on the agenda for decision. *A Preface to Economic Democracy* makes clear that in a society where economic resources translate into political resources, economic inequality must result in political inequality. "Both corporate capitalism and bureaucratic socialism tend to produce inequalities in social and economic resources so great as to bring about severe violations of political equality and hence of the democratic process, and ... we ought to consider whether an alternative more congenial to democratic values might be found." That conclusion may sound tame to some readers, but taken in the context of Dahl's career and of his place in American academic life, it is poignant and powerful.

Dahl's "alternative" is a system of self- governing enterprises, owned and controlled by those who work in them, and subject, within broad limits, to the discipline of the market and regulation by the state. Each worker, or "enterprise citizen," would have one vote and usually (though not always) one equal ownership share in the firm. Large firms would be governed by representative rather than direct democracy; managers and consultants would be hired as needed; the state would regulate externalities and fraud, and perhaps play a role in promoting innovation and allocating credit to new firms; taxation and transfers would correct gross inequalities of income. A transition to this system might be accomplished through something like Sweden's Meidner Plan or Denmark's Social Democratic plan, whereby labor, in a (complicated) sense, buys up the private economy.

Would such a system work? Dahl deploys one argument after another, elegantly, rigorously, and with a deft use of the surprisingly rich literature on the subject, to show that worker self-government would be at least as efficient as private ownership by most of the conventional criteria: investment, productivity, flexibility, innovation. And by unconventional criteria—fostering moral responsibility, solidarity, participatory democracy, job satisfaction—it's likely to be much superior.

A Preface to Economic Democracy is a short book and the title is not coy. It really is a preface, concerned primarily with deducing the legitimacy of worker self-government from common American beliefs about political democracy, and secondarily with sketching out a plan for implementing that ideal. Both parts of this project succeed; but what's most impressive is the ambition. Near the end of his career, John Stuart Mill added a passage to his *Political Economy*, in which he pretty much admitted that he had thought through the moral premises of liberalism and come to the conclusion that workers were entitled to govern themselves economically as well as politically. The quintessential bourgeois liberal declared himself a libertarian socialist. Mill's magnanimity echoes in Dahl's quiet manifesto.

Ernest Callenbach is as far from the academic mainstream as Dahl is central to it. He's not exactly obscure, though: his ecological utopian novel *Ecotopia* (1975)—in my opinion, the best work of social theory in recent years—has a large European following, especially among the Greens. Along with Michael Phillips, he has written an audacious little book arguing that Congress and state legislatures should be chosen by sortition—by lot—rather than by election.

The logic of their proposal is this: in a representative government, the governors ought to be reasonably representative of the governed. This was also the Founders' opinion. James

Madison wrote: "The government ought to possess not only, first, the force, but secondly, the mind or sense of the people at large. The legislature ought to be the most exact transcript of the whole society." John Adams wrote that the legislature "should be an exact portrait, in miniature, of the people at large, as it should think, feel, reason, and act like them." Now, professional politicians as a group are not at all representative of the people at large. In the mid-1980s, fifty-one per cent of the adult population of the US is female; 4.8 per cent of the House of Representatives is female. Eighteen per cent of the population is black or Hispanic, compared with 7 per cent of the House. The average net worth of a Congressperson is greater than that of 95 per cent of the population. And so on.

Furthermore, the "profession" of professional politicians is not making laws but getting reelected. By the authors' calculation, 50 percent of the average Congressperson's working time is devoted to non-legislative activities. In addition, electoral victories can be, and usually are, bought; and as their price increases, campaign funding increasingly determines access to political "representatives." All this is familiar in outline, but Callenbach and Phillips make its extent and implications vividly clear.

Their solution is a 435-member House of Representatives (the same size as the present one) chosen statistically to yield an exact cross-section of the adult population (an easy task, with computer assistance), serving staggered three-year terms, of which the first three months would be spent in training at a nonpartisan academy. In this "transcript" (Madison) or "exact portrait, in miniature" (Adams) of contemporary America, one-half of Congress would be women; one-third would be retirees, students, or housewives; one-quarter would be blue-collar workers; one fifth would be black, Hispanic, Asian-American, or native American; one-tenth would be involuntarily unemployed. There would be nine food-service workers, four farm laborers, three auto mechanics, and one lawyer. There would, at least initially, be majorities for legal abortion, a nuclear freeze, the death penalty, and school prayer; and against busing, open housing, corporate tax privileges and, possibly, many First Amendment freedoms.

Gulp. *A Citizen Legislature* is a moment of truth for radical democrats. It's hard to disagree with Callenbach and Phillips that "living by the considered will of the people is what democracy is supposed to be about" and that "pure intelligence—if there is such a thing—is certainly not directly related to political wisdom; the only reasonable assumption is that both are broadly distributed through the population." But what about the 25 per cent of Americans who are (by Jonathan Kozol's recent estimate) illiterate? Would 25 per cent of a sortition Congress be illiterate; and if not, why not? Doesn't any criterion of exclusion entail a departure from randomness? And doesn't that imply acceptance, in principle, of standards of competence, and therefore of competition?

The question of competence is a delicate one. Callenbach and Phillips solicited comments on their proposal and have appended several to the book. One of the respondents quotes Shaw: "If you ask me, 'Why should the people not make their own laws?' I need only ask you, 'Why should the people not write their own plays?' They cannot. It is much easier to write a good play than to make good law. And there are not a hundred men in the world who can write a play good enough to stand the daily wear and tear as long as a law must." Shaw knew an awful lot about both law-making and play-making. Might there be such a thing as legislative skill, and might it have some relation to legislative experience or to the study of law and public policy? Then again, the respondent who quotes Shaw is, perhaps significantly, a state legislator.

Clearly the risks and difficulties of a sortition system would be considerable. Would they outweigh the vast incompetence, corruption, apathy, and cynicism generated by the present electoral system? Callenbach and Phillips argue persuasively that the shortcomings of our present arrangement, which is based on the supremacy of money, are not reformable. And they argue plausibly that their alternative scheme would provide many incentives to efficiency, integrity, and public-spiritedness among legislators. They then conclude: "Resistance to the sortition idea comes generally, in the last analysis, from an attachment to hierarchy and a lack of trust in the people themselves."

Well, perhaps. But what if "the people themselves" share that distrust and that attachment? This is the deepest of democratic dilemmas: all things are possible if the people trust themselves; nothing much is possible if they don't. But like freedom, self-confidence cannot be conferred.

It may be that the chief value of *A Citizen Legislature* will prove to be heuristic. No reader of this intelligent, offbeat book will ever again take the rightness of electoral democracy for granted. And any democrat who balks at the authors' rigorous interpretation of that noble commonplace, "government by the people," will find herself obliged, perhaps for the first time, to formulate an equally plausible one.

Do the Right Thing

From time immemorial—or at least since Spike Lee's 1989 movie *Do the Right Thing*—men and women have asked, like the subtitle of Michael Sandel's new book, "What's the right thing to do?"* Every year a thousand or so Harvard undergraduates seeking an answer to this question sign up for "Moral Reasoning 22: Justice," Professor Sandel's renowned introductory course and the most popular offering in that university's history. What they learn there is of some consequence for the rest of us. After all, the next most popular course at Harvard is "Social Analysis 10: Principles of Economics," from which legions of students annually emerge, like former Harvard president (and economics professor) Lawrence Summers, utterly sure of themselves, contemptuous of moral reasoning, and primed to lead their country into the financial abyss. Unless "Justice" manages to infiltrate "Principles of Economics"—and not only at Harvard—America is likely to languish in moral and financial bankruptcy for a long time.

The three most common ways of philosophizing about justice emphasize, respectively, happiness, freedom, and morality. Utilitarians think politics should maximize the population's overall welfare, however that is measured. Libertarians counter that the best way to do that is for politics to leave markets alone; that justice is whatever state of affairs results from the sum of all voluntary transactions among free individuals. Communitarians believe that "free individuals" is an incomplete description of human beings; rather, every person, group, institution, and activity has a distinctive purpose (what the Greeks called a *telos*), which politics exists to help them fulfill. Jeremy

*Justice: What's the Right Thing to Do? by Michael Sandel. Farrar, Straus and Giroux, 2009.

Bentham and John Stuart Mill were the founding fathers of utilitarianism. Milton Friedman and Robert Nozick are the best-known exponents of libertarianism. Aristotle was the first important communitarian theorist of justice, while Sandel himself is the most recent.

Straddling these categories are the forbidding grey eminences of moral philosophy, Immanuel Kant and John Rawls. Kant claimed that justice has nothing to do with happiness; that freedom consists solely in doing one's duty; and that to discover our duty we must resolutely disregard consequences, circumstances, sentiments, and attachments—everything contingent, in fact—and instead consider only ideal reason and logical consistency. Rawls, attempting a grand synthesis, allows that we may consider happiness and freedom, but only after we have forgotten, so to speak, who we are. We must choose our society's ground rules as though we were no one in particular, mindful that everything particular about us—our talents and virtues no less than our trust funds—is a lucky (or unlucky) accident. For Rawls justice is, above all, fairness.

Sandel pilots readers skillfully through these philosophical rapids, giving each perspective its due with admirable judiciousness and perspicacity. He is quite right to highlight the moral limits of reliance on the market, since the superior wisdom of minimally regulated markets has been our main civic shibboleth for several decades now. Also illuminating is his argument, following Aristotle, that moral judgments about one or another policy should take into account the way of life and the type of character that the community in question aspires to produce.

Nevertheless, to one who subscribes, as I do, to the James/Dewey/Quine/Rorty tradition of philosophical pragmatism, it is a little difficult to take Aristotle or Kant seriously. (It is, I should think, impossible for anyone at all to take Friedman and Nozick seriously.) Aristotle's impersonal *telos*-es and Kant's transcendental idealism are simply dead in the water, like St. Anselm's ontological proof for the existence of God. They are philosophical relics, as phlogiston and the ether are scientific relics.

And besides, justice isn't solely, or even primarily, a philosophical affair. Correct reasoning can help us define and discriminate among our obligations. But without humane feeling on our part, no obligation will have much force. Solidarity and generosity are the root of the matter, not Socratic dialectics, however stimulating. On this the greatest moral teachers agree, including the poet Shelley ("The great instrument of moral good is the imagination. A man, to be greatly good, must imagine intensively and comprehensively; he must put himself in the place of another and of many others; the pains and pleasures of his species must become his own") and the Jewish reformer Jesus of Nazareth ("Blessed are those who hunger and thirst for justice ... Whatever you do or don't do for the least of your fellow creatures, you are doing or not doing to God Himself").

Perhaps Sandel or a colleague should offer a parallel course: "Moral Imagination 22: Injustice." Rather than nimble reasoning from first principles about intriguing but sometimes farfetched dilemmas, the new course would emphasize imaginative apprehension of actual, intolerable moral horrors. For example: rather than ask (as Sandel and numerous other moral philosophers do) whether one should push a stout person in front of a runaway train in order to save five children playing a little farther down the track, one might ask why the top executives of tobacco companies that bribe Congressmen (legally, of course) in order to avoid restrictions, invest in pseudo-scientific research in order to cast doubt on smoking's lethal effects, and aggressively market their product in Asian and African countries where public-health regulation is weak should not be disemboweled on television by terminal lung-cancer patients. Or why the Forbes 400 should not be politely but firmly relieved of the few percent of their colossal net worth required to drastically reduce river blindness, mosquito-borne malaria, fatal diarrhea, cleft palate, vaginal fistulas, severe chronic malnutrition, and quite a few other principal causes of human suffering.

Undoubtedly the world would be a better place if everyone took Michael Sandel's course or read his book. Still, it is not our theoretical confusion that renders us passive and condemns billions of our fellow humans to needless agony; it is our indifference. Where there's a moral will, there's a political way. But deciding collectively where our taxes and charitable donations should go, and making sure they get there, could get pretty time-consuming. We'd have to give up several hours a week of television, perhaps permanently. Is justice—or democracy, for that matter—really worth so great a sacrifice?

Only Fair

Few words name a quality as central to Americans' self-conception as "fairness"; few idioms in American English are so immediately intelligible, so widely resonant, as "fair and square," "fair dealing," "a fair chance," "fair game," or "a fair fight." No appeal flies so straight from one American heart to another as "It's not fair!" Fairness anchors the American democratic ethos the way honor anchored the European feudal ethos—in effect, fairness *is* an American's honor. So when a slick literary critic turned deconstructionist law professor rides into town and calls fairness "impossible," "incoherent," "a sham and a cheat" ... well, them's fightin' words.

Or would be, if liberals were not largely defined by an unwillingness to fight over mere words. In a liberal polity, everyone has a right to any opinion. A liberal constitution (i.e., one that contains some version of the First Amendment) protects free speech against state interference; academic freedom protects it in the schools; public sentiment supports it strongly. Truth will emerge, liberal citizens firmly believe, from unfettered competition in the intellectual marketplace. All true liberals will defend to the death anybody's right to say anything, however obnoxious—however racist, homophobic, pornographic, religious, or irreligious. Among us, ideas are sacrosanct; the law governs acts, not ideas.

Tosh, says Stanley Fish. There's no such thing as free speech. Obviously one cannot say just anything. One can't publish military secrets; can't libel; can't advertise falsely; can't direct a blind person into the path of a speeding car. Such utterances have prompt, harmful, easily foreseeable consequences—that is, they are for all practical purposes acts—so they are uncontroversially prohibited. But, objects Fish, all speech has consequences, weighty or trivial, proximate or remote; in this sense, all speech shades into action. The consequentiality of speech is after all the very premise of First Amendment doctrine. We permit (in principle) all speech because we cannot know in advance, and the state is therefore not allowed to prejudge, which argument will eventually produce the most desirable consequences—i.e., the truth. This implies that if some instance of speech—say, pornography or hate speech—causes grave harm and has nothing much to do with the search for truth—i.e., has little or no relation to the purpose for which the First Amendment protects speech—then there is in principle no reason not to prohibit it. And sometimes we do, as I've noted.

Of course, the First Amendment enjoins the state from promoting as well as proscribing opinions. The state must be, according to a standard formulation, "neutral among competing visions of the good life"; that is, among religious or moral views. No public resources should further (or hinder) any religious purpose. In educational policy (e.g., curriculum design and textbook selection), health policy (sex education, contraceptive availability, abortion funding), civic architecture and ceremony, and everything else it does, the state is required to be strictly impartial toward religion.

Again impossible, says Fish. Leaving religion out of the common life is something many strong believers are unwilling, indeed are forbidden by their beliefs, to agree to. Nor can schools avoid having an effect on a child's religious development. If the schools are, as the First Amendment requires, indifferent to the claims of sacred authority, the child's spontaneous deference to those claims—in other words, its faith—will thereby be undermined. This is exactly what conscientious religious parents cannot permit. Liberals may reply that the highest purpose of education in a free society is to train children to reason well and to judge for themselves. But the sovereignty of reason and the supremacy of individual judgment are anathema to believers. Secular liberals' highest purposes are emphatically not *their* highest purposes.

Yet another prong of Fish's attack on neutral principles

and procedural fairness is his answer to arguments against affirmative action. In their simplest and most popular form, these arguments condemn all race-conscious policies as discriminatory and therefore invidious. The proceduralist assumption that "any action tinged with race-consciousness is equivalent to any other action tinged with race-consciousness" gives rise to the principle: "favor no group, no matter who the group is or what it has done or what has been done to it"—no matter whether it has, until recently, endured generations of devastating exploitation and neglect or has escaped that misfortune. In its complete (and not at all innocent) disregard of history and context, this allegedly neutral principle becomes, Fish charges, a "device for erasing the difference between oppression and the amelioration of oppression."

That's the trouble with principle: it holds politics to an unattainable standard. This standard—neutrality, impartiality, fairness—is unattainable because no speech is without consequences, no purposes are non-moral, and no policy can equally affect groups with vastly different histories and circumstances. And whenever this standard seems to have been met, it's because some people have succeeded in getting their own values—secular rationality, individual autonomy, sexual privacy, economic productivity—designated as the general good and therefore beyond politics.

So far Fish's argument is not, as he readily acknowledges, entirely original. (Except, it's worth noting, in presentation. *The Trouble with Principle** is not your usual deconstructionist sludge. Fish is one of the most penetrating, agile, witty, and elegant writers around. It is hard to imagine another book on law, politics, and philosophy—or anything else, really—appearing for quite a while that will give as much sheer pleasure to impartial and objective readers of all ideological persuasions as this one does.) But while others also claim to have shown that the philosophical foundations of liberalism rest on sand, Fish's view of

The Trouble with Principle by Stanley Fish. Harvard University Press, 1999.

the consequences of this demonstration is unique. He thinks it has no consequences. The appeal to principle, he observes, is an ubiquitous and inevitable rhetorical strategy. Moreover, it's a legitimate strategy. It's not that principles don't exist or that they do no work; they just don't do the work liberal theorists claim they do: i.e., adjudicate impartially among conflicting substantive views. They've done good rhetorical work in the past: e.g., helping to eliminate slavery and to raise the status of women. But at present they're doing bad work, at least some of the time: e.g., helping to rule out in advance most measures for preventing speech-related harms and at least some measures for remedying racial inequality.

So...? "What's a liberal to do? My answer is simple: forget about the principle (and therefore stop being a liberal), which was never what you were interested in in the first place, and make an argument for the policy on policy grounds, that is, on the grounds that you think it is good and right. Argue that civil rights supporters were not working for a color-blind society (even though it may have been rhetorically effective to use that language) but for better conditions for African Americans, and that today the achieving of better conditions might involve practices of voluntary segregation. Argue that in your view the presence of Marxists on campus is beneficial to education and the presence of bigots and racists is not, and that's all there is to it."

Now many readers will, as I did, find Fish's critique of liberal theory wholly convincing. Liberals should by all means forget about principle and argue for policies on policy grounds. But they should by no means make the arguments Fish seems to be inviting them to make here and elsewhere in *The Trouble with Principle*. Practicing voluntary segregation is about the least useful way imaginable of achieving better conditions for African Americans, followed closely in uselessness by racial redistricting, minority set-asides, hiring and admissions quotas, and special protection against offensive speech. (The most useful ways are: huge and targeted investments in K-12 education; a rise in the minimum wage; basic literacy and numeracy training for welfare recipients who need it; job training, after-school activities, and subsidized summer camp or travel for inner-city youth; and a wealth tax to pay for it all.) The presence of Marxists on campus is indeed beneficial to education (the presence of pseudo-Marxist cultural studies mavens is another matter), but the presence of bigots and racists is even more beneficial, above all to the education of bigots and racists. The latter are, after all, fellow citizens and confused human beings. (And if they are students, they are paying—through the nose, probably—to be enlightened rather than told to shut up.) If such people are stifled, they will not become less dangerous and (eventually) harmful; on the contrary. Liberals owe them, and their potential victims, patient attention and powerful counterarguments.

Of course Fish too is owed more of a counterargument than the above paragraph, but I at least have the excuse of a lack of space. Fish ticks off and disposes of "the nifty nine arguments against affirmative action" with extreme cursoriness—a paragraph each—and sniffs in conclusion: "Sometimes the principled reasons people give for taking a position are just window dressing, good for public display but only incidental to the heart of the matter, which is the state of their hearts." As a response to the very substantial arguments of Shelby Steele, Orlando Patterson, Jim Sleeper, Tamar Jacoby, Stephen and Abigail Thernstrom, and others—historical and statistical arguments, not abstract, philosophical ones—this is unworthy of Fish and even suggests a lack of political seriousness.

Similarly with free speech. Fish's attempted demolition of free-speech absolutism is wholly successful: his analyses of *Collin v. Smith* (the Skokie case) and *American Booksellers v. Hudnut* (the Indianapolis antipornography ordinance case) are masterly, as is his review of the First Amendment literature. But his political conclusion, that "the notion of ... free speech is empty and is thus, at the very least, a questionable counterweight to the harms and injuries permitted in its name," is not thought through. The issue is thought through more deeply and satisfyingly, without recourse to principle, in a recent essay by Ellen Willis, who concludes:

> Symbolic expression, however forceful, leaves a space between communicator and recipient, a space for contesting, fighting back with one's own words and images, organizing to oppose whatever action the abhorred speech may incite. Though speech may, and often does, support the structure of domination, whether by lending aid and comfort to the powerful or frightening and discouraging their targets, in leaving room for opposition it falls short of enforcing submission. For this reason the unrestrained clash of ideas, emotions, and visions provides a relatively safe model—one workable even in a society marked by serious imbalances of power—of how to handle social conflict, with its attendant fear, anger, and urges to repress, through argument, persuasion, and negotiation (or at worst grim forbearance) rather than coercion. In the annals of human history, even this modest exercise in freedom is a revolutionary development; for the radical democrat it prefigures the extension of freedom to other areas of social life.

Willis does here what I wish Fish had done at least occasionally: she explicates and reconciles our conflicting intuitions—in this case, that ideas matter but that words are only words—rather than merely pointing out the conflict.

The debunking of liberalism is urgently necessary; but liberalism is not pure bunk. Here is Fish in full debunking mode: "What, after all, is the difference between a sectarian school which disallows challenges to the divinity of Christ and a so-called non-ideological school which disallows serious discussion of that same question? In both contexts something goes without saying and something else cannot be said (Christ is not God or he is). There is of course a difference, not however between a closed environment and an open one but between environments that are differently closed."

Having attended both kinds of school, I'm reluctant to leave the matter there. When the subject of the divinity of Christ comes up in a sectarian school, a student who expresses the wrong view is rebuked the first time, sent to the principal's office the second time, and expelled the third time. When the subject comes up in a nonsectarian school (it is of course not "disallowed"), everybody has a different view or no view, and the student who persists in returning to the subject after everyone else's interest in it is exhausted is asked to organize a discussion outside of class, attendance optional. Thus are these two environments "differently closed." In the nonsectarian institution, unlike its sectarian counterpart, dissenters are frustrated but not punished, patronized but not stigmatized, ignored but not silenced. This may not be perfectly fair, but it's pretty fair; and that—for most of us, most of the time—is fair enough.

There's something to every intuition, as Fish concedes, indeed insists. And fairness is the mother of all (18th-, 19th-, 20th, and) 21st-century American political intuitions, probably including (he's so canny it's hard to tell) Fish's. I suspect that if Fish ever gets around to laying out his own moral intuitions rather than upbraiding liberal theorists for running away from theirs, he will find himself, on the whole, justifying the ways of liberalism to man.

Notice Thy Neighbor

Five hundred years ago, slavery was the most natural thing in the world. So was the torture of criminal suspects, convicts, and heretics. So was the virtual ownership—and regular physical chastisement—of women by their fathers or husbands. Most of us (I hope) now abhor these things, but anyone time-traveling back to that era who informed a slave-owner, torturer, or wife-beater that his behavior was shameful would have been met with incomprehension, perhaps even indignation.

If someone traveled back from the 26th century to 2009, what would he or she upbraid us for? In what respects would our behavior seem shameful to her, as slavery and torture seem abhorrent to us? If you don't know already, you will after reading Peter Singer's *The Life You Can Save*.* Much of this valuable little book is devoted to detailing how much suffering there is among the world's poor, how easily it could be remedied by the world's non-poor, and how little the latter can be bothered. Our 26th-century visitor would give us an earful.

Singer, a philosophy professor at Princeton, is probably as much of a celebrity as a philosophy professor can be in unphilosophical 21st-century America. His 1975 book, *Animal Liberation*, launched the animal-rights movement, and several of his subsequent books on applied ethics have been bestsellers. Singer is, like Jeremy Bentham and John Stuart Mill, a radical utilitarian, a useful busybody who challenges metaphysical and theological rationalizations of human pain. In particular, he is notorious for contending that human life, although precious, is not sacred; hence the legitimacy, in most circumstances, of

The Life You Can Save: Acting Now to End World Poverty by Peter Singer. Random House, 2009.

abortion and, in extreme circumstances, of infanticide. What matters is to minimize unnecessary suffering.

Preventing unnecessary suffering among the global poor is hardly controversial, of course; just the opposite. And yet, compared with abortion or infanticide, Americans are not very excited about foreign humanitarian aid. We are also not very well-informed about it. Ninety-five percent of Americans think the United States is more generous with aid than other rich countries, when the opposite is true by a large margin. Most Americans think that between 15 and 20 percent of federal spending goes for such aid; the correct figure is less than one percent. Most Americans think their country does too much to help the global poor and should only dedicate 5 to 10 percent of government spending to this purpose—which, as I've just noted, is five to ten times more than we actually do spend on it. Measured against national income, the percentages are even lower. For every hundred dollars of America's national income, our government spends 18 cents on foreign humanitarian assistance and individuals spend another seven cents.

But why should Americans give more? Does foreign aid do any good? Much of it, Singer acknowledges, does not. A good deal is simply stolen by corrupt foreign elites or squandered on poorly conceived mega-projects. And many economists object that aid does not help poor people nearly as much as economic growth.

Nevertheless, Singer makes a convincing case that money wisely spent can save many lives. Smallpox killed several hundred million people in the twentieth century, but thanks to the World Health Organization, an agency of the UN, it will not kill anyone in the twenty-first. Measles, river blindness, malaria, and diarrhea, all easily treated and prevented, still kill millions every year, but there has been progress. Some of the most affecting pages in *The Life You Can Save* describe the low-tech, low-cost programs that have rescued many thousands of children and women from lives blighted by cleft palates and obstetric fistulas and have restored sight to a million people blinded by cataracts.

All this through simple surgical procedures costing between $50 and $400. So little money, apparently, can do so much good.

Singer has heartening stories to tell about some of the exemplary people who've made a difference. A few are famous, like Paul Farmer, the Harvard doctor who moved to rural Haiti and was the subject of a *New Yorker* profile. Most are not: they are obstetricians and ophthalmologists who visited poor countries and could not forget what they saw; or they are hedge fund employees or real estate developers or Silicon Valley entrepreneurs on whom it dawned one day that there must be more to life. He also "outs" a few of the super-rich who spend unconscionable amounts on luxury consumption—"hyper-consumption" would be more accurate. With admirable restraint, Singer refrains from calling for the expropriation and disemboweling of such people, a fate they undoubtedly deserve.

Instead, he asks what the rest of us can do, and why we don't. We don't because inertia is easier than initiative. However generous we are, if it takes some effort to give and no effort not to give, we probably won't give. This is the insight underlying a well-received recent book, *Nudge*, by Cass Sunstein and Richard Thaler. They suggest (and Singer agrees) that, when possible, giving be made the default option: that is, one would have to opt out rather than opt in. This system works extremely well for organ donation; and if one percent, or even less, were deducted from most people's paychecks (unless they opted out) and donated to a non-profit organization of the employee's choice, it could begin to make a dent on global poverty.

For those willing to do more than this bare minimum, Singer has worked out a detailed chart specifying how much everyone at every income level should give each year in order to make possible a minimally decent life for all our fellow humans. To simplify: his proposal comes to 5 percent of gross income for the non-poor but non-affluent (i.e., most of us), 10 percent for the affluent, 15 percent for the rich, and 20 to 25 percent for the super-rich. Is this unrealistic? Maybe. But if we don't, our 26th-century descendants will be heartily ashamed of us.

Camping

In dark times, it sometimes helps to take a longer view. Abolitionists undoubtedly had many reasons to be discouraged in the 1820s and 30s. Let us hope they also found comfort sometimes in reflecting that so immoral and irrational an institution as slavery simply *could* not persist until the end of days. For surely all the people cannot fool themselves all the time?

Economic inequality in the 21st century is not, perhaps, so starkly immoral and irrational as chattel slavery in the 19th. Still, the ownership of 40 percent of the world's wealth by one percent of its inhabitants while 30 or 35 percent—two billion people—live on less than two dollars a day entails (even after translating those two dollars into local currencies) a truly staggering amount of needless suffering. Surely this state of affairs— along with the less desperate but nonetheless substantial misery of the less well-off in developed societies—cannot persist for many more decades, much less centuries?

Perhaps technology will help, although this can no longer be taken for granted. Resources are finite, and in some cases exhausted; and the costs of previous technologies, from climate change to species depletion to air-borne and water-borne pollution to toxic waste disposal, have scarcely begun to be reckoned. In any case, even benign technological development may not prevent the hardening of current inequalities into something like a global caste system, with an enormous and degraded underclass. The only thing that can prevent that is intelligent, humane collective action.

The original name for intelligent, humane collective action was "socialism." During the 20th century, however, the word was commonly used to describe actions that were anything but intelligent and humane, and were not even collective in the relevant sense (ie, democratic). For their different purposes, dictators and plutocrats embraced this usage: the dictators in order to dignify their tyranny with the prestige of a noble ideal; the plutocrats in order to insinuate that tyranny is the inevitable result of trying to realize the ideal. Ideologically, this was a very successful pincer movement. Today the word "socialism" is understandably unpopular among those who take it to mean what Stalin and J. Edgar Hoover agreed that it meant.

Still, you can't keep a good idea down forever. Far from the political or academic mainstream, socialist writers like David Schweickart, John Roemer, Alec Nove, Michael Albert, Ernest Callenbach, Gar Alperovitz, and others have been formulating arguments and even plans. G. A. Cohen, the recently deceased Chichele Professor of Social and Political Theory at Oxford, authored two major books (*If You're an Egalitarian, How Come You're So Rich?* and *Rescuing Justice and Equality*) vindicating socialist morality against the more cautious and far more influential liberalism of John Rawls. They were intricately argued books, dense with the jargon of British analytic philosophy, and probably did not win many hearts and minds to the socialist cause. But Cohen's final, very short book may do just that.*

Imagine a camping trip, he asks us. We are out with a large group of friends, whom we like and trust, along with a few of their significant others and casual companions, whom we don't know but who seem nice enough. Some of us bring tools and provisions; other things we chip in to buy. Some people have relevant skills, like fishing or making campfires or singing. Some people bring nothing but themselves. The purpose of the trip is simply that everyone have a good time. What relations of production and distribution will we adopt?

Clearly, those with food or tools will share them rather than sell or rent them. Those with skills will not charge for helping others or for doing the most demanding tasks. No one will seek to exploit his or her comparative advantage in order

Why Not Socialism? by G. A. Cohen. Princeton University Press, 2009.

to maximize profits or leisure. From each according to her abilities; to each according to her needs: that is camping-trip socialism.

Why can't the rest of life be like that? Some will say: because it's not just. People with more skills or resources deserve higher rewards. Do they, Cohen replies? Our genetic endowment, early environment, and educational opportunities, which are overwhelmingly responsible for our success or failure in the marketplace, are matters of luck rather than desert. Moreover, in a capitalist society, inequality, like interest, compounds over time.

Others will say: because it's not efficient. People need incentives to work hard, and what stronger incentive is there than financial reward? That, Cohen points out, is an empirical question. For some people most of the time, and for most people some of the time, there are indeed stronger incentives than personal gain, just as on the camping trip. Doctors (at least European ones), nurses, teachers, and book reviewers do not tailor their work to expected monetary return. Moral, intellectual, and aesthetic incentives may be rarer than financial ones, but they are no less productive, and they are certainly far less destructive.

Fine, skeptics will say, gifted people may not need extra incentives to work hard, but what about slackers and schlubs— i.e., the great majority of us? As conservatives' horror stories of union featherbedding demonstrate, job security brings out the worst in many people. (Political theorists will recognize this as the famous "collective action problem.") Here, Cohen acknowledges, is the rub. Is there enough virtue in the world—generosity, honor, patience—to make socialism feasible? Not any time soon, of course; all those millennia of scarcity and greed have scarred us deeply. But in the imaginable future? Or is there an evolutionary equivalent of original sin, an irreducible minimum of radical evil in human nature that must rule out socialism forever?

Anyone who offers a confident answer to that question is either a blithe utopian or (more likely) an apologist for the capitalist status quo. Anthropology, biology, and evolutionary psychology are currently in ferment over the question of how deep are the evolutionary roots of cooperation and competition. *A priori* dismissal of the possibility of socialism is evidence of ignorance or bad faith.

But suppose there is, someday, enough virtue—how would socialism work? With the help of a useful distinction between the *informational* and the *motivational* functions of market prices, Cohen canvasses some possibilities. Central planning is out—there's not enough information available to planners. (Though Michael Albert and Robin Hahnel argue intriguingly in *Looking Forward** that decentralized planning is possible with present-day information technology.) But even if we must rely on markets for information, we must also find other motivations than those that markets appeal to: greed and fear.

One option is market socialism. The version Cohen expounds, based on the economist John Roemer's *A Future for Socialism*, allows inequality of income but not of wealth. Every citizen receives a share of the nation's capital assets and can trade shares on the stock market, but not buy or sell them. Their dividends may increase, and their earned income is not limited (though it is progressively taxed), but at death, all their shares are returned to the national treasury. Publicly-owned banks and other financial institutions monitor corporate performance, as major shareholders do now (in theory). Thus the capitalist class is eliminated with, Roemer claims, no loss of economic efficiency.

No doubt the best forms of socialist organization will emerge, like everything else, after much trial and error. But a vast quantity of preliminary spadework is necessary to excavate the assumptions that keep us from even trying. With *Why Not Socialism?*, Cohen has turned over a few shovelfuls, bringing us a little nearer the end of the immemorial—but surely not everlasting—epoch of greed and fear.

*South End Press, 1999

Illfare

Until a year ago, Tony Judt was a prolific historian of twenti-eth-century Europe and a frequent critic of American foreign policy. Then he was stricken with amyotrophic lateral sclero-sis (ALS, or "Lou Gehrig's disease.") As his mobility has dwin-dled, his thoughts have turned from scholarship and polemic to memoir and prophecy. A series of exquisite autobiographical essays have appeared in the *New York Review of Books*, revisit-ing his boyhood and adolescence in post-World War II England. *Ill Fares the Land** is a political valediction, a distillation of his career-long engagement with the vicissitudes of twentieth-century history and ideology.

Thinking back on many conversations in recent years with "young people on both sides of the Atlantic," Judt recalls hear-ing frequently "a general sentiment of frustration: 'we' know something is wrong and there are many things we don't like. But what can we believe in? What should we do?" An intellec-tual could hardly put his or her ebbing energies to better use than by offering, with eloquence and humility, an answer to these questions, as Judt does here.

Anyone of an age to have asked Judt the above questions has lived through a period of decline. For a golden quarter-century, from the late 1940s to the early 1970s, the promise of American life seemed at least partly fulfilled. Thanks to the New Deal, labor unions, and a flexible economic policy aimed at full employment, prosperity was more widely diffused and more solidly based than in any other period of American his-tory. But over the last few decades we have lost—mostly squan-dered—our apparently insuperable advantages and seemingly indestructible national well-being. How?

**Ill Fares the Land* by Tony Judt. The Penguin Press, 2009.

Judt reprints a very striking set of charts showing that, compared with twenty or so other developed countries, the United States, though at or near the top in per capita Gross Domestic Product, ranks at or near the bottom in measurements of mental and physical health, trust, law-abidingness, and intergenerational mobility. (One could also add leisure and job security to the list of things Americans generally have less of than their European, Canadian, Japanese, and Australian counterparts.) The reason for America's poor performance emerges clearly from those same charts: economic inequality is far more acute in the United States than elsewhere in the developed world—except for the UK, which also scores relatively low on most measures of well-being. The lesson of the data is hard to miss: large-scale inequality is not good for a society.

Of course, it's easier to miss this lesson if you agree with Margaret Thatcher's famous dictum: "There is no such thing as society." What explains that apparently puzzling assertion is the second, less often quoted half of Thatcher's remark: "there are only individuals and families." In other words: every man for himself and his kin; others can look out for themselves. On this view, social solidarity is a sentimental fiction; the common good is a bureaucratic hustle. Private enterprise is always more efficient than public; market outcomes are optimal, by definition. Above all, taxes are theft, except for the purpose of funding high-tech weapons and unnecessary wars, subsidizing Big Oil and Big Agriculture, or rescuing Wall Street shareholders and executives.

Although Thatcher and Reagan liked to pose as traditionalists, their (selective) hostility to government was hardly traditional wisdom. As Judt emphasizes, from the 1930s through the 1970s it was generally agreed that the state had an indispensable role: to moderate the business cycle, to insure equal opportunity, to guard the society's natural and cultural heritage, and to help the hapless and helpless. Americans called this set of undertakings the "welfare state"; Europeans called it "social democracy." Judt defines it pithily as "belie[f] in the possibility and virtue of collective action for the collective good."

The trauma of the Great Depression and the authority of Keynes, who explained it more convincingly than anyone else, stood behind that consensus. The shared sufferings of World War II also predisposed European societies, in particular, toward a modicum of trust and cooperation. It paid off handsomely. From roughly 1948 to 1973—that is, from the Marshall Plan to the end of the Bretton Woods international economic regime—social-democratic policies produced unprecedented prosperity and stability.

The main reason for the decline of social-democracy in recent decades is the ascendancy of free-market economic theory, which Judt traces back through Milton Friedman and other University of Chicago economists to the Austrian refugees Friedrich Hayek, Ludwig von Mises, and Joseph Schumpeter. At first Keynesian economists and policymakers paid no attention to their views. "Only when the welfare states whose failure [Hayek and von Mises] had so sedulously predicted began to run into difficulties did they once again find an audience for their views: high taxation inhibits growth and efficiency, governmental regulation stifles initiative and entrepreneurship, the smaller the state the healthier the society, and so forth."

Judt's explanation is mostly right but perhaps leans too heavily on a belief in the causal priority of ideas. He quotes Keynes approvingly: "Practical men, who believe themselves to be quite exempt from any intellectual influences, are usually the slaves of some defunct economist. Madmen in authority, who hear voices in the air, are distilling their frenzy from some academic scribbler of a few years back." True, but there is quite a variety of defunct economists and academic scribblers. Why do some, but not others, prevail?

No, free-market ideology did not triumph because economists and statesmen began to find it more persuasive than they had formerly. It triumphed because a great many businessmen never accepted the New Deal, never stopped trying to roll it back, and eventually found the right strategy: concentrated ownership of the media; increased business funding (and with it, control) of scientific and economic research; the growth of corporate public relations and business-funded think tanks, directing a constant stream of propaganda at Congress and the media; increased spending on electoral campaigns and political debate, especially through new forms like PACs; revolving-door employment of former legislators and regulators; and coordination of these efforts by the Business Roundtable, the US Chamber of Commerce, and industry associations. They became a juggernaut, then simply hired or promoted economists and statesmen with suitable opinions. "In every age," as Marx pointed out, "the ideas of the rulers are the ruling ideas."

Still, however we lost social democracy in the United States, Judt is unquestionably right about the importance of regaining it. He has packed a great deal of wisdom into this short book and leaves us very much in his debt.

Immortal Bees

If you read the newspapers, you may find the timing of Roger Scruton's *The Uses of Pessimism** a little curious. In the first decade of the twenty-first century, the American Right continued its long march through the country's political institutions. Taxes on the rich were slashed; inequality reached Gilded Age proportions; deregulation re-established the law of the corporate jungle; Social Security is under continual assault; the labor movement is prostrate; and proposed legislative reforms of health care and finance have been rendered skeletal by locust-like swarms of industry lobbyists. The last best hope of American liberals was elected president in 2008 and appears to have no other desire than to please Wall Street, the Pentagon, and the Business Roundtable in all things. The most conservative Supreme Court in memory has recently removed all limits on political spending by corporations, guaranteeing the continuation of plutocracy into the indefinite future.

In Europe, governments of every ideological stripe are united in their determination to impose savage austerity on working people in order to placate bankers. The working classes now have a great deal to lose besides their chains: namely, pensions, universal health care, state-supported day care, free higher education, etc. And they may well lose it, or much of it. At such a moment, is there really a pressing need for an eloquent and impassioned manifesto against irresponsible idealism, excessive optimism, and revolutionary left-wing utopianism?

Scruton is a philosopher and may perhaps be forgiven for not taking much notice of purely phenomenal matters. Besides, he is English and very grumpy about the encroachment of the European Union and its rules upon merry, eccentric old

*Atlantic Books, 2010.

England. Perhaps he is right to be, though to perceive in the elite of bankers and conservative bureaucrats who direct the EU a cadre of radicals driving the Continent single-mindedly along the road to socialism is evidence of a very strong imaginative predisposition.

Scruton does indeed have a bee—several bees—in his bonnet. Each chapter in *The Uses of Pessimism* is devoted to chasing after and swatting at a different one of these pesky buzzing creatures, which have names like "The Best Case Fallacy," "The Utopian Fallacy," "The Zero Sum Fallacy," "The Planning Fallacy," and so on. Alas, they are immortal bees, he admonishes us; they swarm again in every generation, plaguing ordinary, sensible people who are just trying to get on with their lives and have no interest in utopia or revolution. Eternal pest control is the price of freedom.

The various fallacies that Scruton hunts down and vanquishes reduce to one prime delusion: "that human beings can either foresee the future or control it to their own advantage." This is the belief of "unscrupulous optimists," who imagine that "the difficulties and disorders of humankind can be overcome by some large-scale adjustment." Their "illusions of mastery" and "abstract schemes for human improvement" invariably come to nothing—or worse, lead straight to totalitarianism. (Lenin and Mao were the quintessential unscrupulous optimists.) Only "personal virtue"—patience, cheerfulness, humility—allows us to "play the small part that it is given to humans to play in bettering the lot of their fellows." Burke, Santayana, and other conservatives were right: "prejudice," the inherited wisdom of custom and tradition, is superior to theory; "piety and caution in worldly affairs" are always more salutary than rebelliousness and large ambitions.

By "pessimism" Scruton means—at least in his calmer moments—moderation, a sense of limits, and a preference for local, small-scale solutions wherever possible. Put that way, who could disagree? Stated carefully and fair-mindedly, Scruton's deep skepticism about radical innovation might indeed have been valuable. In all societies, capitalist or non-capitalist, officials should be accountable to the public they allegedly serve and experts should be able to satisfy the ordinary people whose lives and money they propose to experiment with. This is non-partisan wisdom: it applies to all governments. And not only to governments but also to those more powerful institutions and individuals whom governments today in fact mainly serve: corporations and large investors.

Unfortunately, Scruton's exposition is not careful or fair-minded; it is exasperatingly careless and infuriatingly tendentious—a succession of right-wing talking points such as one might hear from Sarah Palin or Rush Limbaugh. For example, according to Scruton, the cause of the recent global financial crisis was government over-regulation: banks had been "pressured into ignoring the demands of prudence" and forced to issue mortgages to poor people who couldn't afford them. In reality, the regulations in question specifically required lenders to evaluate borrowers' creditworthiness by existing standards. Moreover, only a small fraction of financial institutions at risk were mortgage-issuers; most were large-scale purchasers of derivatives, CDOs (collateralized debt obligations), and other financial gimmicks. The financial crisis—as even Alan Greenspan has acknowledged—was the result of *not enough* government regulation.

According to Scruton, "laws of bankruptcy have been weakened and credit made easier," another government-forced dereliction that contributed to our present woes. Every part of this claim is wrong. First, credit was made "easier" by the aggressive and often deceitful marketing of the credit-card and mortgage-lending industries. Then, to prevent their victims from escaping, these industries pressured Congress to *strengthen* the bankruptcy laws against borrowers and in favor of lenders.

Trade unions and consumer protection agencies are apparently superfluous. Dismissing the "zero sum" fallacy and the very possibility of "exploitation," Scruton writes blandly: "Consensual agreements benefit both parties: why else would they enter into them? And that is as true of the wage contract as it is of any contract of sale." Can Scruton truly believe that dealings between a politically well-connected, lawyer-heavy multi-billion-dollar company and each and every one of its employees or customers are fully consensual in any meaningful sense? If so, then he must believe in the neoclassical dogmas of perfect competition and symmetrical information, which are at least as implausible as the Marxist theory of "surplus value" that he derides.

And so on and on, one right-wing shibboleth after another. Scruton simply will not acknowledge that many contemporary problems—I would say the most urgent ones—are caused not by the utopian zeal of unscrupulous optimists but by the raw greed of investors and executives, who generally have federal, regional, and local governments securely under their thumb. When Scruton intones magisterially that the free market is an "exemplary manifestation of our collective rationality" and "the only peaceful solution to the problem of coordination in a society of strangers," one can only stammer incredulously in reply: "But ... Halliburton? ... Enron? ... Goldman Sachs? ... British Petroleum?"

Pace Scruton, there is another "peaceful solution to the problem of coordination in a society of strangers." It's called democracy. Not the ersatz kind we currently enjoy, which consists of choosing every few years among a narrow range of options determined by those who have power to set the political agenda and manufacture popular consent; but the real thing, in which an active, informed citizenry continually discusses the public business, demands access to all necessary information, regularly instructs its representatives, and monitors the government's performance more diligently than can be done by merely tuning in each night to the evening news.

I daresay Scruton would approve of real democracy. After all, he inveighs frequently against "top-down planning." This shows the right spirit: top-down anything is undemocratic. If only Scruton had the beginning of a clue about who's actually on top in the contemporary world, he might well have written a useful book.

Minimal Democracy

A four-letter word beginning with "f" has tragically corrupted the minds of countless innocent Americans. I mean "free," as in the expressions "free market" and "free enterprise." It is a glorious word, of course, but its association with these morally neutral abstractions generally serves to obscure their often harsh and irrational consequences. In our day, these two catchphrases, illicitly trading on the prestige of "free," are the first resort of scoundrels. The late 20th and early 21st centuries have been scoundrel time, as bureaucrats and legislators of both parties have raced to repeal or nullify longstanding tax, regulatory, labor, environmental, and social welfare policies in the name of market freedoms, for the near-exclusive benefit of the rich.

Charles Lindblom, Sterling Professor Emeritus of Economics and Political Science at Yale, author of the classic *Politics and Markets* and (with the equally eminent Robert Dahl) *Politics, Economics, and Welfare*, has noticed these depredations. *The Market System* is not, however, a topical book. It is an elegant précis of Lindblom's life work; a conceptual inventory, sparing of detail. Throughout most of *The Market System**, Lindblom's dispassion is almost clinical. "I do not try to convince you," he announces, "that you should, taking everything into account, admire or deplore the market system." Even so, he convinces us to do both. "[The market system] can coordinate human behavior or activity with a range and a precision beyond that of any other system, institution, or social process. But it is a harsh and often cruel coordinator. It is both an ally and enemy of personal freedom—ally because it opens up a range of choice for each participant, but enemy because it closes off some major choices

**The Market System: What It Is How It Works, and What to Make of It* by Charles Lindblom. Yale, 2001.

that a free people could otherwise make. It destroys many mammoth historical inequalities and then introduces inequalities of its own. It achieves extraordinary efficiency because it permits participants to make precise and calculated choices. But it is grossly inefficient because of the choices it has closed off. Historically, it has supported democracy—there are no democratic nation-states except in market societies—but it has sabotaged important democratic features of ostensibly democratic states."

Hardly anyone in twenty-first-century America needs to be convinced of the market system's virtues. Lindblom need not, and does not, work up much expository momentum demonstrating them. As with people, the system's vices are more interesting. But even in the second half of the book, largely devoted to examining the market's real or alleged shortcomings, he is a stickler for historical balance and conceptual precision. For example, he suggests persuasively that urbanization, industrialization, and bureaucratization are to some extent independent of market relations and must share the blame for instrumental rationality and the degradation of work. Twentieth-century communism, if good for nothing else, at least made clear how much more than merely reforming the market system will be necessary in order to conserve the best of our pre-modern heritage.

Similarly, when discussing markets and morality, Lindblom makes a useful distinction between universal ethics and role ethics. The market system, the legal system, the state, the family, and other bounded areas of social life have special codes that modify or suspend the requirements of a universal ethic. Forgiveness is a virtue, though not necessarily for a judge

The Market System's most interesting chapters address several perennial claims, now virtually articles of faith: markets are uniquely efficient and fair; markets promote individual liberty; markets are a necessary condition of democracy. These claims are all at least plausible, as Lindblom fully acknowledges. But are they true?

Efficiency is "the relation of valued output to valued input."

Lindblom's lengthy and lucid discussion of this concept convinced me (and half-convinces him) that it is useful mainly for rhetorical purposes. "Whether an allocation is efficient depends on who is doing the evaluations, or on whose evaluations count. Consequently, there is no one allocation that is efficient—it all depends." All transactions have externalities (he calls them "spillovers"); very few of them are fully compensated or even recognized. And the market system relies extensively on supportive public policies, not all of them democratically determined (to put it mildly).

What about the price mechanism—doesn't that guarantee efficiency? Subject to the usual qualifications (information costs, unequal market power, etc.), yes. But here Lindblom introduces the notion of "prior determinations": economist-speak for the fact that people's endowments—financial, educational, and other—differ drastically, that this greatly affects market outcomes, and that these differences are in crucial respects politically determined (e.g., by the law of inheritance). But if that is true, then the claim that market outcomes are maximally fair and efficient is poppycock. They are no more fair than luck is fair. As usual, Lindblom puts it rather more circumspectly. "[In virtue of prior determinations,] market systems, wisely or foolishly, largely give up the possibility of an efficient resource allocation and pattern of production. They settle instead on inefficient allocations improved to the limited degree that voluntary transactions make improvement possible."

The relation of markets to freedom and democracy is complicated. Lindblom's treatment of it is finely balanced. Corporations are central to the market system, yet are internally unfree. Is this a contradiction? Yes and no: managerial authority is regularly abused, but even employee-owners would have to discipline themselves rigorously in response to market pressures. Can occupational choice, consumer choice, and other freedoms exist without a market system? In principle, yes: in a competently planned society, workers would presumably be hired rather than assigned and goods would be sold rather than rationed. But in practice, no: beyond a certain size, competent central planning is impossible.

Near the end of the book, however, Lindblom's dispassion comes close to melting down in the course of twenty quietly smoldering pages. What provokes him is elite manipulation of "mass" (as he calls the rest of us)—that is, advertising, public relations, and sound-bite politics. He actually becomes eloquent:

> A reasonable suspicion—to understate it—is that the messages of market elites constitute a twofold assault on the mind, the effects of which are all the more grave because government elites join in the assault. The first assault might be called distraction.... Market elite persuasion of mass is so persistent and relentless, so widespread, and so inventive in its appeals that one must ask how much room it leaves in the mind for thinking about other things—or thinking at all rather than simply reacting....
>
> The second assault is obfuscation. Politics, it is now often said, is huckstering. As for communication from the market elite on products, its mixture of emptiness, confusion, and deceit may have descended to a level below which there is not much room to drop further....
>
> If we simply look about us at both sales promotion and the political appeals of market elite to mass, especially those now in the hands of specialists in public relations, we cannot escape some fears that they are systematically undermining that respect for truth or honesty long argued to be a requirement of civilized society.

All this distraction and obfuscation, bad enough in itself, has the further effect of preventing popular challenges to elites. Lindblom calls this effect "circularity." Ideological conformity is so carefully nurtured by business and government, and critical thinking so successfully discouraged, that as a practical matter, "even in the democracies, masses are persuaded to ask from elites only what elites wish to give them."

What, then, of the historic connection between markets and democracy? "The democracy to which [the market system] is tied is a minimal or low-grade democracy rather than a highly developed one, blighted as it is by its citizens' incapacity to think. That this minimal democracy exists at all seems to owe a great deal to merchant and entrepreneurial political energies that curbed the powers of the authoritarian state before undertaking an assault on the mind that obstructs a fuller democracy. In all this we find no convincing evidence or argument that, except in the mind, the market system is necessary to democracy."

Surely these conclusions are a little eyebrow-raising, coming from the former president of the American Political Science Association? Is it too much to hope that the rest of the profession will take note?

Outgrowing All That

Everyone loves a good argument; and as we know from the dia-
logues of Plato, few questions are more likely to get an argument going than "what is justice?" In *Economic Justice**, North-
eastern University professor Stephen Nathanson addresses the
economic aspects of this perennial question.

To whittle this immense subject down to size, Nathanson
concentrates on three economic systems—libertarian or laissez-
faire capitalism, statist socialism, and the welfare state—evalu-
ating them by three criteria: productivity, desert, and liberty.
About each system he asks: "How well off does it make people?
Does it reward people in accord with what they deserve? And,
what is its impact on people's liberty?"

Productivity is capitalism's strong suit, and Nathanson
gives it full credit—as did Marx and Engels, who wrote in *The
Communist Manifesto* that "the bourgeoisie, during its rule of
scarcely a hundred years, has created more massive and colossal productive forces than all preceding generations together."
But producing wealth is not the same as producing well-being.
The latter depends at least as much on distributing wealth in
ways that maximize its happiness-producing effects (or, as
economists would say, its "marginal utility"). Severe economic
inequality has been the rule rather than the exception in capitalist societies. Is this a necessary or merely an accidental consequence of the operation of unregulated markets? And if it is a
necessary consequence, can it be justified by capitalism's overall high output?

This is (or at any rate, ought to be) the central political issue
of our day. Nathanson's treatment of it is penetrating and judicious, emphasizing exactly what needs to be emphasized. First

Economic Justice by Stephen Nathanson. Prentice Hall, 1998.

of all, he acknowledges, inequality is not *inherently* unjust. What is immoral is not that some people have too much but that other people have too little; the one is not always the cause of the other. The Soviet, Chinese, and other formerly state-socialist regimes made it a crime to be rich (actually, even moderately well off), which led, as capitalism's defenders point out, to cruelty, inefficiency, and stagnation. So a first approximation to economic justice would seem to be: a decent minimum for everyone, and then let government mind its own business.

Of course, it's not quite that simple. As Nathanson points out, the distinctively dynamic character of capitalism means that inequalities are cumulative. "The rich get richer and the poor get poorer"; "them as has, gets"; "you have to spend money to make money": these are not merely folksy sayings but rigorous and inescapable deductions. As a result, even a decent minimum for everyone will require continuing redistributive efforts by government.

A final point about inequality that Nathanson does well to stress is its effect on liberty. Defenders of capitalism correctly point out that so far, all democratic societies have been market-oriented. But it's also true that in a market-oriented society, political influence is, to some extent, available for purchase like any other commodity. Lobbying, campaign contributions, and media exposure require money, time, and skills that ordinary people don't have and that rich people and corporations can buy. This is undemocratic. Continuing government efforts will be needed to prevent economic inequality from turning into political inequality.

But, some readers will ask, doesn't justice simply mean that people ought to get what they deserve? And don't people who work harder or have more valuable skills deserve to get more than others? When faced with difficult questions, philosophers make distinctions. Nathanson distinguishes between *personal* desert, which is due our individual efforts and achievements, and *human* desert, which is due us simply in virtue of our humanity. In theory, capitalism rewards personal desert, though as Nathanson points out, many people, especially in other countries, work long hours and receive very little, while others receive a great deal through inheritance or investment income, without themselves working. And of course, rich and poor children don't personally deserve their very different life chances. The notion of human desert implies that everyone deserves enough resources to support a minimally decent life. Once this principle is granted, we can haggle over what is "minimally decent" and how much is "enough." What we can no longer do is let the devil take the hindmost—the laissez-faire solution.

Nathanson calls his preferred solution the "comprehensive welfare state." It would rely on the market and would therefore allow considerable inequality; but it would raise enough money through taxation to guarantee every citizen sufficient resources to live a life free from insecurity and acute deprivation, and it would try determinedly to curb the power of money in politics. This may not sound like a radical ideal, but although a few European countries approximate it, the United States still has a long way to go before reaching it.

I could say more in praise of *Economic Justice*, but I don't want to leave the impression that it's flawless. It is a convincing book, but not quite a compelling one. It ought to be livelier—not only because today's undergraduates, raised on television, are scarcely able to sit still for philosophical argument, but also because the case for economic justice must appeal to the heart as well as the head. After all, as Shelley wrote in *A Defense of Poetry*, "the great instrument of moral good is the imagination"—and that means stories. For the benefit of future editions of this excellent little book, I offer Stephen Nathanson an illustration from—of all places—television.

In one memorable episode of *Star Trek: The Next Generation*, the *Enterprise* encounters a derelict starship full of twentieth-century humans in suspended animation. One of them is an ace investor and dogmatic libertarian capitalist. As soon as he is revived, he demands that the *Enterprise* turn around immediately and return him to Earth, where his large fortune (compounded annually for four hundred years) awaits him. Captain Picard demurs, explaining gently that wealth and poverty, luxury and want, became obsolete on Earth long ago. In the twenty-fourth century, each person has enough resources to live a full life and no one's life is wasted.

It is Picard's *tone* that speaks across the centuries to us viewers—the same tone that an educated twentieth-century person would use in explaining to a visitor from an earlier era why, for example, we no longer burn widows or expose girl babies on mountaintops or torture captives or enslave other peoples. We have outgrown all that, we would explain patiently to our visitor; we can no longer, with a good conscience, inflict or ignore suffering on such a scale. And the still more grown-up humanity of the future, Picard seems to be saying, will consider the accumulation of vast wealth and power by some, while the lives of many others are stunted, to be equally benighted. I suspect that a great many *Star Trek* viewers were converted that evening to a belief in the comprehensive welfare state.

Zippie World

In the middle of Thomas Friedman's *The World is Flat** is a long quote that towers over the intellectual landscape of the rest of the book as a mountain towers over low hills. It is Marx and Engels' celebrated prophecy of globalization—"All that is solid melts into air"—from the *Communist Manifesto*. Friedman has apparently just discovered it and is "in awe at how incisively Marx detailed the forces that were flattening the world during the rise of the Industrial Revolution, and how much he fore-shadowed the way these same forces would keep flattening the world right up to the present."

Friedman is right to be impressed, however belatedly. After the long detour of Second- and Third-World pseudo-socialism, capitalism has resumed the path Marx and Engels foresaw: toward one wholly rationalized, seamlessly integrated world; with everything for sale; with no one and no activity exempt from the pressure of competition, the risk of obsolescence, the specter of ruin; with no rest, no external haven, no inner sanctuary. A flat world.

This second great age of globalization began, by Friedman's reckoning, on "11/9." (He means November 9, 1989, when the Berlin Wall came down.) "In the Cold War era," he explained in his bestselling *The Lexus and the Olive Tree†*, "capital could not move across borders the way it can in today's globalization system." Many national governments did not permit foreign ownership of core industries, foreign speculation in their cur-rencies, or unrestricted foreign access to their domestic mar-kets. (For "foreign" read "American.") They could get away with this because, in the pseudo-socialist bloc, people were not free

*Farrar, Straus and Giroux, 2005.
†Farrar, Straus and Giroux, 1999.

and in any case did not know what they were missing, and in the Free World the US was wary of alienating its geopolitical allies. Friedman's account of "the Cold War system" in *The Lexus and the Olive Tree* is accurate and illuminating, as far as it goes. There is no damned nonsense (or very little) about "freedom"—except for the freedom of those with a lot of capital to do anything they pleased with it. That is indeed what the Cold War was about.

The end of the Cold War has made it politically feasible, and computerization has made it technically feasible, to move capital around the world at dazzling speeds and staggering volumes without interference from any but the most determined governments. This allows large investors to buy control of a country's key resources, industries, and infrastructure, to put intense upward or downward pressure on its currency, and to influence, or even dictate, its fiscal, environmental, labor, and tax policies. These new masters of the universe, gathered around computer screens in New York, London, Frankfurt, and Tokyo, are the subject of the most memorable of Friedman's many piquant coinages, the "Electronic Herd."

What lures the Herd to graze in an economy is a favorable investment climate; or, in another charming Friedmanism, the "Golden Straitjacket." Donning the Straitjacket means low social-welfare expenditures; low or no tariffs or subsidies to protect domestic industries; no barriers to foreign ownership, currency speculation, or profit repatriation; and a flexible labor market, i.e., no unions. (If you want to know in detail what a "favorable investment climate" looks like, study the decrees of the Coalition Provisional Authority, which were designed—without consulting any non-rich Iraqis—to fit post-Saddam Iraq for the Straitjacket.) All this is bitter medicine, but salutary, according to Friedman. "Governments which deviate too far from the core rules will see their investors stampede away, interest rates rise, and stock market valuations fall. The only way to get more room to maneuver in the Golden Straitjacket is by growing it, and the only way to grow it is to keep it on tight....

The tighter you wear it, the more gold it produces and the more padding you can then put into it for your society."

Such is the canonical view of globalization. Friedman is exceptionally, exuberantly in-our-face about it, insisting that its harsh discipline is not merely a necessary evil but also fair, economically rewarding, and in fact democracy-enhancing. You can rail at the stampeding Herd for leaving your country's social safety net in tatters, your unemployment rate several points higher, and many people's life savings diminished as the currency plummets. It's no one's fault, though, but yours and your spendthrift government's. "There's no one in charge!" Friedman admonishes. Capital-attraction and capital-repulsion are neutral processes, like laws of nature.

And playing by the "core rules" will not only make your society richer; it will also make you freer. "The democratizations of technology, finance, and information," Friedman enthuses, "are at the heart of the globalization system." You can't keep your population down on the farm, politically speaking, once they're plugged into the Net. Moreover, corruption, nepotism, bureaucratic incompetence, and arbitrary power are bad for business; the rule of law, a professional civil service, accurate and accessible statistics, and a stable, legitimate government are good for business. If your society wants to prosper, it will shape up. This "revolution from beyond" Friedman calls "globalution."

The World Is Flat is an updated report from the field. Whatever one thinks of Friedman as a thinker, he's an energetic reporter and a good storyteller. His new book teems with interesting anecdotes about innovative companies, technologies, and business processes. Everyone's heard by now of the book's opening gambit: his wide-eyed tour of the call centers of Bangalore, India, where adolescents re-christened "Derek" and "Daisy" practice saying "Thirty little turtles in a bottle of bottled water" in order to communicate with Americans frantic about lost luggage or frozen computers. There's also a brief history of open-sourcing: of how Linux and Apache grew, on virtually pure anarchist principles, to become the backbone of the Internet. In counterpoint, one learns how Walmart conquered the world by becoming "the best supply-chain operator of all time," in the words of an awed business consultant.

Supply-chaining is one of the world-flattening forces that are kicking globalization up another level. Outsourcing, off-shoring, work-flow software, digitization—every new organizational and technological development tends to divide, isolate, simplify, and cheapen the production process. An old friend of Friedman's used to be an illustrator. Now, thanks to computer design programs like Quark and Photoshop, he's JAFA ("Just Another Fucking Artist"). His skills have become "vanilla"—Friedmanese for expendable, a mere commodity—so he has "transformed himself into an ideas consultant," supplying drawing concepts that are outsourced for production. This is the fate of a good half the characters who crowd Friedman's book. While unassumingly making a living, they are overtaken by labor-saving technology and turned into inexpensive vanilla ice cream. Fortunately, they somehow manage to reinvent themselves as a pricier "chocolate sauce" or "cherry topping," and the GDP continues its steady ascent.

The book's other characters include dynamic executives who are sponsoring all this outsourcing, off-shoring, and vanilla-ization. The go-go chairman of Rolls Royce Ltd. (which naturally doesn't make cars any more—too vanilla) spouts this choice bit of New Economy-speak, which greatly impresses Friedman: "We own the ability to identify and define what product is required by our customers, we own the ability to integrate the latest science into making these products, we own the route to the market for these products, and we own the ability to collect and understand the data generated by those customers using our products, enabling us to support that product while in service and constantly add value." Can you guess from that babble what Rolls Royce *does* make now?

Perhaps most impressive and intimidating are the "Zippies,"

the alpha fauna of Friedman's brave new flat world. Zippies are "the huge cohort of Indian youth who are the first to come of age since India shifted away from socialism and dived headfirst into global trade and turned itself into the world's service center." An Indian magazine calls them "Liberalization's Children," and they rule: "young city or suburban resident, between 15 and 25, with a zip in the stride. Belongs to Generation Z. Can be male or female, studying or working. Oozes attitude, ambition, and aspiration. Cool, confident, and creative. Seeks challenges, loves risks, and shuns fear ... destination-driven, outward looking, not inward, upwardly mobile, not stuck-in-my-station-in-life." An even bigger cohort of Chinese Zippies, Friedman promises, is only a few years behind them, and together they are going to blow their lazy, spoiled American contemporaries away.

It's tempting to smirk at this ad-copy prose and at the rest of Friedman's hymn to the Grand Global March of Productivity. There are serious empirical and analytical questions about it all, too. As Doug Henwood in *After the New Economy* and Eamonn Fingleton in *Unsustainable* have shown, prophecies of permanent, turbocharged, cyber-digitally-driven prosperity look pretty dubious. Real pay for most US workers, Henwood notes, is lower than in 1973; and as Fingleton points out, "with almost no exceptions, manufacturing-oriented economies have outpaced the United States in income growth" in the 1980s and 90s. And that income growth was more evenly distributed: it's highly plausible that the growth of the information economy has contributed to America's notable income inequality. In fact, virtually the only industry in which information technology has made an unquestioned and substantial contribution to productivity is financial services. And that, from society's point of view, may well be no more beneficial than gains in the gambling industry would be—of which, arguably, the capital markets deserve to be considered a part.

Bringing the blessings of capital markets to the rest of the world was one of the chief benefits of globalization in the 1990s, Friedman wrote in *Lexus*. In one of that book's most obnoxious passages he announced: "I believe globalization did us all a favor by melting down the economies of Thailand, Korea, Malaysia, Indonesia, Mexico, Russia, and Brazil in the 1990s, because it laid bare a lot of rotten practices and institutions in countries that had prematurely globalized." Apart from its callousness, this and Friedman's other comments on the Asian financial crisis of 1997–98 made clear that he had misunderstood its lessons, which are that someone *is* in charge of the Electronic Herd and the capital markets; that it's the IMF (which takes its orders from the US Treasury); and that following the IMF's prescriptions leaves countries more, not less, vulnerable to being whipsawed.

Still, Friedman is not heartless. There's a frank recognition of the pain of globalization in *Lexus*, and even the surprising statement that "you dare not be a globalizer today without being a social democrat." In *The World Is Flat* he writes: "The social contract that progressives should try to enforce between government and workers, and companies and workers, is one in which government and companies say, "We cannot guarantee you any lifetime employment. But we can guarantee you that government and companies will focus on giving you the tools to make you more lifetime-employable.'" In a flat world, "the individual worker is going to become more and more responsible for managing his or her own career, risks, and economic security, and the job of government and business is to help workers build the necessary muscles to do that."

Friedman offers three simple, sensible muscle-building proposals: portable-pension legislation, portable health insurance (with plans negotiated by government, not individual employers), and two years of government-subsidized tertiary education for everyone. (He might, if he were a bit braver and/or less fabulously wealthy himself, have emphasized that all this and much more like it could have been accomplished for a fraction of the amount wasted on the richest 1% by the Bush tax cuts.) He even has a suggestion for the anti-globalization left, whose idealism he professes to admire: form NGOs in Africa, India, and China that will "promote accountability, transparency, education, and property rights" and thus help "ensure that the poor get the infrastructure and budgets to which they are entitled." After all, the poor, too, yearn to join the flat world. "The wretched of the earth want to go to Disneyland, not to the barricades."

I wouldn't presume to badmouth Disneyland to the poor. But one may well feel a bit uneasy about the quality of life in the flat world. Thoreau is said to have replied, when informed excitedly by a mid-19th-century Thomas Friedman that Maine and Texas could now communicate by telegraph: "But what if Maine and Texas have nothing to say to each other?" History does not record Friedman-then's reply, but Friedman-now would have absolutely no idea what Thoreau was talking about. That information technology might have the effect of making life, at least in some respects, less gracious, subtle, sensuous, and profound, but instead more sterile, frenetic, shallow, and routine—there is no inkling of this in *The World Is Flat*, indeed no evidence that Friedman could even comprehend the notion.

"If you are a little too slow or too costly—in a world where the walls around your business have been removed and competition can now come from anywhere—you will be left as roadkill before you know what hit you." It sounds like the war of all against all—"turbocharged," to use one of Friedman's favorite adjectives; and the ultimate weapon, the focus of creativity, the highest achievement of this new stage of civilization is apparently … ever-newer operations-flow software, to optimize your business process. Except for those Third World NGOs, no one in the flat world seems to be doing anything of loftier significance than getting Walmart's suppliers to make deliveries just a few minutes nearer to ship-time or inventing a new radio-frequency identification microchip to track its inventory.

Well, it will be the Zippies' world, not mine. I'm sure they will be fully as cool, confident, and creative, as ambitious, aspiring, and attitudinous, as Friedman promises. I only hope they'll have enough imagination to be bored.

No Respect

Our age is hungry for accounts of inner experience—of what it feels like to have been abused, neglected, or spoiled rotten; addicted to drugs or shopping or love; a child prodigy, schizophrenic genius, gang member, or Satan worshipper. We don't seem equally interested, though, in public or collective experiences, like work and welfare. In a well-known essay a decade ago, Tom Wolfe scolded his fellow novelists for leaving the external world, especially the work world, largely unexplored in contemporary American fiction. On the nonfiction side, Barbara Ehrenreich's recent first-person report, *Nickel and Dimed*, a glimpse into the vast, dim regions of unskilled and temporary labor, is an honorable exception. The *New York Times* and many other major newspapers have a full-time fashion reporter (sometimes even a fashion desk) but not a labor correspondent.

Over the last few decades, some of the best writing on work and its discontents has been done by Richard Sennett. Formerly at New York University and now at the London School of Economics, Sennett is a protean figure: not merely a sociologist of work (and current president of the American Council on Work) but also an urban and architectural historian, an accomplished novelist, founder of the New York Institute of the Humanities, and close friend of Michel Foucault, Joseph Brodsky, Hannah Arendt, and Susan Sontag, while they were alive.

As the child of an Old Left family and a graduate student at Harvard in the late 1960s under the celebrated social theorists David Riesman and Eric Ericson, Sennett was well-equipped to plumb the social psychology of work in America and primed to uncover subtle mechanisms of capitalist exploitation. In a very influential book early in his career, *The Hidden Injuries of Class* (1972), Sennett and co-author Jonathan Cobb interviewed Boston-area blue-collar workers. It was the era of antiwar protests,

Black Power, and expanding welfare programs, and of widespread working-class reaction against those things. As thoughtful leftists, Sennett and Cobb wanted to get past Marxist clichés about "false consciousness," letting workers speak for themselves.

They spoke poignantly. The interviewees repeatedly told Sennett and Cobb that they resented the authority of those above them but did not dispute its legitimacy; that they were dissatisfied with their work but blamed themselves for not having done better in life; that they felt obliged to sacrifice themselves for their families and encourage their children to surpass them but feared thereby losing their authority and their children's respect; that they believed the only basis of dignity and self-respect was to accept responsibility for what one has done or become, yet still felt obscurely unfree or ashamed.

It's striking how little all this had to do with the traditional substance of class politics: poverty, insecurity, overwork, unsafe or degrading working conditions. Instead, the workers' complaint (at any rate, as interpreted by the interviewers) was about the quality and social significance of their work. To Sennett and Cobb, this persistent ambivalence, alternating grievance and resignation, suggested a different, more complicated kind of false consciousness. "The terrible thing about class in our society," they concluded, "is that it sets up a contest for dignity." The prevailing American ethos (or mythos) of individualism and equal opportunity "makes people feel anxious, defeated, and self-reproachful for an imperfect ability to command the respect of others." Society thus "diverts men from challenging the limits on their freedom by convincing them that they must first become legitimate, must achieve dignity on a class society's terms, in order to have the right to challenge the terms themselves." Workers of the world, unite! You have nothing to lose but your self-reproach!

By his own account, Sennett lost interest in the politics of work for two decades, partly, he has said, in reaction to the arrogance and elitism of the New Left. In recent years he has returned to the subject with a pair of books that take up his earlier themes: the effects of work on character, and the bearing of social inequality on self- and mutual respect.

The Corrosion of Character: The Personal Consequences of Work in the New Capitalism* posed some troubling questions about the leaner, meaner corporate environment of 1980s and 90s. The traditional corporate bureaucracy—layered, hierarchical, pyramid-shaped, with clearly demarcated responsibilities and lines of authority—had given way to "flat," "disaggregated," "re-engineered" (it is impossible to speak of current business practices without using jargon) organizations. Mostly, of course, this just meant firing people: either eliminating jobs or exporting them somewhere cheaper, leaving formerly high-wage, unionized employees to scramble for the low-wage, non-union service sector jobs created in great numbers during the 80s and 90s and hailed by successive Presidents as evidence of America's continuing economic vitality.

But "re-engineering" also meant a new relation to those who remained employed. Flexibility, innovation, and risk were the new management watchwords. In the age of mass production and giant industrial firms, efficiency corresponded to scale; in an age of microprocessors and information technology, efficiency is achieved by precisely targeting new market niches, quickly retooling in response to new marketing data, anticipating shifts in consumers' mood and tastes. Decision-making structures changed, as authoritative directives from above were replaced by ad hoc, project-oriented teams, "facilitated" rather than led. The function of top management was no longer to formulate policy and guide operations but to set profit targets and audit performance—in effect, to manage quarterly share prices. In this atmosphere, the older corporate virtues became obsolete. Loyalty, reliability, and institutional memory were out; youth, mobility, a smooth manipulativeness, and a Teflon-like ability to avoid being held responsible for failure were in.

*Norton, 1998.

As Sennett points out, these shifts are bound to have larger consequences. The values of the new economy—"short-term behavior, the meeting mind-set, and above all, the weakness of loyalty and commitment that mark the modern workplace"—are on a collision course with the traditional values of obligation, trustworthiness, fidelity, and devotion to professional standards. Just as surely as television has shortened our attention span and advertising has undermined our impulse control, the new "flexible" capitalism will soften our backbone and corrode our character. (Whether it contributed, for example, to the feeding frenzy among executives for stock options is an intriguing question.)

If the social psychology of work is little-explored territory, the social psychology of welfare is practically undiscovered. Sennett's new book, *Respect in a World of Inequality**, is intended as a companion volume to *Corrosion*. Part of Sennett's childhood was spent on welfare and in public housing (in the Cabrini Green project in Chicago, next to which the notoriously violent Robert Taylor Homes were later constructed). He and his mother were both exceptionally talented, so they soon escaped. But he has gone back often and thought a good deal about those he left behind. What he wants his readers to think about now is: How can those who do not escape dependence and/or whose talents are inferior nevertheless achieve self-respect? And how can the rest of us help?

In the United States, he points out, for an able-bodied, non-caretaking adult to be dependent on public support is considered shameful. Conversely, to be self-supporting is a source of pride and self-respect. Hence the (official) aim of the welfare bureaucracy: to help everyone capable of it become proudly self-supporting. In European social democracies, on the other hand, citizens without a basic income, whether able-bodied

*Norton, 2003.

or not, simply get a check in the mail. Shame and pride do not come into the picture.

Sennett sees pitfalls in both approaches. Welfare agencies cannot avoid making and enforcing judgments about what their clients need. However compassionate the former's intentions, this is, philosophically speaking, to transgress on the latter's autonomy. But a basic incomes policy, which divorces assistance from compassion, does not guarantee autonomy, only anonymity. And besides—philosophically speaking again—"impersonal caregiving is a very pessimistic view of the human condition; it supposes people are likely to do others injury by caring for and about them personally, so that the human elements of judgment and response to need should be eliminated."

I think Sennett exaggerates the importance of treating needy people sensitively and underestimates the usefulness of shoveling money at their problems. Surely—to put the matter crudely—cash without respect is better than respect without cash? How, Sennett asks, can "people in our society express respect so as to reach across the boundary of inequality"? Is this really such a difficult question? Here are three wholly unoriginal suggestions. First, roughly equalize nationwide per-pupil expenditure (not counting costly special education programs, which artificially inflate the spending levels of many poorer districts) in grades K-12. (Private schools would be included in the calculation, so that they may serve the purpose of religious or cultural or pedagogic diversity but not of unfairly privileging the children of affluent parents.) Second, guarantee comprehensive health care to all children under 18. Third, exempt the first $20,000 of income from the payroll tax, to be paid for in full by restoring the estate tax. These three simple, obvious, and expensive measures would go a long way toward producing a nation composed entirely of first-class citizens in a generation or two. In such a society there would be fewer occasions to "reach across the boundary of inequality." Also, perhaps, less need to worry about respect.

Reasons and Passions

The last three decades have been bitter medicine for the left. In the late 1970s, the achievements of the New Deal seemed secure, embraced even by Richard Nixon, the most conservative president since Herbert Hoover. Labor unions were an accepted feature of economic and political life. In the wake of Medicare and Medicaid, inaugurated in the 1960s, the path to universal health care seemed open. Nixon himself had created the Environmental Protection Agency, an important victory for the cause of governmental regulation. Jimmy Carter acknowledged that the corporate-loophole-ridden tax code was a "disgrace" and promised to make human rights the "soul" of American foreign policy. Despite much unhappiness over busing and *Roe v. Wade*, the feminist and civil-rights movements appeared triumphant.

Thirty-something years later ... well, there's no need to call the dreary roll of reverses. In policy and opinion, the country's political center of gravity has shifted far to the right. How has it happened?

Jonathan Haidt's fascinating, important, and exasperating new book* offers one set of answers. A social psychologist at the University of Virginia and a professed liberal Democrat, Haidt was dismayed by liberalism's eclipse. Seeking to understand it, he proposes a new, or at any rate newly formulated, theory of our moral and political judgments, called Moral Foundations Theory.

As we all know and often forget, humans are not purely rational. Or, to put it another way, there's more to rationality than is dreamed of in our everyday philosophies. We have

The Righteous Mind: Why Good People Are Divided by Politics and Religion by Jonathan Haidt. Pantheon, 419 pages, $28.95.

a long, complex evolutionary history, which has left us with a tangled, multilayered psyche and many more motives than we are usually conscious of. With the help of research by a couple of generations of psychologists, anthropologists, and behavioral economists, Haidt has excavated these psychic structures. But before entering on a detailed description, Haidt pauses to emphasize the First Principle of any adequate moral psychology: "Intuitions come first, strategic reasoning second."

Experiments repeatedly show that—to oversimplify only a little—we all believe what we want, regardless of reasons. This certainly tallies with my, and many other liberals', experience of political debate. Changing one's views in response to an opponent's arguments is about as rare as an honest Congressman. (Cases of both are known, but only a few.) Arguments are largely instrumental; they are meant for attack or defense. Most of the time, we argue like lawyers rather than philosophers. Hume was right: "Reason is and ought only to be the slave of the passions, and can never pretend to any other office than to serve and obey them."

Where, then, do our moral judgments come from? According to Moral Foundations Theory, morality begins as a set of evolution-derived intuitions, which each child then learns to apply within his or her culture. Haidt suggests six dimensions or categories or foundations, into which nearly all our intuitions fall: 1) Help those in need and minimize suffering everywhere (the Care/Harm foundation); 2) Reward people according to what they contribute (Fairness/Cheating); 3) Advance the fortunes of your group (Loyalty/Betrayal); 4) Defer to legitimate superiors and protect subordinates (Authority/Subversion); 5) Resist domination by illegitimate authority (Liberty/Oppression); 6) Respect your group's totems and taboos (Sanctity/Degradation).

By Haidt's reckoning, liberals focus too narrowly on the first and a special version of the second foundation. Compassion is the supreme liberal virtue, supplemented by egalitarianism, which relies on a view of contributing that emphasizes effort rather than output. Because it is individuals who suffer and need, liberalism is individualistic.

Conservatives, by contrast, have a more balanced moral matrix, resting more equally on the six foundations. The details of that argument rest to a considerable extent on questionnaires and psychology-lab experiments, but Haidt's main conclusion is overwhelmingly plausible: conservatives are less attuned to individual freedom and fulfillment, more sensitive to and concerned about the cohesiveness and stability of groups. They are instinctive Durkheimians, agreeing with the great French sociologist that every society is unified by sacred, unchallengeable beliefs, and that "to free man from all social pressures is to abandon and demoralize him." Even before "social capital" became a social-scientific buzzword, conservatives understood that communities are fragile and require continual shoring up, sometimes at the expense of individual welfare. "If you are trying to change an organization or a society and you do not consider the effects of your changes on moral capital, you're asking for trouble. This," Haidt affirms, "is the fundamental blind spot of the left." Where liberals see individuals in need, conservatives see social structures at risk.

"Republicans understand moral psychology; Democrats don't," Haidt announces in italics.

> Republicans trigger the full range of intuitions described by Moral Foundations Theory. Like Democrats, they can talk about innocent victims (of harmful Democratic policies) and about fairness (particularly the unfairness of taking tax money from hardworking and prudent people to support cheaters, slackers, and irresponsible fools). But Republicans since Nixon have had a near-monopoly on appeals to loyalty (particularly patriotism and the military virtues) and authority (including respect for parents, teachers, elders, and the police, as well as for traditions). And after they embraced Christian conservatives during Ronald Reagan's 1980 campaign and became the party of "family values," Republicans inherited a powerful network of Christian ideas about sanctity and sexuality that allowed them to portray Democrats as the party of Sodom and Gomorrah. Set against the rising crime and chaos of the 1960s and

1970s, this five-foundation morality [he hadn't yet gotten around to introducing the sixth one—GS] had wide appeal, even to many Democrats.

Some of this has been said before (eg, by George Lakoff), though not so systematically or with so large a background of experimental data and evolutionary theory. What should we make of it? What is true and valuable, in the first place, is the reminder that every utterance is the tip of an iceberg, merely the surface layer of a deep linguistic (Wittgenstein) or psychic (Freud) substrate. To understand someone, even for conversational purposes—much less persuade him or her—takes a lot of patient, skillful work. Of course every non-autistic adult recognizes this to some degree; but most of us, most of the time, to an inadequate degree.

So, for example, an opinion about immigration or the Affordable Care Act may have little to do with that issue or that law and much more to do with the speaker's feeling about his/her interlocutor, or about which group or tribe the opinion associates one with. In that case, facts and reasoning about policy will only get the discussants so far. They must either go deeper, baring their fundamental commitments and identifications to each other, or else save their breath.

How, then, do minds ever change? They rarely do, it appears. "Whether you end up on the right or the left of the political spectrum turns out to be just as heritable as most other traits: genetics explains between a third and a half of the variability among people on their political attitudes. Being raised in a liberal or conservative household accounts for much less." Presumably political campaigns, discussions with friends and co-workers, television programs, books and articles, and even one's education, account for still less.

Are society-wide misunderstanding and mistrust inevitable? Haidt's practical recommendations for avoiding them are not robust. "I believe that psychologists must work with political scientists to identify changes that will undermine

Manichaeism." That should at least attract some foundation funding for psychologists and political scientists. Beyond that, he can only suggest that perhaps if Congressional families all lived in Washington DC and their children played sports together, Congressional Republicans and Democrats might be less polarized.

For secular rationalists (i.e., most politically active liberals and leftists), all this is discouraging. But we get no sympathy from Haidt, who scourges the "rationalist delusion": the idea that "reasoning is our most noble attribute," which usually goes along with "a claim that the rational caste (philosophers or scientists) should have more power" as well as "a utopian program for raising more rational children." We had better reconcile ourselves to religion, Haidt advises—he deplores the New Atheism—and if possible, even join one. Lack of belief is no problem: "it is religious belongingness that matters for [social capital]," he approvingly quotes from a scholarly study, "not religious believing."

Truth or falsity is beside the point for Haidt; the social benefits of religion are too great to allow for quibbling on that score. Religions "help groups to cohere, solve free rider problems, and win the competition for group-level survival"; and they make individuals "less selfish and more loving." Gods and religions are "tools that let people bind themselves together," or in the language of evolutionary psychology, "group-level adaptations for producing cohesiveness and trust." The data strongly suggest, Haidt claims, that religious people are happier, more generous, more productive, and better behaved than the non-religious.

At the very least, unbelievers should keep their skepticism to themselves. "Asking people to give up all forms of sacralized belonging and live in a world of purely 'rational' beliefs might be like asking people to give up the Earth and live in colonies orbiting the moon. It can be done, but it would take a great deal of careful engineering, and even after ten generations, the descendants of those colonists might find themselves with inchoate longings for gravity and greenery." Like the serpent in

Eden, reason promises a brave new world but can only bring homelessness and exile.

The Righteous Mind is an easy book for a defensive liberal rationalist to ridicule. Haidt clearly knows a thing or two about moral psychology and political rhetoric, but apparently very little about current affairs or political economy. For one thing, the recent political polarization he laments is of a peculiar sort: there is only one pole. Since the Republican capture of Congress in 1994, and even before, the Republican side has been characterized by relentless, take-no-prisoners partisanship; the Democratic side by disunity, vacillation, surrender. This is the fundamental fact of recent American political history, and Haidt shows no awareness of it.

For another thing, though some of their electoral success may well result from the fact that "Republicans understand moral psychology; Democrats don't," it's also true—a regrettably partisan point, but it must be made—that Republicans cheat a lot. The Nixon campaign attempted to forestall a peace agreement in October 1968 that might have elected Hubert Humphrey. The Reagan campaign attempted to delay the release of the hostages until Jimmy Carter had left office. A Republican Supreme Court awarded the presidency to George W. Bush in 2000. The Swift Boat campaign against John Kerry in 2004, financed by Republican donors, was based on lies, while the CBS *60 Minutes* report alleging George Bush's evasion of National Guard duty was substantially true, despite a firestorm of successful Republican denial. Lee Atwater's and Karl Rove's dirty tricks are too numerous to catalogue. Currently Republicans across the country are busy with voter-suppression efforts, under the deceitful pretense of combating vote fraud. No doubt the Democrats are hardly political innocents; but compared with the Republicans, they are hapless pikers. Yet oddly, the Republicans' godly supporters do not object to this ungodly behavior.

There are also deeper, less obvious objections to Haidt's critique of liberal hyper-rationalism. Minds *sometimes* change; the voice of reason, though small and soft, as Freud pointed out, does eventually get a hearing. Mightn't it be fruitful to ask how this can happen rather than assuming, as Haidt does, that it hardly ever will? Mightn't there be some material conditions in which rationality is not invincibly more difficult than unthinking allegiance, and in which cooperative inquiry seems as natural as strategic reasoning?

Strategic reasoning is, as Haidt emphasizes, a mechanism of inter-group competition; and competition is premised on insecurity. Universal radical insecurity—the inevitable and intended result of "flexible labor markets" and "minimal government"— is not conducive to imaginative receptivity or disinterested reflection. Upton Sinclair famously observed that it is all but impossible to get a man to understand something when his salary depends on his not understanding it. The same goes for his tax breaks, regulatory exemptions, government contracts, and other matters on which a man's survival, or his accustomed lifestyle, may depend. When the middle class is shrinking and one person in four or five is below, at, or not far from poverty level, most people will hunker down, not open up. Some degree of competition, insecurity, and inequality will probably always be necessary. But the price of our present degree of those things is a lessened ability to reason together about difficult matters.

Another, equally pervasive condition of contemporary life also handicaps collective rationality. Tellingly, nearly all the data Haidt refers to seems to be derived from brief interactions: lab experiments, interviews, questionnaires. There is rarely any occasion for prolonged reflection and relaxed discursiveness in these circumstances, any more than there is on radio and TV talk shows, where the average response is only seconds long and thoughtful pauses are disparaged by the producers as "dead air." Newspaper opinion pieces rarely exceed 700 words. Naturally readers and listeners fall back on preset attitudes and received opinions.

Moreover, we are all increasingly hyperstimulated. The sheer volume of commercial messages, entertainment, and social media makes some inner compensation necessary, so we double down on our inner stabilizers, otherwise known as prejudices. Deep experiences of any kind—grappling with art or philosophy, having one's mind changed about politics, or simply possessing one's soul—require a modicum of silence, slowness, and solitude. For most Americans, that modicum is vanishing.

For secular liberals, the message of Haidt's book is a sobering one: achieving large-scale trust, comity, and mutual aid is hard, very hard. Though it has sometimes been done in the past, secular liberals are barred from using the old methods. We want bonds, we want limits, we want authority; but we don't want illusions. The will of God, the infallibility of Scripture, and the divine right of husbands and fathers seem to us illusions. Even "my country right or wrong" is an illusion if it means, as it frequently does in the mouths of false patriots, "my country can do no wrong." We can't accept these illusions, and we can't ask others to accept them—even if it will make them better behaved—though of course we must live with, and compromise with, people who think otherwise.

But we also owe it to conservatives—and to ourselves—to devise ways of promoting stability and solidarity that don't rely on illusions. Here liberals have indeed failed, though the three centuries since the Enlightenment are hardly a great deal of time in which to resolve the immemorial tensions between reason and instinct or individual and group. Perhaps the best we can do for now is to point out, patiently, persistently, and with as much love for our equally stubborn fellow citizens as we can muster, that some social arrangements make it harder to hear one another.

Copywrongs

In the spring of 1993, when the Chicago Bulls were charging toward their third straight NBA championship, a television announcer mentioned that Los Angeles/New York/Miami head coach Pat Riley was attempting to copyright the phrase "three-peat." If he succeeded, the announcer reported matter-of-factly, then every time an employee said it on the air, the network would have to pay Riley a royalty. This was my introduction to the brave new world of intellectual property law, in which every cultural "product"—every image, every insight, every flicker of wit—would become private rather than common property.

In *Code and Other Laws of Cyberspace* (1999), Lawrence Lessig illustrated this looming iron cage of commercial rationality with reference to the mother of all cultural transactions: buying a book. Today, he pointed out, once you have bought a book you are free to use it pretty much as you please. You can read it once or several times, lend or give it away, photocopy or scan it, write a review of it, sell it, read it aloud to your children, use it as decoration, or throw it across the room. Some of these uses (e.g., reselling it) are guaranteed by statute, but most are simply too difficult to regulate. The "transaction costs" of enforcing any restrictions on them would be prohibitive.

But suppose a new technology drastically reduced these transaction costs. This new technology would allow a purchase agreement to specify "whether you could read the book once or one hundred times; whether you could cut and paste from it or simply read it without copying; whether you could send it as an attached document to a friend or simply keep it on your machine; whether you could delete it or not; whether you could use it in another work, for another purpose, or not; whether you could simply have it on your shelf or have it and use it as well." These restrictions would be enforceable thanks to features of the book's new format that could at virtually no cost monitor, and then either charge for or block, every imaginable use. Similar features would protect CDs, videos, Websites, databases, and anything else that is encoded or transmitted digitally. (As you have probably guessed, "digital" is the name of the new technology.)

Why is this disturbing? One could answer that question from a variety of standpoints. As a matter of justice, one may consider the present, freewheeling World Wide Web analogous to the public library and broadcasting systems, which at least in principle foster social equality by making cultural resources available on equal terms to the rich and non-rich. Or one may borrow Cass Sunstein's perspective in *Republic.com* and worry that ever more particularized consumption decisions will increase cultural fragmentation. One may also feel—unless one is satisfied with the strength of the social fabric, or unless one knows a way to increase the number of hours in a day—that inducing Americans to spend still more time in front of flickering screens calibrating our consumption bundles ever more precisely is not worth distracting us still further from being adequate parents, spouses, neighbors, and citizens, as well as readers, sandlot athletes, hobbyists, and tinkerers. One may even feel slightly uneasy on the score of privacy, since a technology that will meter our every use of every copyrighted cultural product will reveal an awful lot about us to whoever can access it.

None of these is Lessig's chief concern. Whatever other harm the new law of intellectual property will do everyone who is not a shareholder of large media and software companies, it will also, he warns, kill off the remarkable creativity associated with the pre-commercial Internet. "Explosion," "revolution," "transformation," etc., etc.—we are all good and tired of the hype. Nonetheless, it has been quite a ride. New ways of connecting to the Net, communicating across the Net, and perhaps most important, distributing art, ideas, and information across the Net were, in its heroic early phase, devised at an amazing rate.

By and large, this was not done for profit. The GNU/Linux operating system, the Apache server, the PERL programming language, the BIND (Berkeley Internet Name Domain) system, the "sendmail" program, and the protocols of the World Wide Web—"these projects," Lessig writes, "together constitute the soul of the Internet." All of them are "open code" projects. That is, the code in which they are written is unowned or is governed by a General Public License, which allows anyone to modify the code, provided he or she makes those modifications available free to everyone else. The code that enables the Internet is thus common property. It is, to use a traditional term that Lessig adapts to cyberspace with extraordinary rigor and originality, a "commons."

A commons is a resource that is available to everyone (or in some cases, everyone in the relevant community) without permission. The term will be familiar to many readers from Garrett Hardin's well-known argument about the "tragedy of the commons." To take Hardin's example: if a pasture is held in common, the benefits of adding to one's herd will accrue to oneself, while the costs will be shared. The result is overgrazing and a ruined pasture. The solution is exclusive property rights.

This little parable has played a large part in forming contemporary intuitions about political economy. The belief that private control almost invariably produces the most efficient use of scarce resources is part of the common sense of market societies and is regularly invoked in order to oppose state regulation or public ownership. But as Lessig and other dissenting law professors (as well as media studies professor Siva Vaidhyanathan in *Copyrights and Copywrongs**) point out, this maxim does not apply straightforwardly to intellectual resources.

Pasture is what economists call a "rivalrous" resource. One person's (or cow's) consumption leaves less for others. English and American literature is a non-rivalrous resource.

*Siva Vaidhyanathan, *Copyrights and Copywrongs: The Rise of Intellectual Property and How It Threatens Creativity*. New York University Press, 2001.

One person's consumption leaves no less for others. Rivalrous resources can be depleted; non-rivalrous resources cannot. It follows that, from the point of view of efficiency, different kinds of property rights should govern the two kinds of resources. In Lessig's formulation: "If the resource if rivalrous, then a system of control is needed to assure that the resource is not depleted—which means the system must assure that the resource is both *produced* and not *overused*. If the resource is non-rivalrous, then a system of control is needed simply to *assure that the resource is created....* Once it is created, there is no danger that the resource will be depleted. By definition, a non-rivalrous resource cannot be used up."

With a non-rivalrous resource, one can have a commons without the tragedy. In *Code* and *The Future of Ideas**, Lessig shows at great length that the pre-commercial Internet was the site of much rapid and fruitful innovation precisely because it was a commons. And he shows at even greater length that the evolution of intellectual property law, driven by corporate leviathans and their lawyer-gnomes and articulated by free-market ideologues on the judicial bench, is drastically changing the open character of the Internet, enclosing the commons.

The Internet originated as a network connecting computers engaged in military research. A couple of decades later, researchers at a European physics laboratory invented hypertext, the basis of the World Wide Web. Both the Net and the Web employed "end-to-end" architecture. Between the edges, or ends, of the network (i.e., individual users) was a simple, neutral data transport system that would run whatever new applications were programmed in at the ends. This meant that anyone could invent and distribute new applications or modify existing ones. And a great many people did.

This "architecture of freedom" guaranteed progress but not profits. So, as the Internet gradually migrates onto a new

*Lawrence Lessig, *The Future of Ideas: The Fate of the Commons in a Connected World*. Random House, 2001.

physical structure—broadband—large, vertically integrated companies like AOL-Time Warner are moving to substitute an architecture of control, "layering onto the original code layer of the Internet new technologies that facilitate greater discrimination, and hence control, over the content and applications that can run on the Net." Only Federal regulation can preserve the remarkable "innovation environment" of the early Internet. Alas, it won't happen.

Lessig tells similar stories—all of them detailed, illuminating, and depressing—about the cable TV, music, film, publishing, and software industries. In each case, new modes of creation and distribution enabled by the Internet threaten the market share of big players. The behemoths respond by "locking up" their products with encryption software, requiring users to sign away even traditionally protected rights of "fair use," using their ownership of parts of supply and distribution networks to marginalize potential competitors, or simply threatening newcomers with ruinously expensive lawsuits. The courts (by now most federal judges are Reagan/Bush appointees), forgetting to balance private claims against the public interest, give the behemoths what they want. Legislators, intensively lobbied and campaign-funded, also give the behemoths what they want.

This shrinking of the public domain is not at all what the Founders had in mind. Constitutionally speaking, intellectual property is not like other property. The copyright and patent clause in section 8 says: "The Congress shall have Power ... to promote the Progress of Science and useful Arts, by securing for limited Times to Authors and Inventors the exclusive Right to their respective writings and Discoveries." It is clear, as Lessig and Vaidhyanathan show, that the Founders did not intend authorship to confer unlimited ownership rights. Not only did they say so (viz., "for limited Times," which was understood by Congress and the courts until a few decades ago to mean "for limited times"), but they said why. Unlimited exclusive control would stifle progress. The purpose of copyright is to promote innovation; the proper goal of copyright law is to strike a balance between rewarding achievement and facilitating more achievement.

Being sensible and cultivated persons and not Chicago School economists, the Founders recognized that "Science and useful Arts" are to some extent a gift economy. Gratitude, the pleasure of discovery, the impulse to self-expression, and devotion to a common enterprise motivate creators quite as much as lucre. Of course everyone needs to make a living, but the real point is to keep the tune flowing, the conversation humming, the gift in motion. Poets, jazz musicians, filmmakers, physicists, and coders know this. It's not their fault (and it's not for their benefit) that the balance has been lost—that, as Lessig laments, "the ability to propertize culture in America is [now] essentially unlimited ... even though the plain text of the Constitution speaks volumes against such expansive control."

Said Vaidhyanathan's *Copyrights and Copywrongs* covers much of the same ground as *The Future of Ideas*, with more attention to history and sociology, less to technology or legal and political theory. Three chapters on the history of copyright in literature, film, and music (this last with fascinating material on blues and rap) are framed by two analytical chapters, one surveying the common-law roots and constitutional meanings of copyright, the other assessing the likely cultural consequences of the revolution in intellectual property law. Smoothly written and equable in tone, it makes a valuable supplement to Lessig's brilliant but slightly hectic exposition.

"A republic, if you can keep it," Benjamin Franklin is said to have answered someone in the crowd outside Independence Hall who asked what the deliberations inside had produced. We've done an indifferent job, as Christopher Lasch, Walter Karp, Robert Wiebe, and other citizen-scholars have reminded us. An important feature of that republic was a culture of innovation, made possible by laws that found a reasonable balance between commerce and creativity. This feature, like the culture of deliberation that briefly flourished in the early Republic, is being eroded by the pressures of competition and concentration. Lessig himself, as skeptical as Franklin, doubts that these pressures will be successfully resisted in the long run. But at least, thanks to *Code* and *The Future of Ideas, Copyrights and Copywrongs*, Sunstein's *Republic.com*, and the writings of David Shenk, Sven Birkerts, and a few others, we need not be herded altogether passively into the global cyber-playpen.

In Literacy We Trust

Probably every reader of this book has encountered that stirring pronouncement by Thomas Jefferson: "Were it left to me to decide whether we should have a government without newspapers, or newspapers without a government, I should not hesitate for a moment to prefer the latter." Not many people, however, know the sentence immediately following: "But I should mean that every man should receive those papers and be capable of reading them." Nowadays freedom of the press is not in imminent danger (at least not from the government; concentration of ownership is another, and very serious, matter). But less of the populace, arguably, now reads substantive, intellectually demanding newspapers than a hundred or even two hundred years ago.

Nor do "substantive" and "intellectually demanding" describe contemporary electoral politics. Commenting on the Lincoln/Douglas debates, Christopher Lasch wrote: "By current standards, Lincoln and Douglas broke every rule of political discourse. They subjected their audiences (which were as large as fifteen thousand on one occasion) to a painstaking analysis of complex issues. They spoke with considerably more candor ... than politicians think prudent today. They took clear positions from which it was difficult to retreat. They conducted themselves as if political leadership carried with it the obligation to instead of merely getting elected." Comparison with present-day debates between political candidates is, to put it mildly, unflattering to us.

How did we become a nation of political illiterates? Part of the answer is to be found in the work of Lasch and other historians such as Robert Wiebe and Jackson Lears, who have traced the effects of mass production and political centralization on American character and culture. Another compelling line of explanation emerges from the analysis of mass culture by Neil Postman, Todd Gitlin, Mark Crispin Miller, and others.

And then there are the schools. The following anecdotal report (cited by E. D. Hirsch in *Cultural Literacy: What Every American Needs to Know**) can stand for innumerable others. A pollster who conducted frequent focus groups among Los Angeles teenagers in the early 1980s observed: "I have not yet found one single student in Los Angeles, in either college or high school, who could tell me the years when World War II was fought. Nor have I found one who could tell me the years when World War I was fought. Nor have I found one who knew when the American Civil War was fought.... Only two could even approximately identify Thomas Jefferson. Only one could place the date of the Declaration of Independence. None could name even one of the first ten amendments to the Constitution or connect them with the Bill of Rights.... On and on it went." Egad. What will political debates be like in 2050?

Ignorant and uncurious students become incompetent, economically insecure workers and passive, gullible voters (or, more often, nonvoters). On this all educational reformers can agree. What is to be done? In *Cultural Literacy*, and more recently in *The Schools We Need and Why We Don't Have Them†* Hirsch, a professor of English at the University of Virginia, broached the seemingly modest and uncontroversial notion that "a mastery of national culture is essential to the mastery of the standard language in every modern nation." That is, without knowing a great many particular—perhaps even specifiable—facts that most other English-speaking people also know, one cannot effectively speak (or read or write) English.

This proposition did not, of course, turn out to be uncontroversial. The venerable distinction, long enshrined in pedagogical theory, between skill and content, between "knowing how" and "knowing that," was put in question. The assumption that

*Houghton Mifflin, 1987.
†Doubleday, 1996

reading, writing, "critical thinking," "problem-solving," "creativity," and so on are discrete, content-neutral skills, capable of being transferred from one subject-matter to another, has been central to American educational philosophy since Dewey. In "Lectures on the Philosophy of Education" (1899) Dewey wrote:

> I do not wish to make a plea for ignorance, but the amount of information that a person requires in existing society is comparatively a small thing. The necessary amount of training, of control of his powers, of judgment, observation, and action is very great, but any person who has got that control can ... get on with a comparatively small amount of actual information. When we give up the encyclopedia or dictionary ideal of education and substitute for it the ideal of growth ... it will mean a revolution in the present educational ideals and practices.

And so it did. The "ideal of growth," based on an organic conception of human nature derived from the European Romantics and American Transcendentalists, and the belief that a child's formal abilities, or "control of his powers," preceded and enabled the acquiring of mere "information," together constituted educational "progressivism." In the hands of Dewey's crusading colleagues at Teachers College, Columbia, it swept the field.

Part of its attraction was its apparently close fit with the ethos of American democratic individualism. There seemed a whiff of collectivism and authoritarianism—not to mention Mr. Gradgrind—about the insistence that all children should learn certain facts in a certain order, presumably determined by some remote bureaucracy. The educational progressives believed that every child has unique capacities and must learn at his or her own pace, free of regimentation and coercion, and that self-directing elementary school students would grow up into self-directing citizens. All this seemed axiomatic, and what's more, downright American.

Hirsch demurs. In the first place, on empirical grounds: the research results are in and the evidence is undeniable that American schoolchildren perform poorly on language and mathematics tests compared with children in other developed nations, most of which have more standardized, content-oriented curricula than we do. No one, in fact, does deny this; it is Hirsch's conclusions that evoke furious rebuttals. Briefly, he proposes that every school have explicit content requirements for each grade (K–12) and that schools make these available to parents. No child can advance without meeting those requirements, and every child will get all the compensatory help that is needed. Even more specifically and emphatically: "Because of the sensitivity of academic progress to early conditions, this single, attainable goal—every child reading at grade level by the end of first or second grade—would do more than any other single reform to improve the quality and equity of American schooling."

What's so controversial about that? Perhaps it's the specter of objectivity—the assumption that academic achievement is significantly measurable; or of elitism—the assumption that some kinds of knowledge are more important than other kinds. In any case, the opposition comes mainly from professors and administrators. As Hirsch repeatedly points out (and as Jonathan Kozol noted in *Savage Inequalities**), most poor, working-class, and minority parents favor traditional, content-based curricula over the progressive, "process"-based variety. And they're not dupes; on the contrary, they appear to understand that—as Hirsch continually emphasizes—the children of affluent, educated parents will absorb at home far more of the background knowledge necessary for cultural literacy than their less advantaged peers. Ineffective public education not only isn't (in Horace Mann's hallowed phrase) a "great equalizer"; it actually amplifies inequality.

Still, what about freedom and individuality? Doesn't standardization inevitably promote conformism? Doesn't an emphasis on authority and discipline in the curriculum send children the wrong message, even if only subliminally, about

*HarperPerennial, 1992.

the importance of autonomy and initiative? Culturally literate robots are not, after all, democratic citizens.

Hirsch has an answer to these objections. "Children can express individuality only in relation to the traditions of their society, which they have to learn. The greatest human individuality is developed in response to a tradition, not in response to a disorderly, uncertain, and fragmented education. Americans in their teens and twenties who were brought up under individualistic theories are not less conventional than their predecessors, only less literate, less able to express their individuality."

Hirsch's point can be generalized, it seems to me. Freedom has value, indeed has meaning, only in relation to constraint. We are our constraints: The limitations (i.e., capacities) imposed by infantile dependence, territoriality, scarcity, and mortality among them define human nature. Human development is determinate: first identification, then differentiation. Early, intense local identifications—with particular persons, objects, places, stories, rites, creeds—are our core. Personality, like puberty, comes later, in evolutionary sequence, and had better not be rushed.

Progressive educational theory, for all its benefits, has neglected the tragic aspect of freedom. Psychological freedom requires the gradual mastery of terrifying fantasies about internalized omnipotent adults. Intellectual freedom requires gradual emancipation from inherited religious and political myths. In both cases, eliminating these painful struggles against the constraints of socialization also eliminates the possibility of depth, emotional or imaginative. Mature freedom and individuality are the result of successfully waging these unavoidable conflicts. There are no shortcuts.

Here is another tragic fact, perhaps even more relevant to the debate over educational reform: Money is the root of all good. Hirsch's program, if he is serious—as I believe he is—about bringing all disadvantaged children up to grade level, cannot work on the cheap (a fact that has apparently eluded Secretary of Education William Bennett, whose opportunistic support cost Hirsch so much liberal good will). "It will be a great day," the old New Left slogan went, "when the schools have all the money they need and the Air Force has to hold a bake sale to pay for a new bomber." Perhaps traditionalists and progressives can agree on this, at least.

Republic or Empire?

A future historian comparing America in 1945 with America in the second decade of the twenty-first century might well conclude that the intervening epoch—the "American Century," in period-speak—had been a real bender. From globe-bestriding colossus, producing 50 percent of world output, fully employed, militarily unrivalled, financially prepotent, culturally vibrant, internationally admired, even beloved, to a banana republic, indebted up to the eyeballs, with an obscenely rich upper class, a corrupt and mediocre political class, an unorganized and insecure workforce, one in six adults un- or underemployed, one in six citizens uninsured, one in four children living at or near the poverty line, plummeting rates of scholastic achievement, and, among developed nations, the lowest rate of social mobility, the lowest life expectancy, the highest rates of infant mortality, obesity, and mental illness, the highest homicide rate, and the highest incarceration rate. Among non-Americans, love for the United States– as distinguished from a desperate desire to escape even worse circumstances by emigrating here—is scarce indeed

How did we blow it? The best explanation I know of is Robert Kuttner's *The Squandering of America* (2007), a sure-handed, many-faceted account of the political economy of our decline. Morris Berman's *Dark Ages America* (2006) and *Why America Failed* (2011) set the story in the larger, quasi-Spenglerian context of a narrative about instrumental rationality and possessive individualism. It will soon, no doubt, be a crowded genre. An early and, one may hope, influential entry is *The Short American Century*, a rich and various collection by eight leading historians and political scientists, assembled and introduced by the prominent analyst and critic Andrew Bacevich.*

In February 1941 Henry Luce, the master huckster of mid-century America, published an instantly famous essay in his shiny new magazine, *Life*, entitled "The American Century." His immediate purpose was to enlist the United States in World War II. More generally, he exhorted his countrymen to stop minding their own business and assume the burdens and glories of world leadership. Because of its surpassing power and virtue, the United States was the indispensable nation, Luce proclaimed, many decades before the hapless Madeleine Albright actually coined that unfortunate phrase. As the "inheritors of all the great principles of Western civilization—above all Justice, the love of Truth, the ideal of Charity," Americans had a duty and an obligation to exert our influence "for such purposes as we see fit and by such means as we see fit." We must create a "vital international economy" and an "international moral order." There was no need to obtain the consent of the rest of the world, since "what we want will be okay with them."

In retrospect it is easy to mock this compendium of breezy fatuities (faithfully echoed, with far less excuse than one can find for Luce, in the 1997 founding manifesto of the Project for a New American Century). But the contributors to *The Short American Century* take Luce's essay with proper seriousness, as a template for post-World War II planning and policy. What Luce provided policymakers and pundits was a splendid lesson in how to cloak selfish and partisan goals in moralizing and universalistic rhetoric. Though hypocrisy of this sort was already a specialty of American diplomacy, Luce's background as the child of Protestant missionaries in China lent his exhortations an extra evangelical fervor. And as impresario-in-chief of the Good Life, bringing Americans monthly bulletins from the brave new worlds of automobiles, home furnishings, movies, cosmetics, and fashion, Luce saw that American consumer

The Short American Century: A Postmortem, edited by Andrew Bacevich. Harvard University Press, 287 pp. $25.95.

culture and mass entertainment could win friends and influence people abroad.

As Emily Rosenberg's essay, "Consuming the American Century," points out, exporting consumerism was an essential part of Cold War strategy. "Export expansion meshed neatly with the new global battle against Communism." The State Department arranged global distribution for "Advertising: A New Weapon in the World Wide Fight for Freedom," helpfully produced by the Advertising Council. It was not merely a matter of competing for prestige against Soviet-style societies or of luring Third World populations with capitalism's kitchen appliances and TV shows away from the less glamorous progress in mass literacy, public health, and heavy industry promised by state-led development. It was even more important to create markets in the developed countries for the vastly expanded productive capacity with which America emerged from World War II. Without such new markets, a return to prewar economic stagnation was widely feared in government and business circles.

The strategy worked all too well. The "globalized culture of consumption" took root above all in the United States. "From being the world's principal producers, Americans became its central consumers. An open-trading world and global advertising expertise that had once provided American *producers* with an antidote to fears about inadequate markets now presented American *consumers* with access to cheap, attractively promoted goods made beyond their shores." The once-mighty American "empire of production," hungry for export markets, became an "empire of consumption," hungry for inexpensive goods produced abroad, frequently by American manufacturers using low-wage Third World labor. The result was a catastrophic growth in Americans' indebtedness, along with robust profits for American multinational corporations. As Bacevich observes, it is long past time for a national debate about "whether the hedonistic, consumer-oriented definition of freedom" that America has preached and practiced is "sustainable or even desirable."

The ambitions and illusions that motivated the American Century had deep roots in American history, and Eugene McCarraher's witty essay, "The Heavenly City of Business," sets out to excavate them. The "eschatology of corporate business," he writes, has "long been central to American identity." From the Puritans to the early-19th-century "prophets of prosperity" to the Social Darwinists and their Christian counterparts to the Progressive imperialists from Theodore Roosevelt to Walter Lippmann, Henry Luce's predecessors in every generation had urged Americans to make use of their "pecuniary and moral power to evangelize the world." Tocqueville's *Democracy in America* is full of astonished remarks about Americans' distinctive combination of cupidity and self-righteousness; Melville's *The Confidence-Man* was a *Heart of Darkness* of America's merciless expansion. A brief, savage reprise of the writings and doings of Thomas Friedman, Newt Gingrich, Alvin Toffler, and others brings McCarraher's "imperial trajectory of techno-eschatology" full circle. The short American Century was, it seems, at least three centuries in the making.

There are other essays in this collection with a primarily domestic focus: Nikhil Pal Singh on the "unfinished dialectic of color and democracy" that "continues to distort and undermine the development of an ethical relationship to the wider world" and Akira Iriye on "transnationalism," or the evolution of "non-state, non-national" identities, communities, and organizations in the US and other developed nations. But the main purpose of *The Short American Century* is to revise common—largely triumphal—understandings of the Cold War and American hegemony.

Walter LaFeber has done a great deal to challenge this received wisdom, and his "Illusions of an American Century" is a blisteringly alternative reading of postwar history. The American Century was born in anxiety rather than overweening confidence, LaFeber claims. "Fear, not Henry Luce's optimism, forged the … Cold War consensus": fear of renewed economic collapse; fear of Communist political victories in Europe; fear of ideological pollution at home. And especially at first, disaster followed disaster: the Communist victory in China, the unpopular war in Korea, the French defeat in Indochina, and unrest in Latin America, culminating in the Cuban Revolution. The disasters continued in the sixties and seventies, though they were easier to ignore in the blaze of American prosperity. By now, however, on the other side of prosperity, they have become more difficult to ignore.

Andrew Bacevich's eloquent concluding essay takes aim squarely at American exceptionalism, the conviction that "the United States as a great power differs from every other great power in history. It stands apart: unique, singular, *sans pareil....* Seeking neither dominion nor empire, the United States uses its power to advance the cause of all humanity.... Its purposes are by definition beyond reproach." That this belief is alive and well is obvious from the storm of partisan criticism that greeted President Obama's avowal that of course he was an American exceptionalist, just as "Brits are British exceptionalists, and Greeks are Greek exceptionalists"—a deplorable lack of patriotism, his critics charged. More subtle (or equally crude) expressions of the true faith may be found every day, on every op/ed page and talk show.

What this assumption of America's exceptional nobility ignores, Bacevich points out, are the many ignoble exceptions: the savage suppression of popular uprisings in the Philippines, Haiti, and elsewhere; the blatant hypocrisy of enforcing an Open Door policy in one hemisphere and a Monroe Doctrine in the other; the unleashing of the CIA on Iran, Guatemala, Indonesia, Chile, and any number of other unfortunate countries; the long history of "assassination plots, dirty tricks gone awry [or worse, successful], cozy relations with corrupt dictators"; and more recently, torture, rendition, and domestic surveillance. America has neither the ability nor the right to stamp its image on any century's history. Instead Bacevich issues a ringing call to humility, based on a chastening catalogue of our current incapacities and a sage reminder of the inescapable limits of any nation's wisdom and power.

With all its considerable merits, *The Short American Century* also displays a mildly troubling defect. I mean euphemism. Several of the essays employ language that betrays a residual belief in good intentions somewhere behind American foreign policy, an unwillingness to judge American actions and motives as harshly as those of other nation-states, a reluctance to reckon with the fact that America is—like every other nation in modern history—a class society.

The worst offender is David Kennedy, whose "The Origins and Uses of American Hyperpower" sits a little uneasily in this collection. Kennedy believes that until the second Bush administration spoiled everything, the American Century was "on the whole, a laudably successful affair," which "made the world safer, healthier, and happier." After World War II,

> a notable cohort of American leaders now at last gave its answer to a pointed question that Woodrow Wilson had posed some three decades earlier. "What are we going to do with the influence and power of this great nation? ... Are we going to play the old role of using that power to our aggrandizement and material benefit only?" In the wake of World War II, American leaders set out to use US power in ways that finally set in motion the transformation Wilson had sought in vain.... On the occasion of the first gathering of the UN ... President Harry Truman used words that could have been Wilson's—or Thomas Jefferson's or Tom Paine's: "The responsibility of great states is to serve, and not dominate the peoples of the world." And while it is undeniable that the United States continued to pursue what Wilson had scorned as its own "aggrandizement and material benefit" (considerations never absent from American foreign policy, nor should they be), what is most remarkable is the way that Washington exerted itself to build what [one] Norwegian scholar has called an "empire by invitation."

Though Henry Luce would probably nod in approval, this is a seriously flawed picture. Much post-World War II policy planning documentation is available from the State Department, the Council on Foreign Relations, and other elite groups. It is perfectly clear that the overriding goal of American policy was to integrate the postwar world economy under US leadership, severely restricting, if necessary, the ability of foreign governments to control US business activities within their borders or to set economic objectives incompatible with US priorities. The US needed export markets in Europe, and the US, Europe, and Japan needed raw materials from the less developed world. And we needed docile, business-friendly governments everywhere. These, overwhelmingly, were the preoccupations of postwar American planners, not "to serve ... the peoples of the world."

Kennedy rebukes the Bush administration for trying to spread democracy forcibly, reminding us magisterially that Wilson, Roosevelt, and Truman "asked only that the world be made *safe* for democracy." That is nonsense. A democratic façade was always welcome, but what US policymakers asked—demanded—was that the world be made safe for foreign direct investment.

Jeffry Frieden's "From the American Century to Globalization," a brisk survey of the international economy from Bretton Woods until today, is similarly plagued by euphemism. For example, explaining the success of postwar economic integration, he writes: "World War II and the Cold War had effectively lopped off the political extremes: the Far Right discredited by its fascist connections, the Far Left tainted by its association with the Soviet Union. As a consequence, neither the extreme right-wing nationalism of interwar business and agricultural groups nor the extreme left-wing redistributionism of interwar labor could get a hearing." I suppose that's one way of describing the situation in postwar Europe. A less reflexively conventional formulation might have emphasized that the left (including the Communists, who were frequently prominent in the anti-fascist resistance) was quite popular in France, Italy, Japan, and Korea. There was a very real prospect in these countries of left-wing governments with trade-union and Communist participation or even leadership. The US mobilized all its resources—including the newly-created CIA—to thwart this possibility and barely managed, with bribes—both legal (the Marshall Plan) and illegal (CIA payments to politicians and journalists)—threats, and repression, to beat it back and install pro-business governments (often including fascist collaborators) in power. There was no "discrediting," and the only "consensus" was among US policy-makers and their foreign clients.

Likewise, Frieden characterizes Reaganism/Thatcherism with fine academic blandness: "The Bretton Woods order gave way to a more unqualified belief in the desirability of removing barriers to international economic exchange and to a generalized skepticism about heavy-handed government intervention in national economies." What the Bretton Woods order actually gave way to was unbridled rapacity on the part of the international investor class, riding roughshod, with the help of the World Bank and International Monetary Fund and multilateral free trade agreements, over the policymaking autonomy of developing nations with respect to labor markets, resource ownership, capital flows, taxes, social welfare, and the environment, and at home launching an ideologically-driven assault on labor unions, regulation, and progressive taxation. Surely Frieden knows all this; couldn't he hint at even a fraction of it?

Even the sterling essay by Jackson Lears, perhaps the best in the collection, is at fault in this regard. Lears's "Pragmatic Realism and the American Century" expertly traces an undervalued tradition of American thought: the tough-minded, pragmatic anti-interventionism of William James, Randolph Bourne, and, in their later phases, Walter Lippmann, Reinhold Niebuhr, George Kennan, and William Fulbright. In opposition to the first phase of American imperialism—McKinley's, Theodore Roosevelt's, and Wilson's—which chronically conflated manliness and militarism, James and Bourne rejected the "mindless cult of national vitality" and wisely countered that "heroism might come in many forms—some of them having nothing to do with military adventure." While others—TR, the young Lippmann, Dewey, and the *New Republic*—were losing their heads, James and Bourne, and their successors in similar circumstances, stubbornly insisted that "war is the least predictable of human enterprises and the least subject to management and control."

Pragmatic realists "counseled war only as a last resort—the least desirable alternative in the policymaker's arsenal." Lears's skillful rehabilitation of pragmatic realism, and of the misunderstood isolationist tradition of Charles Beard and Robert Taft, is just what is needed to help drive a stake through the heart of contemporary neoconservative (and liberal) interventionism.

Still, I wish Lears were a little less prone to see in American foreign policy a history of "intrusive moralism" or "virtue unleashed" or "messianic dreams" or (quoting William Fulbright) "the crusades of high-minded men bent on the regeneration of the human race." Likewise, I wish he had not written that the United States was "mistakenly fighting indigenous nationalism" in Vietnam. America's shameful history of military intervention in the Third World has not been based on hubris or moralism, nor was there any mistake about what we were fighting in Vietnam or elsewhere. Business-friendly states in societies thoroughly integrated into a US-dominated global economic system—this has been the consistent goal of US foreign policy. It has regularly entailed subverting democracy, popular sovereignty, and indigenous nationalism. US policymakers—certainly including Kennan, who was a wise and decent man only when compared with monsters like Kissinger—knew exactly what they were doing. Whatever they may have said (usually for public consumption) about their depredations, they were not high-minded men bent on the regeneration of the human race.

Bacevich himself, in his very fine concluding essay, pulls a punch. About the last decade's interventions in the Middle East he writes: "The prospects of the United States 'ending tyranny' anytime soon, as George Bush promised, appear less than promising. ... Whatever democracy's prospects in the Islamic world, they depend not on what Washington prescribes and attempts to enforce but on what Arabs, Iranians, Afghans, and Pakistanis demand and struggle for." Does Bacevich actually believe that the Bush/Cheney administration sincerely desired to end tyranny or enforce democracy in the Middle East, rather than merely to impose dependable clients, if possible with a democratic façade, though without genuinely empowering Middle Eastern populations, with their unpredictable priorities? I hope not.

Declining empires are dangerous. Popular enlightenment is urgent, and this book, whatever its flaws, will help. That the United States is a rogue state, recklessly militaristic, grossly hypocritical and self-serving in its professions of devotion to democracy and human rights, and the chief promoter and beneficiary of investor-friendly and worker-unfriendly forms of economic development—this is the lesson of the American Century. It is well understood in the rest of the world, even among America's allies. Only in the United States is it unmentionable, indeed unthinkable, at least in the academic mainstream and the major media. This, alas, is the true American exceptionalism. Because *The Short American Century* takes exception, even if less forcefully than one might wish, to this exceptionalism, it is a valuable step toward the self-knowledge Americans will need if we and the rest of the world are to survive the long centuries ahead.

II. Thinkers

The Workingman's Friend

In the "Overture" to his grandly symphonic *The Enlightenment: An Interpretation*, Peter Gay describes the "international type" of the *philosophe* as a "facile, articulate, doctrinaire, sociable, secular man of letters." On this definition, was Adam Smith a *philosophe*?

Yes and no. Unlike his French counterparts and even his bosom friend David Hume, he led a retired life, much of it in the small Scottish town where he was born, and he lived with his mother until she died at a very advanced age. He was shy, destroyed most of his letters, and did not seem to relish giving brilliant performances, either in print or in conversation. He never fell afoul of civil or religious authority, had no mistresses, and engaged in no public quarrels. (A semi-public one, though. Shortly after Hume's death, Smith met Samuel Johnson at a party. Johnson spoke slightingly of Hume, Smith defended him, and their exchanges grew increasingly heated until Johnson exclaimed, "Sir, you lie!" To which Smith retorted, "Sir, you are the son of a whore!" and stalked out.)

On the other hand, Smith was modestly sociable—he had warm relationships with Turgot, Quesnay, and Condorcet. Like most of the *philosophes*, he was prolific and versatile, publishing much-admired essays on law, literature, and the history of science as well as his masterpieces on moral philosophy and political economy. And although he was not openly irreligious like Hume and Voltaire, he had as little use for the Calvinist superstitions of Scotland as his French contemporaries had for Roman Catholic ones. Perhaps the main point of difference lies in that slightly ambiguous word "doctrinaire." Smith was a critic and reformer, and there are plenty of doctrines in his writings, some of them strikingly original. But he was detached and scholarly by temperament, rather than ardently polemical. If he was a *philosophe*, he was an exceptionally philosophical one.

Adam Smith was born in 1723 in Kirkcaldy, Scotland. His father, a lawyer and civil servant, died six months before Adam's birth. He left his family well off, and young Adam's mother devoted the rest of her life to her son, who reciprocated her devotion. The first and only adventure in Smith's life took place in his childhood, when he was snatched while at play by some strolling vagabonds but was shortly afterwards rescued by his uncle and a search party. He was sent to the excellent local grammar school and then, at fourteen, to Glasgow University. After three successful years there, he won a scholarship to Oxford, which was then sunk in intellectual torpor and futile scholasticism. Smith loathed it and returned to Scotland halfway through the term of his scholarship.

The academic job market was considerably brighter then than now. The 25-year-old was invited to give two series of lectures, on rhetoric and jurisprudence, at Edinburgh. They were a rousing success, leading to Smith's appointment as Professor of Logic and Metaphysics at Glasgow University in 1751 and Professor of Moral Philosophy in 1752. He remained there happily until lured away, for a princely fee, to tutor and travel with a young duke. From 1767 to 1776 he largely secluded himself in Kirkcaldy, composing *The Wealth of Nations*. He returned to Edinburgh in 1778 as Commissioner of Customs, an important and lucrative post, and died there in 1790.

As Nicholas Phillipson dryly observes at the beginning of his—unavoidably—rather dry biography*: "There is a general lack of visibility in Smith's life." Smith burned his letters, notes, and unpublished manuscripts; we don't even have a likeness till he was past forty. Phillipson makes up for this by sketching—in sometimes gratifying and sometimes tiresome detail—the social and cultural background of the Scottish Enlightenment, the remarkable environment in which Smith's development

---

*Adam Smith: An Enlightened Life by Nicholas Phillipson. Yale University Press, 2010.

thrived. Scotland's early-18th-century prosperity produced an eager audience for lecturers like the young Smith, and generous patrons for prominent public intellectuals like the mature Smith. Perhaps equally important, Phillipson suggests, the bustle of Kirkcaldy and Glasgow, growing market towns, may have first planted in Smith's mind the image of incessant activity, continually expanding needs, and harmonious haggling that lurks everywhere in the background of his writings.

Most important for Smith, and central to the Scottish Enlightenment, was David Hume. Smith discovered Hume while at Oxford (he was officially reprimanded when discovered reading Hume's *Treatise on Human Nature* in his rooms in Balliol College) and became first a disciple, then a close friend. Smith's brief, eloquent memorial tribute to Hume offended the orthodox and, Smith complained, "brought upon me ten times more abuse than the very violent attack I had made [in *The Wealth of Nations*] upon the whole commercial system of Great Britain."

Hume figures prominently in Phillipson's biography. Smith's lifework, he writes, was essentially to "develop a science of man on Humean principles." Hume declined to derive claims about morality and justice from reason or from metaphysical notions about the nature of being. He looked instead to the way moral sentiments were acquired in the course of social life, to the refinement of passions by conversation and commerce, and to the growth and quickening of "sympathy" or moral imagination. Hume was an astute moral psychologist but, Phillipson writes, never went on to use those insights to formulate a theory of the social origins of morality. That was Smith's ambition.

The Theory of Moral Sentiments (1759) was Smith's "account of the processes by which we learn the principles of morality from the experience of common life." This approach—a natural history of sociability—was both a response to and a continuation of Smith's predecessors, Hutcheson, Hume, and Rousseau. But Smith added something new: he replaced the solitary voice of conscience and the collective voice of mankind with a hybrid: the "man within the breast," an imaginary, impartial spectator whose judgments are not innate but formed by experience and whose sympathy is allocated with scrupulous, almost Stoic, fairness. There is perhaps a foreshadowing of Rawls's "veil of ignorance" in Smith's conception. Even this contemporary echo, however, cannot much enliven Smith's treatise, at least for this reader. It takes the literary genius of a Hume or Rousseau to make eighteenth-century moral psychology engaging. Equally, perhaps, it takes the scholarly flair of an Albert Hirschman or Deirdre McCloskey to make the intellectual history of moral theory absorbingly interesting. Phillipson, though amiable, is a bit pedestrian.

Even more disappointing is that, although Phillipson does an admirable job of recounting what is known of Smith's life, he refrains from offering opinions about Smith's afterlife, which is, after all, far more interesting. Smith has become, along with Milton Friedman and Friedrich Hayek, one of the deities in the libertarian-conservative pantheon. I suspect Smith would have firmly declined this honor, even before his more zealous devotees, the proponents of the "efficient markets" hypothesis, nearly succeeded in wrecking the economies of the United States, Britain, and their unfortunate imitators.

The Wealth of Nations appeared in the eventful year 1776. The title page described the author as "formerly professor of Moral Philosophy in the University of Glasgow." His principal influence, Francois Quesnay, chief of the Physiocrats, was a distinguished physician. They were both amateurs, generalists, and reformers—*political* economists, far removed in outlook and purpose from today's "specialists without spirit." The celebrated sarcasms and exhortations in *Wealth of Nations*—"All for ourselves, and nothing for other people, seems, in every age of the world, to have been the vile maxim of the masters of mankind," for example, or "People of the same trade seldom meet together, even for merriment and diversion, but the conversation ends in a conspiracy against the public, or in some contrivance to raise prices"—are not incidental but central. The book might equally well have been titled *The Welfare of Nations*.

Everyone knows, of course, what Adam Smith stood for: free trade, the division of labor, the minimal state, the invisible hand, the illimitable growth of wants and needs. "It is not from the benevolence of the butcher, the brewer, or the baker that we expect our dinner, but from their regard to their own interest." "Every individual ... intends only his own gain, and is in this, as in many other cases, led by an invisible hand to promote an end which was no part of his intention." "Little else is requisite to carry a state to the highest degree of opulence from the lowest barbarism, but peace, easy taxes, and a tolerable administration of justice; all the rest being brought about by the natural course of things." Case closed.

What everyone knows is seldom altogether wrong; but remarkably often it is not the whole story, either. As Emma Rothschild notes at the outset of *Economic Sentiments,* her superb study of Smith and Condorcet: "They think and write about self-interest and competition, about institutions and corporations, about the 'market' and the 'state.' But the words mean different things to them, and their connotation is of a different, and sometimes of an opposite, politics." It is far from obvious that Smith would have entertained cordial feelings toward Alan Greenspan or Margaret Thatcher.

For one thing, Smith roundly mistrusted businessmen. In addition to the sallies already quoted, he insisted that businessmen, for all they may talk of freedom and fairness, "generally have an interest to deceive and even oppress the public." Two examples out of many from *The Wealth of Nations*:

> Our merchants and master-manufacturers complain much of the bad effects of high wages in raising the price, and thereby lessening the sale of their goods both at home and abroad. They say nothing concerning the bad effects of high profits. They are silent with regard to the pernicious effects of their own gains. They complain only of those of other people.

Not infrequently merchants sought favorable changes in trade or currency policy using "sophistical" arguments.

Such as they were, however, those arguments convinced the people to whom they were addressed. They were addressed by merchants to parliaments, and the councils of princes, to nobles, and to country gentlemen; by those who were supposed to understand trade, to those who were conscious to themselves that they knew nothing about the matter. That foreign trade enriched the country, experience demonstrated to the nobles and country gentlemen, as well as to the merchants; but how, or in what manner, none of them well knew. The merchants knew perfectly well in what manner it enriched themselves. It was their business to know it. But to know in what manner it enriched the country, was no part of their business. The subject never came into their consideration ...

Smith did not by any means deny or gloss over class conflict. On the contrary, he was unflinchingly clear-eyed about the unscrupulousness of employers and the connivance of governments. The U.S. Chamber of Commerce is invited to choke on the following passage:

What are the common wages of labour, depends everywhere upon the contract usually made between those two parties, whose interests are by no means the same. The workmen desire to get as much, the masters to give as little as possible. The former are disposed to combine in order to raise, the latter in order to lower the wages of labour. It is not difficult to foresee which of the two parties must, upon all ordinary occasions, have the advantage in the dispute and force the other into a compliance with their terms. The masters, being fewer in number, can combine much more easily; and the law, besides, authorizes, or at least does not prohibit their combinations, while it prohibits those of the workmen. We have no acts of parliament against combining to lower the price of work; but many against combining to raise it. ...

We rarely hear, it has been said, of the combinations of masters, though frequently of those of workmen. But whoever imagines, upon this account, that masters rarely combine, is as ignorant of the world as of the subject. Masters are always and everywhere in a sort of tacit, but constant and uniform combination, not to raise the wages of labour above their actual rate.... We seldom, indeed, hear of this combination, because it is the usual, and one may say, the natural state of things which nobody ever hears of. Masters too sometimes enter into particular combinations to sink the wages of labour even below this rate. These are always conducted with the utmost silence and secrecy, till the moment of execution, and when the workmen yield, as they sometimes do, without resistance, though severely felt by them, they are never heard of by other people. Such combinations, however, are frequently resisted by a contrary defensive combination of the workmen; who sometimes too, without any provocation of this kind, combine of their own accord to raise the price of labour.... But whether the workmen's combinations be offensive or defensive, they are always abundantly heard of.... They are desperate, and act with the folly of desperate men, who must either starve, or frighten their masters into compliance with their demands. The masters upon these occasions are just as clamorous upon the other side, and never cease to call aloud for the assistance of the civil magistrate, and the rigorous execution of those laws which have been enacted with so much severity against the combinations of servants, labourers, and journeymen.

Like Hume, Smith was firmly on the side of the workers, a robust partisan of full employment and high wages.

What improves the circumstances of the greater part can never be regarded as an inconveniency to the whole. No society can surely be flourishing and happy, of which the far greater part of the members are poor and miserable. It is but equity, besides, that they who feed, clothe, and lodge the whole body of the people, should have such a share of the produce of their own labour as to be themselves well fed, clothed, and lodged.

And another sarcasm against early capitalist apologetics, which applies equally well to later ones:

That a little more plenty than ordinary may render some workmen idle, cannot well be doubted; but that it should have that effect upon the greater part, or that men in general should work better when they are ill fed than when they are well fed, when they are disheartened than when they are in good spirits, when they are frequently sick than when they are in good health, seems not very probable.

Smith straightforwardly supported the principle underlying progressive taxation:

The subjects of every state ought to contribute towards the support of the government, as nearly as possible, in proportion to their respective abilities; that is, in proportion to the revenue which they respectively enjoy under the protection of the state.

Nor was Smith a proponent of the minimal state. Government has the duty of "erecting and maintaining those public institutions and those public works which may be in the highest degree advantageous to a great society," but which "are of such a nature that the profit could never repay the expense to any individual or small number of individuals." And as Emma Rothschild points out: "Of Smith's great diatribes in *The Wealth of Nations*, only one is concerned with what would later have been understood as a principally economic activity of national government."

Smith was, in short, a *mensch*. He would definitely not feel at home in the American Enterprise Institute or the Heritage Foundation.

But although Smith's heart was in the right place, he was wrong about three large matters. Two of them have to do with the quality of life, and so are invisible to most contemporary economists. But one of them is central to their concerns: his advocacy of free trade, based on the theory of comparative advantage. No developing country, Smith asserts, should try to nurture particular "strategic" (as we now say) industries:

> By means of such regulations, indeed, a particular manufacture may sometimes be acquired sooner than it could have been otherwise, and after a certain time may be made at home as cheap or cheaper than in the foreign country. But though the industry of the society may be thus carried with advantage into a particular channel sooner than it could have been otherwise, it will by no means follow that the sum total, either of its industry, or of its revenue, can ever be augmented by any such regulation.... Though for want of any such regulations the society should never acquire the proposed manufacture, it would not, upon that account, necessarily be the poorer in any one period of its duration.

This is from perhaps the most influential section of *The Wealth of Nations*, the one containing the reference to the "invisible hand" and the now hoary old chestnut, "What is prudence in the conduct of every private family can scarce be folly in that of a great kingdom."

But Smith was wrong. Every successful economy—without exception—has prospered by subsidizing key industries and protecting them from foreign competition. And nearly without exception, every developed society has then, with consummate hypocrisy, preached free trade to less-developed countries. Friedrich List first refuted Smith's development theory. For a thorough review of this issue, see the work of the contemporary Oxford economist Ha-Joon Chang, in particular *Kicking Away the Ladder* and *Bad Samaritans*.

The other important—to humans, if not economists—matters about which Smith was wrong were, first, his notion of indefinite progress. Smith recognized that only economic growth could sustain high wages and widely diffused prosperity without society-wide planning and cooperation. Unsurprisingly, he failed to recognize that there are inescapable limits to growth.

Second, Smith acknowledged that work in a capitalist society was liable to be stultifying for most people.

> In the progress of the division of labour, the employment of the far greater part of those who live by labour, that is, of the great body of the people, comes to be confined to a few very simple operations.... The man whose whole life is spent thus ... naturally loses the habit of exerting his understanding or invention, and generally becomes as stupid and ignorant as it is possible for a human creature to become ... [hence] not only incapable of relishing or bearing a part in any rational conversation, but of conceiving any generous, noble, or tender sentiment, and consequently of forming any just judgment concerning many even of the ordinary duties of private life [as well as] of the great and extensive interests of his country ... This is the state into which the great body of the people must necessarily fall, unless government takes some pains to prevent it.

Which is, of course, what a civilized and humane society would do. Ours has failed miserably, indeed scarcely tried. Education in America, like virtually every other institution here, serves the purposes of American business.

Still, these failures of vision are hardly Smith's fault. He at least *had* a moral and social imagination, unlike most of those who now claim his legacy. Perhaps the finest tribute to Smith came from his noblest successor, John Stuart Mill:

> For practical purposes, political economy is inseparably intertwined with many other branches of social philosophy ... Smith never loses sight of this truth ... [A] work similar in its object and general conception to that of Adam Smith, but adapted to the more extended knowledge and improved ideas of the present age, is the kind of contribution which political economy at present requires.

It still is.

What Would Orwell Say?

Perhaps it is time to stop asking "what would Orwell say?" Christopher Hitchens, an ardent admirer and astute interpreter of Orwell, thinks so. "I am no longer interested," he wrote a few years ago, "in whether or not Orwell would take my view or anyone else's if he were still with us ... We have to say goodbye to him as a contemporary." Few of us, though, are as sure of ourselves as Hitchens. And even he admitted that it would be nice to talk things over with Orwell now and then, to "find out what he thought and more importantly how he thought" about whatever vexes us, his stumbling successors. "It would be a pleasure to disagree with him," Hitchens allowed—and, it goes without saying, an even keener pleasure to agree.

A new two-volume reissue of Orwell's essays, selected by the *New Yorker*'s George Packer and introduced by Packer and the novelist Keith Gessen, is an opportunity to talk things over with Orwell.* It's a well-judged selection, serviceably introduced and very helpfully annotated. All the great essays are here, and most of the near-great ones: "A Hanging," "Shooting an Elephant," "My Country Right or Left," "England Your England," "Looking Back on the Spanish War," "Why I Write," "How the Poor Die," "Such, Such Were the Joys," "Inside the Whale," "The Prevention of Literature," "Politics and the English Language," "Writers and Leviathan," "Reflections on Gandhi," and critical essays on Swift, Dickens, Tolstoy, Wells, Kipling, Eliot, Chaplin, Dali, boys' weeklies, and seaside postcards. To those who treasure every page of the four-volume *Collected Essays, Journalism, and Letters,* edited by Sonia Orwell and Ian Angus,

Facing Unpleasant Facts: Narrative Essays by George Orwell. Compiled, with an introduction, by George Packer. Harcourt, 2008. *All Art is Propaganda: Critical Essays* by George Orwell. Compiled by George Packer, with an introduction by Keith Gessen. Harcourt, 2008.

with its innumerable *Tribune* columns, "London Letters" to *Partisan Review*, quotidian book reviews, and letters to friends, *Facing Unpleasant Facts* and *All Art Is Propaganda* will probably not seem indispensable. But since (inexplicably) not everyone does own the more complete four-volume edition, these two elegantly produced newcomers are welcome.

The emphasis in *Facing Unpleasant Facts* is on the personal essayist more than the polemicist. Packer, a reporter who has also written fiction and memoir, perceptively contrasts Orwell's extroverted, observant narratives with contemporary "creative nonfiction."

> The essays in this volume could not be farther from the kind of autobiographical writing that has been fashionable over the past ten or fifteen years, in which the writer puts the reader under the spell of pure novelistic storytelling, all emotional vibration without an insight anywhere. The narrator of this type of memoir drifts helplessly on the surface of events in an eternal present tense, which takes away the power and the responsibility of retrospection: It just happened—don't ask me what it means. Orwell's essays are the opposite—transparent and accountable. He is both character and narrator, and in the distance that comes with looking *back* at his own experience in the past tense he manages to raise it out of the narrow circle of private confession and into the sphere of universal revelation.

Packer also pays some apt compliments to Orwell's inimitable directness of voice and "puritanical bias" toward simplicity. Whether or not it's true that "the soundness of Orwell's political judgment is of a piece with the clarity of his sentences," it's certainly worth thinking about the possible relation. (Unfortunately, Packer cites as evidence of Orwell's "soundness of judgment" what is perhaps his most notable misjudgment: his harsh criticism of Auden's "Spain." As E. P. Thompson showed in "Outside the Whale," Orwell's hectoring response to the phrase "necessary murders" mistook Auden's meaning, which was not that Stalinist liquidations were justified but that, more generally, revolutionary violence in the Spain of the 1930s was justified.)

Perhaps because neither is an academic, both Packer and Gessen give the back of their hand to Orwell's left-academic critics. Packer writes, a little gruffly: "A generation of students has gone to school on the banal truth that all literature is 'constructed,' and learned to scoff at the notion that words on the page might express something essentially authentic about the writer. The usefulness of this insight runs up against its limits when you pick up Orwell's essays." Gessen is a shade more genial. "You can tie yourself in knots—many leftists have done this over the years—proving that Orwell's style is a façade, an invention, a mask ... that by seeming to tell the whole story in plain and honest terms, it actually makes it more difficult to see, it *obfuscates*, the part of the story that's necessarily left out; that ultimately it rubber-stamps the status quo. In some sense, intellectually, all this is true enough; you can spend a day, a week, a semester proving it. There really are things in the world that Orwell's style would never be able to capture. But there are very few such things." If the shoe fits, post-structuralists must wear it. It is also true, however, that many academic leftists remain true to Orwell's stylistic admonitions and liberal values.

Packer and Gessen are illuminating about Orwell the prose writer; neither is out to "steal" Orwell politically, in the way Orwell's essay on Dickens famously noted that Left, Right, and Center had all tried to "steal" that novelist. But I find myself unable to imitate their and Hitchens's restraint. What would Orwell say about ... oh, the 2008 election?

One clue: in 1938, explaining why he had joined the Independent Labour Party, Orwell affirmed, as he did from first to last, that he was a socialist, incorrigibly suspicious of "capitalist democracy," and that it was "vitally necessary that there should be in existence some body of people who can be depended on ... not to compromise their Socialist principles." In the 1970s and 80s he would likely have voted for Dave Dellinger, Jesse Jackson, and Barry Commoner in preference to even the most liberal Democratic Party candidate. Another clue: the ILP also recommended itself to Orwell because it "is not backed by any moneyed interest, and is systematically libeled from several quarters"—which sounds very much like Ralph Nader in 2008.

But what about lesser-evilism? "I do not mean," Orwell assured his less radical readers, "that I have lost all faith in the Labour Party. My most earnest hope is that the Labour Party will win a clear majority in the next General Election. But we know what the history of the Labour Party has been"—i.e., very disappointing. This is precisely the attitude of most Nader voters toward the Democratic Party: exasperation, mistrust, and earnest good wishes. Orwell, it is true, left the ILP two years later in disagreement about the war, which he strongly supported. But he also confidently hoped, and frequently predicted, that the war would put paid to capitalism and class society: that "the Stock Exchange will be pulled down, the country houses will be turned into children's holiday camps, the Eton and Harrow match will be forgotten," and much else not at all in the spirit of any Democratic Party platform. My own conclusion is that as long as America was not fighting for its life, as England had been in 1940, Orwell would probably not have voted for a Democrat, even an awfully winsome one.

And whomever he voted for, he would surely not have joined in the reflexive disparagement of Nader since the 2000 election. That year, a corrupt and irrational electoral system inflicted the worst president in its history on the United States; yet for the following eight years, not a single prominent Democratic politician or liberal intellectual had the courage or imagination to champion thoroughgoing electoral reform. It was so much easier to revile Nader—for which reason alone (though there are plenty of others), Orwell would have refrained. Here as elsewhere, he was not only too intelligent to swallow the conventional wisdom; he also had too much self-respect to swell a chorus—any chorus.

Orwell was not a contrarian; he simply tried to say what most needed saying. In the late 1930s, the Nazis were a far greater evil than England's Stalinist intelligentsia. But few of Orwell's readers had any illusions about the Nazis, while many did not know how untrustworthy most Stalinist publications were, so Orwell devoted considerable energy to telling them. In the 1950s and after, Soviet imperialism may have been as great an evil as American repression at home and support for repression abroad. All but a handful of Americans, however, firmly believed that because the "Free World" was menaced by a ruthless and implacable international Communist conspiracy, criticism of national-security policy (except for not being aggressive or expensive enough) was anti-American. An American Orwell would not have wasted his breath denouncing Communism to readers who (like me) already knew all about it from *Reader's Digest*, J. Edgar Hoover's bestselling *Masters of Deceit*, and the popular TV show *I Led Three Lives*—readers who had absorbed anti-Communism through their pores, as the vast majority of Americans did. Instead he would have recognized his primary obligation to the victims of American foreign policy in Central and South America, the Middle East, Africa, and Southeast Asia. He would have debunked Cold War mythology—*that's* what most needed saying in the decades when belief in America's virtue was seldom challenged at home and the CIA and IMF wrought havoc abroad.

Conor Cruise O'Brien, introducing his own fine essay collection, *Writers and Politics* (1965), defined the responsibility of intellectuals in a way that I imagine Orwell would have endorsed—and practiced—if he had lived during the Cold War. It is a long paragraph; but then, it is a delicate subject.

> All criticism, all political analysis, involves a quest for truth, but few critics, few analysts, could give a philosophically respectable or coherent answer to the question: what is truth? Yet we can identify lies readily enough, and can reasonably hope that, when we have chipped away at these, what remains will be closer to the indefinable truth. A certain amount of chipping away goes on in the pages that follow. It will be seen that the chipping is mainly, though not exclusively, at the expense—or for the benefit—of Western cultural and political edifices. There are, I think, adequate reasons for this. The English-speaking critic and analyst is—or should be—led to criticize and analyze the phenomena of his own contemporary

culture, which is increasingly dominated by values prevalent in the United States of America. The distortions and misleading façades which he will most often encounter ... are pro-American and anti-communist distortions and façades. He will, of course, be aware that in the communist world, and in the poor world of Asia and Africa, there are also distortions and façades, usually much more blatant, and therefore less insidious, than those prevalent in the West. As far as outside criticism can do something to demolish the mendacities of the communist world and the poor world, that effort is being vigorously made by many writers, and I have not felt any great need to add my amateur efforts to those of the numerous professional critics of communist practice. My own guess is that the liberation of the communist world, and of the poor world, from their crude forms of mendacity, will have to proceed from within and that the liberation of the Western world from its subtler and perhaps deadlier forms of mendacity will also have to proceed from within. Whether these liberations make much progress or not will obviously depend mainly on mighty economic and social forces, but also a little on the efforts of individuals. From the other side we can hear a few writers, Poles, Russians, Hungarians, and others, busily chipping away. Our applause can neither encourage nor help them. What might help would be that, from our own side also, should be heard the sound of chipping.

In 1967 Arthur Schlesinger Jr. reluctantly concluded that American attempts to crush the Vietnamese resistance would probably not succeed at an acceptable cost to ourselves. He acknowledged, however, that he might well be wrong, in which case he and other "responsible" critics of the war "may all be saluting the wisdom and statesmanship of the American government." Likewise, if attempts to suppress the Iraqi resistance had not cost thousands of American lives and hundreds of billions of dollars, liberals would very likely have joined conservatives in saluting the wisdom and statesmanship of the Bush administration. Would Orwell?

Keith Gessen is afraid he might. "It must have been clear to [Orwell] on some level that the world was going to use [*Animal Farm* and *1984*] in a certain way"—that is, to discredit in advance all radical criticism of American society or policy. It was not entirely bad faith, not "devious propaganda by the right," that turned Orwell into a "bludgeon" against "the anti-war, anti-imperialist left" during the Cold War. And in our time, Gessen sorrowfully acknowledges, "it was under the banner of Orwell ... that some of the best intellectuals in Britain and the United States cheered on the 2003 invasion of Iraq."

I think Gessen's concern about Orwell's possible complicity in his appropriation by contemporary pro-war intellectuals is misplaced. And "best intellectuals" is altogether too generous. To have supported the US invasion of Iraq was to fail, as Orwell would not have failed, to face several unpleasant facts. The first was the war's criminal nature. Unless authorized by the UN Security Council or in response to imminent armed attack, the use of force in international affairs is illegal. The United States has disregarded this most solemn of international obligations so often and so blatantly that foreign policy "realists" now only smile indulgently when this is pointed out. But Orwell was a genuine realist: he understood that it is from the behavior of the stronger that the weaker learn either respect or contempt for the law, and that a stable culture of law-abidingness is a greater contribution to international security than a new generation of space weapons.

Other unpleasant facts Orwell would not have overlooked include enthusiastic US support for Saddam during the most oppressive periods of his rule, even to the extent of assisting his development of WMD, as well as contemporaneous US support for various Saddam-like crimes, including Turkish atrocities against the Kurds, Indonesian atrocities against the Timorese, and Salvadoran and Honduran atrocities against their own populations. Orwell would doubtless have pointed out that all of these lethal relationships were presided over by exactly the same freedom-loving, democracy-promoting defense and foreign policy officials who more recently assumed charge of liberating Iraq. Finally, Orwell would have marveled at pro-war intellectuals' power of waving away such crucial unpleasant facts as Hans Blix's uncompleted UN weapons inspections and the four mega-bases in the Iraqi desert on which construction began immediately post-invasion—bases capable of projecting full-spectrum military dominance of the Middle East's energy-producing regions and which the Bush administration fought stubbornly, though apparently unsuccessfully, to retain in the recent Status of Forces Agreement.

Sophisticated pro-war intellectuals scoffed at such slogans as "No Blood for Oil"; but Orwell was not so sophisticated. On the contrary, he was, as we know, remarkably downright. For example, if a terrorist enemy declared emphatically that its antipathy to America was based on the enormous and threatening US military presence in the Middle East, on US manipulation of Middle Eastern politics to secure friendly clients at the head of resource-rich states, and on unstinting US support for the dislocation and dispossession of millions of people indigenous to the Middle East, it is unlikely that Orwell would have come up with a name for that antipathy that so effectively obscures these unpleasant facts as "Islamofascism" does.

Orwell's "power of facing unpleasant facts" would have allowed him to see through the containment doctrine, nuclear deterrence, the myth of American exceptionalism, the clash of civilizations, and other rationalizations for American dominance that took possession of so many intellectual Cold Warriors, both liberal and conservative. And beneath the surface of British and American domestic politics, he would have discerned similar ugly facts: the unrelenting efforts of the business classes to roll back the meager protections of workers, consumers, and the environment won between the 1930s and the 1960s. Orwell would, beyond a doubt, have devoutly wished to hang the last capitalist in the entrails of the last commissar, while cursing flag-burners, postmodernists, libertarians, and identity-politics hustlers as irrelevant nuisances. If you want a picture of his likely political evolution from 1949, when he died, to 2009, imagine him stamping on a composite portrait of Norman Podhoretz and Karl Rove—forever.

* * *

If I could talk over one or two things with Orwell today, it would not be to pin him down on the left or right in respect of one issue or another. Instead I'd try to get at "how he thought" (as Hitchens put it) in one or two curious and revealing instances.

For example, Orwell defended the bombing of German civilians. He was not, of course, merely bloody-minded, like Churchill, who continually brayed about "killing Huns." Instead, Orwell sounds a little like D. H. Lawrence to anyone who has read the latter's remarkable essays in *Phoenix*.

> Now, it seems to me that you do less harm by dropping bombs on people than by calling them "Huns." Obviously one does not want to inflict death and wounds if it can be avoided, but I cannot feel that mere killing is all-important. We shall all be dead in less than a hundred years, and most of us by the sordid horror known as "natural death." The truly evil thing is to act in such a way that peaceful life becomes impossible. War damages the fabric of civilization not by the destruction it causes (the net effect of a war may even be to increase the productive capacity of the world as a whole), nor even by the slaughter of human beings, but by stimulating hatred and dishonesty. By shooting at your enemy you are not in the deepest sense wronging him. But by hating him, by inventing lies about him and bringing children up to believe them, by clamouring for unjust peace terms which make further wars inevitable, you are striking not at one perishable generation, but at humanity itself.

Does this paragraph sanction the slaughter of innocents, as long as it is done in the right spirit? Are Orwell's qualifications— "if it can be avoided," "all-important," "in the deepest sense"— inadequate? Is "humanity itself" uncharacteristically (for Orwell) evasive, an escape into abstraction? I think, on the contrary, that Orwell is here defending the sacredness of human life, but with emphasis on "human." Viz: an early, even if unnecessary, death in a (relatively) just war is less of an evil than a degraded public life, saturated with hatred and lies, which themselves make a great many more unnecessary deaths inevitable.

If that is Orwell's contention in this squib (part of a *Tribune* column about, as usual, several unrelated topics), I think it is defensible. By the same reasoning, it is arguable that even greater than the evil of millions of Indochinese and Iraqis killed or wounded and millions more displaced is the deadly blow that American aggression in Vietnam and Iraq has struck at the very notion of a duty to obey international law. This mindless sabotage of civilized morality makes future, perhaps even more horrible, military catastrophes more likely.

One might also try to coax him—strictly off the record—into saying a few encouraging words about the future. Orwell was a socialist with a distaste for utopias and a polemicist with a distaste for rhetoric. He wrote vividly about individual features of English landscape, national character, even cookery, but never tried to evoke the good society in persuasive detail. He seemed to think that was impossible in principle. Individual scenes of happiness—the Cratchit family Christmas, for example—could convince, but "all efforts to describe *permanent* happiness, on the other hand, have been failures, from earliest history onwards." Wells's high-tech utopias were "nightmares," and even William Morris's lovely pastoral *News from Nowhere* only managed to induce "a sort of watery melancholy." (I like to hope, though with no great confidence, that my own favorite, Ernest Callenbach's *Ecotopia* (1975), would have gotten a rise out of him.)

I had assumed the problem was temperamental. Orwell was simply a stoic—a noble grouch. But *All Art Is Propaganda* includes an essay, "Can Socialists Be Happy?", not found in the four-volume collection, which points out that in the popular imagination, happiness has always been associated with a relief from effort or want or pain—a holiday from real life. "Nearly all creators of Utopia have resembled the man who has toothache, and therefore thinks that happiness consists in not having toothache." This is why utopian writers failed: "they wanted to produce a perfect society by an endless continuation of something that had only been valuable because it was temporary," and of course the palliatives they offer—leisure, food, sex, play, even political participation—eventually came to seem boring or oppressive to most people.

Cold War heroes and liberal sages like Isaiah Berlin and Leszek Kolakowski—equating utopia with static perfection, as no utopian has ever done—regularly demonstrated the impossibility or perniciousness of all utopias. Orwell's verdict is wiser and more generous than theirs. Socialists "want a world in which human beings love one another instead of swindling and murdering one another. And they want that world as a first step. Where they go from there is not so certain."

There's still more than enough swindling and murdering around to keep a contemporary Orwell too busy to think much about "where to go from there." All the same, it would be nice now and then to talk over the remoter prospects with him.

Socialist Without a Party,
Christian Without a Church

Though the Cold War ended only twenty years ago, Communism now seems a distant memory. So thoroughly did the Soviet and Chinese Communists betray the ideals in whose name they seized power, and so ruthlessly did they silence nearly everyone who protested that betrayal, that the ideals themselves are in danger of being forgotten. But many of the wisest and bravest men and women of the 20th century began by embracing Communism, and some of the century's best political writing was occasioned by their efforts later in life to understand what, if anything, of that youthful commitment remained valid.

The original allegiance of these ex-Communists was not to a party or ideology but to ordinary working people. Facing the harsh, sometimes lethal conditions of early industrialism, workers gradually organized themselves, usually against ferocious opposition from above. Their struggle for a modicum of comfort, security, and dignity won the support of many sensitive compatriots from other social classes. Some of these sympathizers joined the struggle as spokesmen or even leaders. One was Ignazio Silone, the subject of Stanislao Pugliese's excellent biography.*

In the stark physical and moral landscape of rural southern Italy, a boy named Secondino Tranquilli grew up during the first years of the 20th century observing the travails of the peasants, or *cafoni*. His father died when he was 11, and his mother and all but one of his siblings died four years later in an earthquake that devastated the region. He was a rebellious and melancholy

Bitter Spring: A Life of Ignazio Silone by Stanislao Pugliese. Farrar, Straus and Giroux, 2009.

adolescent, but he came under the influence of a saintly priest who, unlike every other priest the boy had known, actually practiced Christianity. The experience left young Secondino with what the Gospels call "a hunger and thirst for justice."

World War I and its aftermath generated waves of revolutionary activity in Europe. Secondino joined the Italian Socialist Party and, before he was out of his teens, became one of its leaders. When that party split, he became one of the leaders of the new Communist Party. A year later, Fascism descended on Italy and "Pasquini" (his Party name) went underground.

Throughout his 20s, he travelled widely on assignments for the Communist International, besides editing numerous Party publications. There were several sojourns in Spanish, French, and Italian prisons, and many pseudonyms. "Ignazio Silone" was the one that stuck.

The intolerance and deceit of Lenin, Trotsky, Stalin, and the other Russian Communist leaders increasingly disturbed Silone. In 1927 he attended a meeting of the Executive Committee of the Communist International, where Stalin's manipulations shocked and disgusted him. (He told the story in his most famous essay, "Emergency Exit," reprinted in the influential Cold War anthology *The God That Failed.*) Two years later, gravely ill with tuberculosis, he went on medical leave from the Party, and two years after that he was expelled.

Exiled in Switzerland, warned by his doctors that he had only a year or two to live, Silone began writing a story about his hometown, "so that I might die among my own people." The resulting novel, *Fontamara* (Bitter Spring), made him internationally famous. Unexpectedly he recovered, and a few years later came *Bread and Wine,* his best novel and some critics' choice for the finest political novel of the century. During the Second World War, he divided his energies between fighting Fascism and fighting Communism, advising Allied intelligence and trying to keep the Italian Socialist Party from merging with the Communists.

After the war, and after 20 years in exile, he returned to Italy a hero. He remained highly visible, as a novelist, essayist, and editor of the leading Italian literary/political journal, *Tempo Presente,* until his death in 1978. Communist intellectuals never forgave him, but among the best of his contemporaries—Orwell, Camus, Macdonald, Chiaromonte—he was revered. Camus, on his way to receive the Nobel Prize in 1957, told a friend that the award should really have gone to Silone.

Why, now that both the commissars and the *cafoni* have disappeared, are Silone's writings still valuable? Perhaps because of his unusual combination of earnestness and skepticism, of lofty idealism and earthy humor. The peasants in his novels are exploited and deceived, but they are also, at times, a stitch, their wry fatalism tempering the reader's high-minded indignation on their behalf with frequent smiles at their expense. The same ability to see from all sides served Silone well as a combatant in the Cold War. Even among the minority of intellectuals who tried to maintain a critical distance from both sides, everyone lost his balance at one time or another—but Silone less often than most. He was unyielding in his criticism of Soviet-bloc unfreedom, but he also criticized McCarthyism, racial discrimination, and American military interventions.

Idealism without illusions, an unsentimental passion for justice—this is Silone's legacy. He called himself "a Socialist without a Party, a Christian without a Church." What he meant by both Socialism and Christianity, he explained, was "an extension of the moral values of private life"—generosity, solidarity, candor—"to all of social life." It is a simple vision but still a very long way from realization. Few people in his time did more than Silone to keep it alive.

A few last, anticlimactic words must be added. In recent years, two Italian historians have accused Silone—one of the best-known and most hated opponents of Fascism—of having been a Fascist informer. Stanislao Pugliese reviews their case and the subsequent controversy with scrupulous fairness. The evidence is slender, but it seems clear that Silone had a correspondence with a Fascist police official. What is not clear is that Silone ever told him anything of importance. If he did, it may have been a desperate attempt to save the life of his brother, who died in a Fascist prison. How significant is any of this? Not very, I'd say; but the reader must decide.

The Common Fate

A stanza from Bertolt Brecht's poem "To Those Born Later" might have served as an epigraph for Victor Serge's memoir*:

I came to the cities in a time of disorder
When hunger reigned there.
I came among men in a time of revolt
And I rebelled with them.
So passed my time
Which had been given me on earth.

Victor Kibalchich ("Serge" was a *nom de guerre*) was born in 1890 to Russian revolutionary exiles, in Brussels because "my parents, in quest of their daily bread and of good libraries, were commuting between London (the British Museum), Paris, Switzerland, and Belgium." His upbringing insured that he would be a rebel and outsider from early youth: "On the walls of our humble and makeshift lodgings there were always the portraits of men who had been hanged. The conversations of grown-ups dealt with trials, executions, escapes, and Siberian highways, with great ideas incessantly argued over, and with the latest books about those ideas." It was a hard life; his eight-year-old brother starved to death.

Like other young rebels (I. F. Stone and Seymour Hersh, for example), Serge left school early and hung about on the fringes of journalism. At 20 he began editing an anarchist newspaper in Paris. When a group of anarchist acquaintances staged a robbery and were caught, Serge was arrested, framed, and sentenced to five years of solitary confinement. On his release he traveled to Barcelona, where an unsuccessful anarchist uprising was in

Memoirs of a Revolutionary by Victor Serge. Translated by Peter Sedgwick with George Paizis. Foreword by Adam Hochschild. New York Review Books, 2012.

preparation, after which he was again arrested. Serge's early chapters on the pre-World War I European ultra-left milieu and French and Spanish prison camps are, like the rest of the book, wonderfully vivid, but also have a charm and occasional lightness that the later ones, more sublime and tragic but shadowed by the darkness and taut with the unbearable tensions of the Russian years, lack.

At the end of the war Serge was transferred to France and, along with some other political prisoners, sent to newly revolutionary Russia in exchange for captured French military officers. He arrived in 1919, during the Civil War. With the monarchist and aristocratic officer corps, supplied and reinforced by the British, French, and American governments, attacking on several fronts, and the peasantry torn between promises of land and residual loyalties to the old regime and the Church, the Bolsheviks' survival was in grave doubt. Serge threw himself into the battle for Petrograd, for several months on the verge of being conquered by White (ie, counter-revolutionary) forces. Besides helping organize the defense of the city (an experience depicted in one of his several superb novels, *Conquered City*), he acted as a liaison to European parties and publications and also took charge of the archives of the Tsarist secret police, which lent extra authority and keenness of perception to his subsequent analysis of the role of police repression in the decay of Bolshevism.

After the Reds' narrow victory, Serge worked under Zinoviev in the Communist International. The Bolsheviks knew that their hold on power was precarious and believed that the survival of the Revolution depended on successful workers' uprisings in Central and Western Europe. There was plenty of working-class discontent in those countries, and the Russians brought the leadership to Moscow for encouragement and advice. Serge was squarely in the middle of this intense activity, both in Moscow and in Berlin, where he worked in the Communist underground. His magnanimous but unsparing portraits of the European revolutionary leadership and intelligentsia, including

Gramsci, Lukacs, Souvarine, and Andres Nin, as well as such old Bolsheviks as Trotsky and Radek and Russian writers like Gorky and Yesenin, are a large and unforgettable part of the *Memoirs*.

Revolution failed everywhere, most crucially and disappointingly in Germany. The Soviet Union was isolated—encircled—and the results were catastrophic: a desperate obsession among the leadership with Party unity, internal security, and rapid military and economic (in practice, heavy-industrial) development. And by the late 1920s, ten years after the Revolution, the leadership was ... Stalin.

The descent of the Stalinist darkness on the Soviet Union and the international Communist movement has been described many times, but rarely, perhaps never, with such intimate knowledge and moral discrimination as in Serge's memoirs and novels. Serge the novelist is as lyrical as Pasternak, as shrewd as Koestler, as humane as Silone. *The Case of Comrade Tulayev*—written, like most of Serge's novels, at odd moments, with only remote prospects of publication—is one of the best novels about Stalinism, and indeed one of the best political novels of the 20th century. The murder of a Party official, in reality a random act of street violence, metastasizes in the imagination of the secret police into an elaborate treasonous conspiracy. Figures of every stature, lofty, middling, and insignificant, all innocent and most of them fervently loyal, are swept into the investigation's maw, while the investigators and their bureaucratic superiors are, without exception, of a chilling mediocrity and cynicism. There is even a scene with Stalin himself, which manages the extraordinary—but for Serge, characteristic—feat of rendering the dictator's ordinary, even impressive, qualities without lessening our horror.

Progressively disillusioned, Serge leads for several years the twilight existence of an Oppositionist: still inside the Party, but mistrusted and mistrustful. His wife's family is persecuted, partly on his account; she goes mad, and he is left to care for their young son. He is expelled from the Party. Finally, inevitably, comes his arrest. As usual in such cases, he is presented with fantastic allegations and pressured to confess to at least some of them, for his own good and the good of the Party. Unlike most people in his position, he categorically refuses. He is exiled anyway, to a town in the Urals.

His fellow exiles (portrayed in Serge's novel *Midnight in the Century*, as well as in the *Memoirs*) are a lively bunch, though there are no jobs and hunger is incessant. Here and elsewhere in the book, Serge frequently ends a paragraph with a terse resumé of the subject's eventual fate: "Stetsky disappeared into jail in 1938." "Lominadze will kill himself around 1935; Yan Sten, classed as a 'terrorist,' will be shot around 1937." Very effectively, these individual death knells toll the death of the Revolution as well.

In the mid-1930s, Stalin was courting French intellectuals as part of his Popular Front strategy. Some of Serge's novels and essays had been published in France, so André Gide, Romain Rolland, and others succeeded in winning his release, or rather expulsion. Throughout the late '30s, first in Belgium, then in France, closely watched by the government, slandered by the Communists, admired by a few free spirits like Orwell and Dwight Macdonald, he tried simultaneously to defend what the Revolution had started out to be and to criticize what it had become. When France fell to the Nazis, his life was in danger. So dangerous a radical naturally could not be admitted to the United States, so he spent his last years in Mexico, impoverished and isolated, writing his marvelous final novel, *Unforgiving Years*, and this imperishable memoir.

Two passages, one early in the *Memoirs* and one late, give one a sense of the man. In 1917, just released from a French prison, he arrives in Barcelona.

> The treadmill that crushed human beings still revolved inside me. I found no happiness in awakening to life, free and privileged alone among my conscript generation, in this contented city. I felt a vague compunction at it all. Why was I there, in these cafés, on these golden sands, while so many others were bleeding in the trenches of a whole continent? Why was I excluded from the common fate?

I came across deserters who were happy to be beyond the frontier, safe at last. I admitted their right to safety, but inwardly I was horrified at the idea that people could fight so fiercely for their own lives when what was at stake was the life of everyone: a limitless suffering to be endured commonly, shared and drunk to the last drop.... I worked in print shops, went to bullfights, resumed my reading, clambered up mountains, dallied in cafés to watch Castilian, Sevillan, Andalusian, or Catalan girls at their dancing, and I felt that it would be impossible for me to live like this. All I could think of was the men at war, who kept calling to me.

Twenty-five years later, he looks back over a life of exhilarating struggle and betrayed hopes.

The only meaning of life lies in conscious participation in the making of history. One must range oneself actively against everything that diminishes man, and involve oneself in all struggles that tend to liberate and enlarge him. This categorical imperative is in no way lessened by the fact that such an involvement is inevitably soiled by error; it is a worse error merely to live for oneself, caught within traditions which are soiled by inhumanity. This conviction has brought me, as it has brought others, to a somewhat unusual destiny. But we were, and still are, in line with the development of history, and it is now obvious that, during an entire epoch, millions of individual destinies will follow the paths along which we were the first to travel. In Europe, in Asia, in America, whole generations are in upheaval, are ... [learning] that the egoism of "every man for himself" is finished, that private enrichment is no fit aim for life, that yesterday's conservatisms lead to nothing but catastrophe, and sensing the necessity for a fresh outlook tending towards the reorganization of the world.

It was never obvious, alas; and seventy years later, with plutocracy triumphant nearly everywhere, it is less obvious than ever. Still, this testimony from someone who, like few others in the twentieth century, never sacrificed either liberty or solidarity deserves profound respect.

Brecht's "To Those Born Later" concludes:

But you, when the time comes at last
And man is a helper to man,
Think of us
With forbearance.

When—if—that time comes at last, few of those born earlier will be remembered with more forbearance, even love, than Victor Serge.

An Enemy of the State

Even before Barack Obama took the oath of office in January 2009, the ghost of I. F. Stone was weeping bitter tears. Asked on ABC News about the possible prosecution of Bush Administration officials for violating domestic and international laws on the surveillance of citizens and the treatment of prisoners, the President-elect replied that "what we have to focus on is getting things right in the future as opposed to looking at what we got wrong in the past." Thus did our new Conciliator-in-Chief implicitly declare Stone's forty-five-year, 3.5-million-word effort to look at what our rulers got wrong irrelevant to forcing them to get things right in the future. All that is "in the past."

Mr. Obama could not be more wrong. In American politics, as elsewhere, the past is not dead; it isn't even past. The greed and callousness Stone exposed week after week behind America's domestic and foreign policy throughout the last century had their source in institutions that remain in place, and the difficulty of penetrating the screen of business and government propaganda is undiminished. If Obama cares to know what he is up against—he seems, most of the way through his first year in office, still largely clueless—a quick trip through *The I.F. Stone's Weekly Reader**, or better, a leisurely trip through Stone's invaluable five-volume collection, *A Nonconformist History of Our Time†*, would help orient our personable President to America's deeper political realities.

The facts of Stone's life have been told well and often, most recently by D. D. Guttenplan in *American Radical: The Life and*

*Edited by Neil Middleton, 1971.

†*The War Years: 1939–1945; The Truman Era: 1945–1952; The Haunted Fifties: 1953–1963; In a Time of Torment: 1961–1967;* and *Polemics and Prophecies: 1967–1970.* All published by Little, Brown.

Times of I. F. Stone (Farrar, Straus and Giroux, 2009).* He was born on Christmas Eve 1907, in Philadelphia, and christened Isadore Feinstein. His parents had a dry goods store, which prospered modestly during Izzy's boyhood and adolescence, and his cheerful, bustling mother doted on him. He was inordinately bookish, starting very young. (And continuing throughout life—he was, for what it's worth, far more literate, in his unostentatious way, than William F. Buckley Jr.) But he didn't care much for school, or succeed very well. He was also moonlighting from schoolwork as a reporter for local newspapers, and after a year he left college to work full-time as a journalist. He never looked back, at least until retirement, when he learned Greek, investigated Socrates, and discovered that that universally revered martyr for free speech was actually a good deal more hostile to democratic freedoms in Athens than most of Senator McCarthy's victims were to democratic freedoms in America.

Neither Stone's inner nor his outer life seems to have been particularly complex or dramatic. He was a dutiful son: when his father's business suffered in the Depression, and his mother intermittently became mentally ill, Izzy, who was well-paid by then, helped. He met a lively, popular girl, not much given to reading but much taken with his ebullience; they stayed happily married for sixty years. He was an enthusiastic and good-humored but often distracted father. He had few but loyal friends, was close to his siblings and on good terms with his relatives and in-laws, and—especially during his years in Washington DC—was not much of a partygoer. He led a full life, professionally and domestically, with few storms, and had a sunny and feisty personality, with few shadows or enigmas. The one moment of high drama was his decision in 1953, amid the ostracism that followed his fierce denunciations of the Smith Act

---

*See also Robert Cottrell, *Izzy: A Biography of I. F. Stone* (Rutgers, 1992) and Myra MacPherson, *"All Governments Lie": The Life and Times of Rebel Journalist I. F. Stone* (Scribner, 2006).

and the publication of *The Hidden History of the Korean War*, to found *I. F. Stone's Weekly*. A lesser man would have folded his tent, or at least lowered his voice.

Stone was cursed all his life with interesting times, boiling over with war, depression, revolution, and totalitarianism. He covered these calamities not on the scene but behind the scenes, where policy was made. Some journalists could bring political action to life; Stone was one of the few who could bring political causation to life. He read official reports, studies, speeches, press conferences, Congressional testimony, and budget documents, voraciously, analytically, skeptically. He found the threads, connected the dots, brought the substructure of real causes and motives to light.

An early example, which made Stone's reputation in Washington, was his coverage of American unpreparedness for World War II. Long after it became obvious that US involvement in the war was likely, American industry simply would not stop doing business with Germany and Japan, even in strategic commodities like oil, rubber, metals, minerals, chemicals, and machine parts. The trade was too profitable, and the ties between German cartels (by then an arm of the Nazi regime) and American banks, corporations, and law firms (including Sullivan and Cromwell, where John Foster Dulles represented a great many German clients) were too close. Stone tracked down the figures on industry after industry and hammered away at the story until even the Senate committee investigating war preparedness commended him. The additional German and Japanese war production enabled by the delivery of these materials may well have cost the lives of thousands of American and Allied soldiers—more damage, arguably, than was caused even by Communist infiltrators in the State Department.

Equally important were Stone's reports on how greed and incompetence retarded industry's conversion to wartime production. General Motors could not be induced to stop making cars in record numbers even after its factories and workforce were needed for tank, truck, and aircraft production. Alcoa

Aluminum would not increase supply of this vital component for fear that an early end to the war would result in a surplus, hence lower prices. Major oil companies would not open their pipelines to independents; and in general, dominant companies would not cooperate with smaller rivals. All this profitable foot-dragging was aided and abetted by the "dollar-a-year men," the business executives and corporate lawyers "loaned" to the federal government in order to keep an eye out for the interests of their employers and clients. And these, of course, were precisely the "responsible" people, the men of substance—bankers, executives, and lawyers, along with professional diplomats and military officers—to whom Walter Lippmann proposed entrusting real power in a democracy, while the fickle public meekly registered its preferences every four years and hoped for the best.

Another high-profile demolition was Stone's reconstruction of the Gulf of Tonkin episode, which had prompted Congress to authorize the use of force against North Vietnam. Piecing together information from Senate and UN debates and from European and Vietnamese news reports, Stone showed that the official account was false. The US boats deliberately entered what they knew the North Vietnamese claimed as territorial waters; they were supporting, perhaps directing, a South Vietnamese military operation; there was no second attack, as claimed; and the Pentagon had detailed plans already drawn up for the extensive bombing reprisals that followed the North Vietnamese "attack" (which had not caused any injuries or damage), suggesting that the US was hoping for, if not actually attempting to provoke, an incident.

As with the Korean War fourteen years earlier, Stone was virtually alone at the time in challenging a misleading official justification for an undeclared war. And once again, millions of lives were lost because Congress and the press were not equally conscientious.

Far more than a few million lives would have been lost in case of a nuclear war, and Stone was rightly obsessed with the arms race. It was plain to him that the US remained far ahead of the USSR through most of the nuclear era and could have had a far-reaching arms-control agreement at virtually any time. It was equally plain that the prospect of "limited nuclear war" adumbrated in Henry Kissinger's influential *Nuclear War and Foreign Policy* was "poisonously delusive." And amid much high-minded hand-wringing about the malignant but mysteriously self-sustaining momentum of the arms race, Stone kept pointing out the extent to which it was not some "tragic" historical imperative but rather sheer, unstoppable bureaucratic self-aggrandizement by the armed services that drove the progress of weapons technology.

To expose corporate fraud, diplomatic obfuscation, budgetary sleight-of-hand, and wartime propaganda required the investigative enterprise for which Stone is renowned. To write about two other preoccupations, the internal security panic of the Truman era and the struggle for racial equality in the Eisenhower and Kennedy years, required only common decency—as uncommon in these cases as in most others. Stone harried—there is no other word for it—Senator McCarthy and J. Edgar Hoover. "Melodramatic bunk by a self-dramatizing dick" was his entirely typical comment on a speech by Hoover to the American Legion, and he was hardly less scathing about McCarthy. Walter Lippmann and Arthur Schlesinger Jr, by contrast, wrote little about McCarthy and barely a word about Hoover. Stone had his reward, however. The FBI read his mail, searched his garbage, tapped his phone, and monitored his public appearances, while the State Department denied him a visa and tried to confiscate his passport. These marks of distinction were denied to his more circumspect contemporaries. About race, Stone simply said the obvious—now obvious, that is—repeatedly and eloquently. His columns on the subject are still bracing.

Stone was an ardent Zionist in the 1940s and was the first American journalist to report on the Jewish exodus from Europe and the creation of the state of Israel. In 1944 he penned an open letter to American newsmen urging pressure on President Roosevelt to admit more displaced Jews into the United

States. In 1945, when it was still feasible, he advocated a binational Arab-Jewish state. Beginning immediately after the 1948 war, he pleaded for the swift resettlement of Palestinian refugees. Immediately after the 1967 war, he warned Israel against occupying the West Bank and Gaza. From the start—and even before—he was right about Israel/Palestine.

Above all, he was right about the Cold War. He ridiculed the notion that the Soviet Union, bled dry by World War II, was poised to overrun Western Europe, or that it controlled every popular movement from Latin America to the Balkans to the Middle East to Southeast Asia. And he pointed out how much US-Soviet tension was the result of America's insistence on rearming West Germany and integrating it into a hostile European military alliance. The cornerstone of Cold War ideology—that US actions were primarily reactive and defensive, dictated by unrelenting Soviet aggressiveness—took no account of Stalin's fundamental conservatism or of American designs on Mideast oil and on Southeast Asian markets for its Japanese ward. Nor did it allow Americans to perceive how arrogant and threatening the rest of the world considered America's claim that Taiwan was our "first line of defense," a notion Stone sent up superbly in a satire, "The Chinese 7th Fleet in Long Island Sound." Finally, Stone recognized the role of defense spending in America's economic management, both as a subsidy for advanced technology and as a fiscal stimulus that entailed no government competition with private producers—what would later be called "military Keynesianism."

All governments lie, Stone reminded his readers, and none act morally except when forced to by an aroused public. This moral universalism is his most valuable legacy. It is true that Stone worked harder than most other journalists and hobnobbed less. But what set him apart was something else: that he applied to his own government the same moral standards we all unhesitatingly apply to others. No reporter would accept at face value a Communist or even non-Communist government's account of its own motives and intentions. Japan's insistence that it sought only to bring prosperity and order to the rest of East Asia in the 1930s, or the USSR's protestations that it invaded Czechoslovakia and Afghanistan at the request of their legitimate governments to save those countries from subversion by the international capitalist conspiracy, were met with ridicule or simply ignored in favor of explanations based on Japanese or Soviet self-interest, and in particular on the interests of their ruling elites. But very few journalists were equally skeptical (in public, that is) about the motives of American intervention in Indochina, Central America, or the Middle East. Those actions may have been deemed unwise for one reason or another; criticism in this vein was "responsible." But to question America's good intentions—to assume that the US is as capable of aggression, brutality, and deceit as every other state, and that American policy, like that of every other state, serves the purposes of those with preponderant domestic power rather than a fictive "national interest," much less a singular idealism—was to place oneself beyond the pale. Then as now, such skepticism was the operative definition of "anti-Americanism." By that definition Stone was anti-American, and America needs more such enemies.

In recent years students of Soviet espionage in the United States have found what they judge to be evidence of Stone's collaboration with the KGB. Two leading scholars, summarizing this evidence in *Commentary* magazine, conclude that "in the light of these revelations, Stone's entire legacy will have to be reassessed." One can see why neoconservatives would welcome an opportunity to call Stone's "entire legacy" in question. But— leaving aside for a moment the validity of the charges—is there any sense in this demand? Orwell's essays are no less admirable because on his deathbed he offered British intelligence some advice about the ideological soundness of some fellow writers; nor Silone's novels because he may have passed information about Communist activities to Fascist police. Gunter

Grass's, Milan Kundera's, and Peter Handke's writings are no less impressive because Grass remained silent for so long about his youthful service in an SS fighting unit, Kundera may have informed the Czech secret police about a political refugee, and Handke defended Slobodan Milosevic. Our judgments of Heidegger's philosophy and Paul de Man's literary criticism are not (or should not be) affected by revelations about their various degrees of sympathy with Nazism. Irving Kristol's critique of liberalism is no more or less valid because he concealed CIA sponsorship of *Encounter*. Arthur Schlesinger Jr's interpretations of Jacksonianism and the New Deal are no more or less valid because he lied to the press about the Bay of Pigs invasion. Noam Chomsky's views on American foreign policy would be no more or less valid if it were discovered that the Viet Cong or the Sandinistas had paid his children's college tuition. Even Henry Kissinger's scholarly history of diplomacy is no more or less valuable because its author is an authentic war criminal. If Stone, rather than Julius Rosenberg, had given American atomic secrets to the Soviets, he would still be the finest political journalist of the twentieth century; and if Rosenberg had actually written everything that appeared under Stone's byline, then Rosenberg would be the finest political journalist of the twentieth century. It is simply good intellectual hygiene to reject politically-motivated demands to devalue art or arguments by citing the real or alleged failings of their author.

Nevertheless, whatever their significance may be, what are the charges against Stone, and how valid are they? Stone's harshest critics are Herbert Romerstein and Eric Breindel in *The Venona Secrets* and John Earl Haynes and Harvey Klehr in *Spies*.* Based on the FBI's Venona transcripts of intercepted

*The Venona Secrets: Exposing Soviet Espionage and America's Traitors, Regnery, 2000; Spies: The Rise and Fall of the KGB in America, Yale, 2009. For a lengthy and impartial examination of the Stone "case," see Max Holland, "I. F. Stone: Encounters with Soviet Intelligence," Journal of Cold War Studies 11:3 (2009). For a persuasive rebuttal of Haynes and Klehr, see D. S. Guttenplan's review of Spies in the Nation, 5/25/09.

Soviet cable traffic, on the notebooks of Alexander Vassiliev, who had research access for some years to KGB archives, and on speeches and interviews by former KGB general Oleg Kalugin, these critics infer that Stone was a "spy," a "fully active Soviet agent" who "worked closely with the KGB" for several years during the 1930s and 40s and remained an occasional contact and source until 1968; that he was paid for his work; and that he "really produced." What this production consisted of is not specified, with three exceptions: 1) "A group of journalists, including Stone, provided Pravdin [an undercover KGB officer] with information about the plans of the US General Staff to cope with the German counteroffensive in the Battle of the Bulge and resume the Allied offensive. Though the other journalists identified, Walter Lippmann [!] and Raymond Gram Swing, did not know that Pravdin was an intelligence officer rather than a fellow journalist, Stone knew full well." 2) Stone reported that William Randolph Hearst had friendly relations, and perhaps even business dealings, with Nazis. 3) Stone was asked to tell an American in Germany how to get in touch with a (presumably Communist) anti-fascist organization.

This seems like a very meager haul for decades of "close" and "active" collaboration with the KGB. There had better be a great many more, and considerably more damning, revelations from the KGB archives, or else the charges against Stone will need to be taken down several pegs. In addition, some of his critics' descriptions of Stone's public career raise doubts about their judgment and fairness. Stone was alleged to be an "openly pro-Communist journalist" in the 1940s; he was "an enthusiastic fan of Stalin" until the Soviet invasion of Hungary in 1956; and after a period of disillusionment, he fell back into his old ways until the 1968 invasion of Czechoslovakia "caused the KGB to lose Stone again." His "most outrageous" performance was *The Hidden History of the Korean War*, in which Stone "used bizarre reasoning" to prove "that the South Koreans attacked North Korea."

In fact, Stone was never a fan of Stalin or the Soviet Union.

He sympathized with its effort at independent development and criticized its lack of political and intellectual freedom. After the Hitler-Stalin pact of 1939, he declared himself an ex-"fellow traveler." I strongly doubt (his pre-1939 writings are unfortunately more difficult of access than the later ones) that he was ever an uncritical or dishonest one.

After 1939, in any case, he was sharply—though not, given the horrors already known, adequately—critical of the Soviet Union. He never referred to the USSR as anything but a "dictatorship." There is very little praise: Soviet communism is "the greatest social experiment of our time"—little more than boilerplate in 1937. Stalin, he wrote in an obituary, was a "giant figure"—though he seems to have meant this only in the sense that Napoleon and Bismarck and Churchill were giant figures and Harry Truman was not. In his collected writings at least, unfavorable references to the Soviet Union are very much more frequent than favorable ones. A sample:

· "The FBI is carrying out OGPU tactics." (1937)

· In "the Russia of 1937," there is "a hunt for and extermination of dissident elements that has left the outside world bewildered." (1937)

· Stalin has unleashed "an old-fashioned Russian orgy of suspicion of foreigners, intellectuals, and any kind of dissent." (1948)

· "No political dissident in the USSR could hope to get as much fair treatment as has been accorded the Communists even in the hysteria-haunted US of this date." (1949)

· "To picture Russia as a democratic utopia is only to store up explosively bitter disillusion." (1950)

· "I [have been] represented as saying there was more freedom in the Soviet Union than in the United States. I consider a statement of that kind wholly untrue and politically idiotic." (1951)

· "What was wrong with Stalin's regime that such miscarriages of justice could occur under it? And how many unjustly accused or framed political prisoners may there be in the penal labor camps of the USSR?" (1953)

- "[Many observers], friendly to socialism, with a great respect for the Russian people, have been shamed and antagonized by much that has occurred since the Revolution. Amid the gigantic achievements ... there has also been an indifference to mass suffering and individual injustice, a sycophancy and an iron-clad conformity, that has disgraced the socialist ideal." (1953)

- "[By World War II], communism in practice had become not a brotherly society working for the common good, but an authoritarian hierarchical system run by a bureaucratic caste, on the basis of unquestioning obedience by subordinates." (1957)

- "The snoopery that goes on in our own country is still a long way from the perpetual surveillance to which the Russian people are subjected by their own political police." (1958)

- I well remember thirty years ago how the Communists boasted that freedom of the press in Russia under the Constitution promulgated by Stalin was broader than in the United States.... Thirty years later this is still a bitter hoax." (1967)

- "Fifty years after the Revolution, there is still neither free discussion nor free press in the Soviet Union. It has become a gigantic caricature of what socialism was meant to be." (1967)

But perhaps all this criticism was merely an elaborate cover, so that Stone could serve the KGB more effectively.

As for the Korean War, six weeks after it began, Stone told a left-wing audience:

> You won't like what I have to say, so better prepare your tomatoes. I'm sorry to report to you that I couldn't find any proof to justify the Communists' claim that South Korea started this war. ... North Korea started the war, and North Korea was well-prepared for such a war. ... Where did a little power like North Korea get such a strong war machine? The Soviet Union equipped North Korean Communist forces, and the Soviet Union is behind the North Koreans in this war.

Nowhere in *The Hidden History of the Korean War* does Stone claim to "prove that the South Koreans attacked North Korea," only to show that the provocations preceding the war were mutual. His final judgment on the war's origins is spelled out plainly in the book's preface: "I believe that in Korea the big powers were the victims ... of headstrong satellites itching for a showdown, which Washington, Moscow, and Peking had long anticipated, but were alike anxious to avoid." What was "hidden," and what he claimed to have brought to light, was not a South Korean attack but rather "the operations of MacArthur and Dulles, the weaknesses of Truman and Acheson, the way the Chinese were provoked to intervene, and the way the truce talks were dragged out and the issues muddied by American military men hostile from the first to negotiations." He might have added that the book, published in 1952, was one of the first to call attention to the barbaric American bombing campaign, which foreshadowed the holocaust in Indochina.

The book's deeper purpose was to serve as "a study in war propaganda, in how to read newspapers and official documents in wartime. Emphasis, omission, and distortion rather than outright lying are the tools of the war propagandists, and this book may help the reader learn how to examine their output—and sift out the facts—for himself." Which was, *mutatis mutandis*, Stone's purpose in everything he wrote.

The case against Stone reduces to: he did not see, or at any rate acknowledge, the full horror of Soviet totalitarianism in the 1930s. Robert Cottrell summarizes admirably:

> [Stone] did not view the Soviet Union uncritically, acknowledged that there was a stench behind the judicial proceedings in place there, had little liking for the American Communist Party, was no celebrant of any brand of totalitarianism, and certainly did not genuflect toward Moscow. Nevertheless, there was something disingenuous in his unwillingness to criticize still more forcefully the terror that was being played out in Soviet Russia.... Stone, like many of his political and intellectual counterparts, continued to afford Russia and even Stalinist communism something of a double standard, fearing that to do otherwise would endanger the Popular Front and the very possibility of socialism.

Stone's stance toward the Soviet Union in the 1930s rested on three premises. First that the dictatorship had achieved remarkable economic growth and greatly improved the country's standard of living, including consumption, health, and literacy. Second, that, given Hitler's apparent determination to crush Bolshevism, the USSR would be a reliable and powerful ally in case of a European war. Third, that the United States and Britain would be secretly (in fact, it was no secret) pleased if Germany and Russia went to war and destroyed, or at least exhausted, each other.

These premises were at least plausible and together justified Stone's criticism of American hostility toward Russia in the 1930s. Unquestionably, he should have been more forthcoming about Soviet crimes. He seems to have feared that, given the rancor and dishonesty of his ideological opponents, such candor would unduly complicate his arguments against American policy; and moreover, that the situation was desperate. Plausible fears, but still he was wrong. It would have been more effective as well as more honest to have said, perhaps at the beginning of every column on the subject: "The Soviet Union is indeed a bloody tyranny. Of course that is not at all why our rulers are hostile to it. American policy is often friendly toward bloody tyrannies. But a country that tries to withdraw from the global economy, which we dominate, and develop under its own auspices, restricting the scope of American business, is a threat. And a country that seems to be making a success of it, and may thereby arouse that dangerous and perverse inclination in other countries, is an intolerable threat."

Stone did say this, in effect, but far too implicitly. His anxieties about authoritarianism at home and anti-Semitism in Nazi Germany got the better of him, along with an undiscriminating sympathy for what he and many others who should have known better called "socialism." Like his ideological opponents, both Communist and capitalist, Stone seems to have identified socialism with state control of the economy. Hence his frequent insistence that "socialism" and "democracy" were *both* indispensable. But socialism—an ideal long predating the Russian Revolution—simply means popular, democratic control of social life, including economic life. The Bolsheviks were no socialists:

immediately on taking power they destroyed all independent factory councils, local councils ("soviets"), and popular assemblies and remained as hostile to them as any plutocrat or archbishop. The Communist Party owned the economy; socialism was outlawed and persecuted even more fiercely in the Soviet Union than in the United States. Impressing this distinction on conservatives (and liberals) was no easier in the 1930s than it is today. But Stone, who was by instinct a genuine and not (like Lenin and Trotsky) a pseudo-socialist, should have been more careful with the word.

Although not much of the right-wing attack on Stone stands up, it has succeeded nonetheless. Every word spent defending Stone against attacks on his character is one not spent drawing renewed attention to his powerful criticisms of American political economy, foreign policy, and civic culture. These criticisms are Stone's real legacy, which his attackers are understandably far from eager to reassess.

Above all, right-wing hostility to Stone betrays a shallow understanding of republican virtue and the nature of freedom. More than anything else, what makes totalitarianism possible is a people's submissiveness to authority: its slowness to perceive and unwillingness to resist injustices committed not by distant villains and official enemies but at home, by those with the power to make resistance dangerous. Niebuhr, Lippmann, Schlesinger, Hook, and Cold War liberals generally, whatever their other merits, did little to discourage such submissiveness in the American public. They were, instead, fierce in urging resistance to evils to which their readers would never have either occasion or inclination to submit, such as the advent of Communist rule in the United States or the conquest of the rest of the world by the Soviet Union. To warn the populace against remote and implausible threats, toward which incessant government and business propaganda had in any case already rendered them implacably hostile, was not much of a contribution to preserving the spirit of freedom. Stone, in contrast, by regularly exposing the mendacity, greed, callousness, and incompetence of their rulers, did more to unfit the American people for totalitarianism than all the Cold War liberals combined. Of non-liberals—*National Review, Human Events, Readers' Digest*, the Luce publications, and their conservative and neoconservative descendants—it is unnecessary to speak.

"I know," Stone joked, "that if the Communists come to power I'd soon find myself eating cold *kasha* in a concentration camp in Kansas *gubernya*." Actually, it is possible to imagine a Soviet America with a Soviet Reinhold Niebuhr as the regime's favorite moralist, a Soviet Sidney Hook as chief ideological arbiter, a Soviet Arthur Schlesinger Jr as court historian, and a Soviet Walter Lippmann as high pundit and counselor. But it is impossible to imagine an unfree society of any political hue that would not send an I. F. Stone to prison and keep him there.

Just a Journalist

It's said that Art Tatum's technique persuaded a great many young pianists to become insurance salesmen. Edmund Wilson's chops were equally phenomenal; not as sheerly, immediately dazzling, perhaps, but in range, erudition, penetration, clarity, and unfussy elegance, no less jaw-dropping. And just as Tatum's multi-volume *Complete Solo Masterpieces* (Pablo) is one of the summits of piano jazz, the Library of America's new two-volume issue of Wilson's essays and reviews from the 1920s, 30s, and 40s is one of the summits of twentieth-century literary criticism.*

Edmund Wilson's life story is well known from his many published journals (*The Twenties* through *The Sixties*), memoirs ("The Author at Sixty" and *Upstate*), and letters (a superb collection, *Letters on Literature and Politics,* edited by Elena Wilson, his fourth wife), other people's remembrances, and two good biographies by Jeffrey Meyers and Lewis Dabney. He was born in 1895—with difficulty, because he already had an unusually large head. His father was a reforming lawyer and Attorney General of New Jersey but was disabled for much of his later life by hypochondria and depression. Young Edmund got an extraordinary education at the Hill School in Pennsylvania and a decent one at Princeton, especially after he encountered the literary scholar and peerless teacher Christian Gauss. At Princeton he also (like Dwight Macdonald at Yale) began several life-long literary friendships, notably with F. Scott Fitzgerald and the poet John Peale Bishop.

Literary Essays and Reviews of the 1920s and 1930s: The Shores of Light, Axel's Castle, Uncollected Reviews by Edmund Wilson. Edited by Lewis Dabney. The Library of America, 2008. *Literary Essays and Reviews of the 1930s and 1940s: The Triple Thinkers, The Wound and the Bow, Classics and Commercials, Uncollected Reviews* by Edmund Wilson. Edited by Lewis Dabney. The Library of America, 2008.

During World War I, Wilson served as a hospital orderly in France. Afterwards he freelanced for *Vanity Fair* and *The Dial*, and in 1925 he became literary editor of the *New Republic* until 1931, then traveled around Depression-era America as a correspondent. (His reporting is available in a marvelous collection, *The American Earthquake.**) In 1935 he spent some months in the Soviet Union, about which he was ambivalent. The second half of the decade he researched and wrote *To the Finland Station*, his brilliantly idiosyncratic history of revolutionary socialism. In 1940 he rejoined the *New Republic*, though not for long. Like Randolph Bourne before him and others more recently, Wilson fell afoul of that magazine's perennial enthusiasm for American military intervention.

In 1944 he began writing regularly for the *New Yorker*, where most of his subsequent work first appeared, except for *Memoirs of Hecate County*, a collection of stories and novellas, and *Patriotic Gore*, a study of American writing around the time of the Civil War. Besides literary criticism, Wilson produced a great deal of travel writing (much of it, as Lewis Dabney notes, "verging on cultural anthropology") about Europe, Russia, Israel, the Caribbean, and the American Southwest, as well as a widely read and admired book about the discovery of the Dead Sea Scrolls. He was present at the creation of the *New York Review of Books* and first proposed The Library of America.

Wilson's love life was as busy as his writing life. He was married four times, most spectacularly to Mary McCarthy, and had (or attempted) romantic liaisons with Edna St. Vincent Millay, Louise Bogan, Anais Nin, Mamaine Koestler, and other celebrated women, most of whom remained good friends, as did Dawn Powell and Janet Flanner, who escaped his amorous attentions but keenly appreciated his encouragement and help with their careers.

*   *   *

*Da Capo Press, 1996.

T. S. Eliot wrote that in literary criticism, "the only method is to be very intelligent." This was Wilson's method. He made use of Marx and Freud, but pragmatically, as though their importance was not as system-builders or scientific innovators but as astute fellow-critics who had extended our chronically limited understanding of economic and psychological motives. These new approaches took their place in the critic's traditional repertoire alongside the biographical, formal, impressionistic, and others; and the choice of approach was dictated by the individual character of the work or author. The notion of literature as a body of evidence, a corpus over which to fit a conceptual grid, rather than a field for judgments about artistic merit, would have seemed to him perverse—a queer idea of theory.

His characteristic approach was biographical, comparative, historical. In "The Literary Worker's Polonius," a witty and trenchant "brief guide for authors and editors," he is apparently describing himself when he writes:

> ... a reviewer should be more or less familiar, or be ready to familiarize himself, with the past work of every important writer he deals with and be able to write about an author's new book in the light of his general development and intention. He should also be able to see the author in relation to the national literature as a whole and the national literature in relation to other literatures.

"But this," he adds dryly, "means a great deal of work." Wilson was famously indefatigable, vacuuming up new authors and even languages at a rate apparently unimpaired by his sexual and alcoholic indulgences. Mary McCarthy related wonderingly to one of his biographers that "after drinking in his study late into the night, he emerged 'in his snowy-white BVDs in the morning,' freshly bathed and ready to go back to work."

Where energy and the large view were requisite, Wilson was unfailing. Correcting Irving Babbitt about Sophocles, estimating the relative merits of English comic writers from W. S. Gilbert to Kingsley Amis, paying a well-informed tribute to Houdini (Wilson was an amateur magician), comparing Poe's reception in Europe and America—each of these (and perhaps a hundred and fifty others from *The Shores of Light* and *Classics and Commercials*), compact but spacious, authoritative but not bullying, was a week's work (two at most) during the crowded decades these volumes cover.

Wilson was rarely starchy and sometimes quite funny, as in "The Delegate from Great Neck," an imaginary dialogue between Scott Fitzgerald and Van Wyck Brooks; "A Letter to Elinor Wylie," signed "Sam. Johnson" and perfectly pitched in the Doctor's epistolary style; and his dead-on parody in *Axel's Castle* of Eliot's hyper-magisterial critical prose:

> "We find this quality occasionally in Wordsworth," Eliot will write, "but it is a quality which Wordsworth shares with Shenstone rather than with Collins and Gray. And for the right sort of enjoyment of Shenstone, we must read his prose as well as his verse. The 'Essays on Men and Manners' are in the tradition of the great French aphorists of the seventeenth century, and should be read with the full sense of their relation to Vauvenargues, La Rochefoucauld, and (with his wider range) La Bruyère. We shall do well to read enough of Theophrastus to understand the kind of effect at which La Bruyère aimed. (Professor Somebody-or-other's book on 'Theophrastus and the Peripatetics' gives us the clew to the intellectual atmosphere in which Theophrastus wrote and enables us to gauge the influences on his work—very different from each other—of Plato and Aristotle." At this rate ... we should have to read the whole of literature to appreciate a single book, and Eliot fails to supply us with a reason why we should go to the trouble of doing so.

Of course Wilson revered Eliot, and in the same essay he praised Eliot's criticism, though in terms that throw light on their differences. Eliot "has undertaken a kind of scientific study of aesthetic values: ... he compares works of literature coolly and tries to distinguish between different orders of artistic effects and the different degrees of satisfaction to be derived from them." In spite of his "occasional dogmatism" and the "meagerness of his production," Eliot "has become for his generation a leader ... because his career has been a progress, because he has evidently been on his way somewhere," unlike "many of his contemporaries, more prolific and equally gifted."

Unlike, for example, Wilson. "On his way somewhere" meant that Eliot had a critical program, a large view of how all of literature fit together; that he aimed to work out and propagate a comprehensive philosophy of culture. Wilson's aims were nearly always more modest: to describe, to compare, to assess. It's not that he lacked philosophical interests; but he was satisfied with the Enlightenment, with science, with the main current of secular modernity, as Eliot was not. Wilson was a temperamental pragmatist and positivist, comfortable enough in his own philosophical skin to be able to muster at least an undoctrinaire sympathy, if not always much enthusiasm, for romantic and metaphysical heterodoxies.

Besides, he was, he insisted, just a journalist, whose beat was literature (with frequent excursions into politics, popular culture, and travel). He wrote to inform and edify contemporary readers and encourage (or, when necessary, discourage) contemporary writers, rather than, like Eliot, *sub specie aeternitatis*, or like Auden (the first volume of whose collected criticism has just been published* by Princeton University Press), to find out what he thought.

The closest Wilson came to a critical manifesto was "The Historical Interpretation of Literature" in *The Triple Thinkers*. There he distances himself respectfully not only from Eliot's unhistorical aestheticism and from the impressionism of Edwardians like George Saintsbury ("his attitude toward literature was that of the connoisseur: he tastes the authors and tells you about the vintage; he distinguishes the qualities of the various wines") but also from the sociological, Marxist, and Freudian approaches ("The problems of comparative artistic value still remain after we have given attention to the Freudian psychological factor just as they do after we have given attention to the Marxist economic factor and to the racial and geographical factors").

*The Complete Works of W.H. Auden, Vol. III: Prose, 1949–1955, 816 pp., $49.50.

Wilson was not one to shrink from confronting an implied question, however daunting. "And now how, in these matters of literary art, do we tell the good art from the bad?" Among the things named at one time or another as a defining characteristic of art are "unity, symmetry, universality, originality, vision, inspiration, strangeness, suggestiveness, improving morality, socialist realism." All plausible enough, as a first approximation; but how is it possible to judge objectively of these qualities, and why are their effects so valuable?

Wilson answers these questions very much as William James would have. Art, like all other intellectual activity,

> is an attempt to give a meaning to our experience—that is, to make life more practicable ... The writer who is to be anything more than an echo of his predecessors must always find expression for something which has never yet been expressed, must master a new set of phenomena which has never yet been mastered. With each such victory of the human intellect, whether in history, in philosophy, or in poetry, we experience a deep satisfaction: we have been cured of some ache of disorder, relieved of some oppressive burden of uncomprehended events.... This relief that brings the sense of power, and, with the sense of power, joy, is the positive emotion which tells us that we have encountered a first-rate piece of literature.

But this is a subjective reaction; what about objective judgment? Not everyone will feel the same "ache," the same "joy"; and "crude and limited people [will] feel some such emotion in connection with work that is limited and crude." True, but "the man who is more highly organized and has a wider intellectual range will feel it in connection with work that is wider and more complex." And if you ask,

> how can we identify this elite who know what they are talking about? Well, it can only be said of them that they are self-appointed and self-perpetuating, and that they will compel you to accept their authority. Impostors may try to put themselves over, but these quacks will not last. The implied position of the people who know about literature (as is also the case in every other art) is simply that they know what they know, and that they are determined to impose

their opinions by main force of eloquence and assertion on the people who do not know.

The pragmatist's answer is the same for art as for science and philosophy: truth is enduring consensus. That is all we know on earth, and all we need to know.

This conclusion—that all criticism is practical criticism—is persuasive, to me at least. And how good a critic, practically speaking, was Wilson? James Wood's brilliant essay on Wilson (*New Republic*, 9/22/05), tactful but unsparing, is the best assessment. With all respect for Wilson's "glinting, pugnacious clarity," his "comprehensive and solitary scholarship," and his "beautifully restrained and classically elegant expository prose," Wood nevertheless finds that he is "sometimes, in the major essays, disappointing as a literary critic." The meaning, background, and comparative worth of works and authors are reliably propounded, but "it is hard to find any sustained analysis of deep literary beauty"—the kind of analysis Wood excels at—"in his work."

> Wilson's literary criticism, with its introductory relish, its recourse to biographical speculation, and its swerve away from aesthetic questions, now looks more journalistic than it once did. Pritchett seems to me to have had a more literary sensibility and a more natural understanding of how fiction works its effects; Empson explains poetry with a far richer respect for ambiguity; Trilling imbricates ideas and aesthetics with greater skill; and Jarrell accounts for beauty with more devoted vivacity.

It is a fair enough judgment, even if it only means that Wilson didn't do everything equally well.

One thing he did extremely well was make political judgments. This is not, however, the conventional view. His political books are widely praised for their literary qualities. Everyone acknowledges Wilson's superb Depression-era reporting in *The American Earthquake*, his incomparable dramatization of intellectual history in *To the Finland Station*, and his far-ranging scholarship in *Patriotic Gore*. But everyone, it seems, has an unkind word for his political views, or what they take to be his views.

The principal charge is that Wilson idealized Lenin in *To the Finland Station*. James Wood refers to Wilson's "willful romanticizing of Lenin ... who is seen as the gentlest and most selfless of men." David Remnick too refers to Wilson's "romanticized portrait of Lenin" and complains that "to turn Lenin into an author, and to see him almost solely as an author or artist instead of an architect of power, with incredible talent for grasping that power, is a great problem and a self-deception." Paul Berman finds an "enormous enthusiasm for Lenin" and claims that, in Wilson's view, "the reason that Russia had indeed turned out quite badly ... was the mystical element in Marx. It was not because of Lenin—Lenin was the good guy, Marx the bad guy." Louis Menand concurs, seeing a "lack of enthusiasm for Marx" and "enthusiasm for Lenin."

This consensus will probably endure, alas. But I found, along with a vivid portrait of Lenin's many genuinely remarkable personal qualities (and flaws), plenty of lack of enthusiasm for Lenin as a political leader in *To the Finland Station* and no failure to notice Lenin's disastrous "grasping" for power. "Marxism at the End of the Thirties," originally the last chapter of *Finland Station* but later moved to *The Shores of Light*, contains these two forthright condemnations of Lenin's politics:

> The takeover by the state of the means of production and the dictatorship in the interests of the proletariat can by themselves never guarantee the happiness of anybody but the dictators themselves. Marx and Engels, coming out of authoritarian Germany, tended to imagine socialism in authoritarian terms; and Lenin and Trotsky after them, forced as they were to make a beginning among a people who had known nothing but autocracy, also emphasized this side of socialism and founded a dictatorship which perpetuated itself as an autocracy.

And again:

> Lenin's ultimate aims were of course humanitarian, democratic, and anti-bureaucratic; but the logic of the situation was too strong for Lenin's aims. His trained band of revolutionists, the Party, turned into a tyrannical machine which perpetuated, as heads of a government, the intolerance, the deviousness, the secrecy, the

ruthlessness with political dissidents, which they had had to learn as hunted outlaws. Instead of getting a classless society out of the old illiterate feudal Russia, they encouraged the rise and the domination of a new controlling and privileged class, who were soon exploiting the workers almost as callously as the Tsarist industrialists had done, and subjecting them to an espionage that was probably worse than anything under the Tsar.

When Trotsky, jeering at Martov, coins the phrase "the dustbin of history," Wilson rejoins that Martov was right after all:

Today...his croakings over the course [the Bolsheviks] had adopted seem to us full of far-sighted intelligence. He pointed out that proclaiming a socialist regime in conditions different from those contemplated by Marx would not realize the results that Marx expected; that Marx and Engels had usually described the dictatorship of the proletariat as having the form, for the new dominant class, of a democratic republic, with universal suffrage and the popular recall of officials; that the slogan "All power to the Soviets" had never really meant what it said and that it had soon been exchanged by Lenin for "All power to the Bolshevik Party." There sometimes turn out to be valuable objects cast away in the dustbin of history.

And in the chapter on "Lenin at the Finland Station," Wilson gives the last word to the anti-Bolshevik revolutionary Bogdanov, who, revolted by Lenin's authoritarian declarations, "furiously scolded the audience: 'You ought to be ashamed to applaud this nonsense—you cover yourselves with shame! And you call yourselves Marxists!'"

It seems to me that, notwithstanding his later self-criticism about *To the Finland Station*, Wilson was as clear-sighted about the evils of Leninism as his critics.

The other usual occasion for condescending to Wilson is his Introduction to *Patriotic Gore*, with its rejection of belligerent nationalism, which prompted Hilton Kramer to sniff that Wilson "was not really a political thinker" (unlike, say, Norman Podhoretz). True, Wilson oversimplifies a little in the Introduction:

In a recent Walt Disney film showing life at the bottom of the sea, a primitive organism called a sea slug is seen gobbling up smaller organisms through a large orifice at one end of its body; confronted with another sea slug of an only slightly lesser size, it ingurgitates that, too. Now, the wars fought by human beings are stimulated as a rule primarily by the same instincts as the voracity of the sea slug.... The difference in this respect between man and other forms of life is that man has succeeded in cultivating enough of what he calls "morality" and "reason" to justify what he is doing in terms of what he calls "virtue" and "civilization." Hence the self-assertive sounds he utters when he is fighting and swallowing others: the songs about glory and God, the speeches about national ideals, the demonstrations of logical ideologies.... This prevents us from recognizing today, in our relation to our cold-war opponent, that our panicky pugnacity as we challenge him is not virtue but at bottom the irrational instinct of an active power organism in the presence of another such organism, of a sea slug of vigorous voracity in the presence of another such sea slug.

This requires a slight qualification. The aim of American foreign policy is not to "ingurgitate" (i.e., conquer and occupy) other countries but to drain their vital fluids (i.e., to insure unrestricted inflow of American goods and investments and outflow of profits). Once this small correction is made, Wilson's view is far superior to the views of his critics, who upbraid him for insufficient appreciation of American virtue or of Niebuhrian tragic irony.

(Arthur Schlesinger Jr., an admirer of Niebuhr, also opined that Wilson "wasn't really a man of politics." But Wilson's great, and still relevant, 1931 essay "An Appeal to Progressives"— included in *The Shores of Light*—is a more useful contribution to American politics than all of Schlesinger's loyal service in the corridors of the White House and at the dinner tables of Manhattan and Georgetown.)

Will there be another Wilson? Not for a while, certainly. There's too much to master and too many electronic distractions. Reading Greek and Latin for pleasure is practically unheard of now. The very ideal of cultural authority is, rightly or wrongly, suspect. Most important, the freelance life is less and less possible in an economically rationalized, hyper-managerial society. Investors want twenty percent returns; we know what that means for literary journalism. Tenure committees are not impressed by "comprehensive and solitary," idiosyncratic scholarship of Wilson's sort. And where can a freelancer live? Even Hackensack will soon be gentrified. On the Web? Yes, but one wants, if not to be at the center of things, at least to know where it is. Or *that* it is.

Oh well, let's hope that, even in a decentered world, Wilson's temperament and critical method—curious, energetic, humane, and, of course, very intelligent—will keep their appeal.

The Impresario

Matisse said he wanted his art to have the effect of a good arm-chair on a tired businessman. Irving Kristol seems to have wanted his writing to have the effect of a good martini on a beleaguered corporate executive. The executive's prejudices, widely scorned among the young and the educated (in the 1960s and 70s, that is, when Kristol began offering this therapy), were eloquently reaffirmed; his feelings, wounded by impertinent criticism, were tenderly soothed; his conscience, feeble but occasionally troublesome, was expertly anaesthetized. The executive's gratitude knew no bounds; in return, he and his foundations showered their faithful servant with the money and favors that made Kristol so prominent a figure in American intellectual life.

Born in Brooklyn in 1920, Kristol attended City College in the 1930s. There he was part of an unusual cohort of left-wing students, avid readers of Trotsky and *Partisan Review*, an astonishing proportion of whom eventually became leading American intellectuals: Daniel Bell, Nathan Glazer, Irving Howe, Seymour Martin Lipset, and Kristol, among others. After college, he tells us in the engaging "Autobiographical Memoir" that concludes *The Neoconservative Persuasion**, he became an apprentice machinist but, alas, did not persevere. A stint in the Army "had the effect of dispelling any anti-authority sentiments" (along with his socialist ideals), since he thought his fellow GIs—representing the common man—were pretty poor stuff, while Army regulations were generally rational and fair. After World War II he followed his wife (now the eminent historian Gertrude Himmelfarb, who edited this collection) from

**The Neoconservative Persuasion: Selected Essays, 1942–2009* by Irving Kristol. Edited by Gertrude Himmelfarb. Foreword by William Kristol. Basic Books, 2010.

one graduate program to another until they settled in New York and Kristol became an editor at *Commentary*.

At *Commentary* Kristol found himself in another stellar cohort, this time including Elliot Cohen, Clement Greenberg, Robert Warshow, and Richard Clurman. After a few years he moved on to become executive director of the American branch of the Congress for Cultural Freedom, and then, in 1953, co-editor of the Congress's London-based journal, *Encounter*. The Congress was secretly financed by the CIA. Kristol may not have known that and probably wouldn't have cared. In any case, England seemed provincial after New York, so in 1958 he returned to edit *The Reporter*, the project of a wealthy but imperious European émigré. Soon he found himself an executive at Basic Books.

Kristol had tried to write a book (on American democracy) but given up. "I was not a book writer. I did not have the patience and I lacked the intellectual rigor." He also lacked the patience for book publishing and was eager to start another magazine. A rich ex-CIA-agent-turned-stockbroker whom Kristol knew from the Congress for Cultural Freedom agreed to finance *The Public Interest*, beginning in 1965. Critical of the Great Society, and particularly of the War on Poverty, *The Public Interest* attracted much interest and support from *The Wall Street Journal*, the Olin, Bradley, and Smith Richardson foundations, and the American Enterprise Institute. Money was never again a problem, especially once Kristol became field marshal of William Simon's long march through the institutions of New Deal liberalism on behalf of big business.

* * *

Every "-ism" has its truth. What was neoconservatism's? *The Public Interest*'s critique of social policy had a dual thrust: assessment and diagnosis. The bottom line of the assessment was: the more active and interventionist the policy, the less successful. Social Security and Medicare, which simply mailed out checks, worked; more ambitious efforts, such as welfare, education reform, public housing, or juvenile delinquency and prisoner rehabilitation programs, did not. As a first sustained and scholarly review of postwar social policy in America, *The Public Interest* was a genuine public service.

The explanation offered for the failures discovered was another matter. It boiled down to: underreliance on markets and their incentives; overreliance on efforts by a new, self-aggrandizing class of policymakers and service professionals to change attitudes and behavior among the disadvantaged. There were nuggets of insight here, but hostility to the "new class"—a category soon expanded to include practically anyone critical of the status quo—eventually took on an independent ideological momentum. The fact that most of the failed policies had been, as Daniel Patrick Moynihan acknowledged in a burst of candor (or perhaps sheer loquacity), "oversold and underfunded" in the first place was not seriously considered.

Kristol, however, was not a writer to look to for painstaking discriminations. The typical Kristol essay was a relaxed affair—just what the tired businessman required. There are a few long pieces in *The Neoconservative Persuasion*, but most are around 2000 words. First comes the liberal conventional wisdom, larded with scare quotes, about "root causes" or "participatory democracy" or "American imperialism" or "international law." The liberal fantasy in question is refuted by a combination of one-liners, daringly commonsensical contrarianisms, and historical allusions or statistical snippets. By way of conclusion, the deeper, perennial conservative wisdom is restated. It is all genial, effortless, tension-free. Never does Kristol struggle to find his way through some tangled thicket of arguments or to reconcile some apparently contradictory lessons of history. Never does he dive deep into a familiar (or unfamiliar) text, revealing unsuspected patterns, implications, ambiguities. Never does he bring before his readers a sustained procession of historical facts or economic statistics. He appears to write on cruise control.

Kristol's breezy certainty, moreover, is a thing to be envied. His ideological comrade Joseph Epstein wrote wonderingly of Kristol's "commanding tone, supremely confident about subjects that are elsewhere held to be still in the flux of controversy, assuming always that anyone who thinks differently is perverse or inept." In *The Neoconservatives* (1979)—still the definitive treatment—Peter Steinfels skeptically remarked "the frequent appearance of 'always,' 'all,' 'ever,' 'whole,' 'only' [I would add 'of course']" in Kristol's prose:

> Indeed, as soon as Kristol announces something as obvious ("Obviously, socialism is an 'elitist' movement") or the plain truth ("The plain truth is that it is these [liberal, individualist] ideals themselves that are being rejected" by the dissident young) or the simple truth ("The simple truth is that the professional classes ... are engaged in a class struggle with the business community for status and power"), one immediately suspects that the matter is not obvious or plain or simple at all. As soon as he announces something as demonstrably the case—"the proposition (demonstrably true) that the salaries of professors compare favorably with the salaries of bank executives"; "It is a demonstrable fact that in all modern, bourgeois societies, the distribution of income is also along a bell-shaped curve"—one suspects that the matter is either undemonstrable or demonstrably false.

Kristol led the attack on the "new class." Fundamentally, he charged, liberal and radical intellectuals were an anti-democratic elite, seeking to impose their "ideals" on the sensible, materialistic majority. They did this by capturing the state, expanding its powers, and interfering everywhere. "This movement, which seeks to end the sovereignty over our civilization of the common man, must begin by seeking the death of 'economic man,' because it is in the marketplace that this sovereignty is most firmly established." Keynesian fiscal policy, the consumer-protection movement, and the environmental movement were all aspects of this "reactionary revulsion against modernity," against "the kind of civilization that common men create when they are given the power."

Among the many problems with this theory, one might mention: 1) The assumption of consumer—or any kind of popular—sovereignty in the marketplace. On the contrary, the creation of needs and the management of demand are essential to the functioning of a mature capitalist economy. 2) The assumption that demands for reform will never originate among, or strike roots in, a democratic majority. 3) The assumption that government is the natural antagonist of business. This was hardly true in the 1960s and 70s; since then the reverse has been so completely and obviously true that only a helpless addiction to Fox News could persuade anyone otherwise. But these objections were beside the point: the "new class" theory did wonders for ruling-class morale. The identification of progressive reform as the project of a scheming, undemocratic elite has proved to be an ideological zombie, impossible to kill.

It is important, in passing, to distinguish the neoconservatives' critique of intellectuals as a new class from the far deeper and richer critique developed by Christopher Lasch. In *Haven in a Heartless World* (1977), *The Culture of Narcissism* (1979), and *The Minimal Self* (1984), Lasch traced the evolution of a new set of functions called forth by the rise of mass production and industrial organization. The new work force had to be educated; for that very reason, its autonomy and initiative had to be curbed. The varieties of social control exercised by industrial relations specialists, social workers, psychotherapists, educators, public relations and advertising personnel, and numerous other professionals formed, in Lasch's account, a synergy of epic proportions. But Lasch's analysis revealed a profound tension between democracy and corporate dominance, so neoconservatives paid him no attention.

Though Kristol jeered at the supposed idealism of the "new class," he was an energetic preacher of public virtue, notably in "Republican Virtue and Servile Institutions" (1974). Our wise Founders, unintimidated by "democratic dogma," doubted the people's "innate capacity for self-government." They were concerned about what they called "luxury" and we would call affluence—not about the effect of affluence on affluent people's characters but about the effect of the desire for affluence on ordinary people's characters. They conceived of republicanism as "something which involves our making painful demands on ourselves," and of republican virtue as "self-control," a willingness to "subordinate one's own special interests to the public interest," particularly when it came to the "expression of material grievances."

The Founders' stern admonition to popular self-restraint has gone by the board—nowadays, Kristol scoffs, we can scarcely even comprehend it:

> Dostoevsky predicted, in *The Brothers Karamazov*, that when the anti-Christ came, he would have inscribed on his banner: "First feed people, and then ask them to be virtuous." We have improved on that slogan to the extent of adding decent housing, good schools, free medical care, and adequate public transportation as necessary preconditions of virtue.

Consider (as Kristol apparently did not) what this sally implies. If we are justified in demanding virtue—"self-control" and self-denial—from people who do not yet enjoy sufficient food, decent housing, good schools, free (or any) medical care, and adequate public transportation, then what painful sacrifices for the common good are we justified in demanding of those who enjoy not merely all these basic goods in superabundance but also riches beyond the dreams of avarice: that is, the one percent of the American population who receive 23 percent of the national income and own 40 percent of the national wealth? Colossal sacrifices, beyond a doubt. A serious moralist would treat this question as central to any discussion of public virtue. It never seems to have occurred to Kristol.

"Human Nature and Social Reform" (1978) diagnosed the alleged failure of most social reform in the 1960s and 1970s. Kristol's diagnosis turns on the distinction between "opportunity reforms," like tuition subsidies for night school, which build on existing motivations for self-advancement or on proven traditional motivators like religion or family; and "environmental reforms," like welfare or prison reform, which "enable us (in theory) to change everyone's motivations for the better, through the practical exercise of our unadulterated compassion, our universal benevolence, our gentle paternalistic authority." The former always succeed; the latter always fail. The reason is obvious to everyone but liberal intellectuals: "Our reformers simply cannot bring themselves to think realistically about human nature. They believe it to be not only originally good, but also incorruptible; hence the liberal tolerance for pornography."

Does this analysis hold water? Kristol acknowledged "one important exception": those who are unavoidably dependent—"the old, the halt, the blind, the infirm." Programs that "throw money" (though not "too much money") at such people are "perfectly appropriate." This grudging exception seems to me nonetheless large enough to drive a tank through. For children too are unavoidably dependent, and the environment we collectively provide them (or fail to provide them) will shape their later motivations just as much as their genetic endowment (which is what "human nature" means, if it means anything) will. In fact, environments shape *everyone*'s motivations, including those of juvenile delinquents, repeat criminals, and welfare cheats, Kristol's prime exhibits of the failure of social reform. Perhaps the most salient feature of the environment in each of these cases, as Michael Harrington pointed out in a reply to Kristol, is the lack of a unionized, full-employment economy. No doubt many people are simply bad eggs, as Kristol is happy to remind us. But the lack of decent employment prospects helps, in many cases, to turn bad eggs into criminals. Full employment constrains profits, however, so attention must be deflected elsewhere, preferably in a metaphysical direction. In debates about social reform (before we decided, as a society, to more or less give up on the whole project), "human nature" was usually the first and last resort of scoundrels. Kristol worked that dodge relentlessly.

* * *

It is in foreign policy that neoconservatism has done the most damage with the least intellectual authority. Neoconservatives prided themselves on their moral realism and geopolitical astuteness. But their views—especially Kristol's—on Communism and the Cold War were superficial and crudely partisan. Kristol first became notorious for an essay in *Commentary*, "Civil Liberties—1952." There he argued that because Communism was (unlike, say, the US State Department and CIA under the Dulles brothers) "a conspiracy to subvert every social and political order it does not dominate," there could be no question of "complete civil liberties for everyone." All that Communist Party members and their sympathizers could hope for was some recognition of "the expediency in particular cases of allowing them the right to be what they are."

Himmelfarb bravely and usefully includes this essay in *The Neoconservative Persuasion*. It certainly deserves all the opprobrium it has attracted over the years. Kristol's guiding principle—that a mass political organization may be declared an illegal conspiracy to overthrow the government by force without its having either advocated or attempted the overthrow of the government by force, and that any or all of its members may therefore be denied "complete civil liberties"—is as invidious as it is illogical. Rhetorically, the essay is impressive: a masterly guide to assuming a pose of tough-mindedness while courageously confronting "liberal pieties." But in fact, if your liberal pieties are shaken by Kristol's illiberal blasphemies, they must have been very shaky to begin with.

Kristol's view of the Cold War was about equally judicious and fair-minded. The Soviet Union was an "immoral, brutal, expansionist power"; it had always been and—given the nature of the regime—could be nothing else. For America, on the other hand, "*realpolitik* ... is unthinkable": "every American administration has felt compelled to use our influence" to promote "individual rights as the foundation of a just regime and a good society." This benevolence was part of *our* nature, "the very grain of our political ethos." Kristol's superior grasp of the opposing essences of our side and their side made it unnecessary to consider evidence that might have complicated the picture: e.g., American use of atomic weapons at the end of World War II in an attempt to gain leverage over the USSR in negotiating the postwar settlement; American insistence on rearming Germany as part of a hostile military alliance, rather than acceding to Soviet proposals for a neutralized and disarmed Central Europe; and American military intervention or political interference in Western Europe and former European colonies whenever popular movements challenged governments subservient to the United States. "The United States," Kristol wrote, "will always feel obliged to defend, if possible, a democratic nation under attack from non-democratic forces, external or internal." This, after the US-supported overthrow of democratically-elected regimes in Iran in 1953, Guatemala in 1954, Brazil in 1964, Indonesia in 1965, Chile in 1973, and Argentina in 1976. One admires his brazenness.

Kristol's pronouncements about international law were likewise simultaneously self-assured and fact-free. As expressed in the United Nations Charter, international law was an absurdity, "one vast fiction"; a fiction, moreover, that has been "abused callously, or ignored ruthlessly, by those nations that, unlike the Western democracies, never took it seriously in the first place." Alas, whoever may have taken the United Nations seriously from its inception, the US certainly did not, consistently ignoring near-unanimous General Assembly resolutions on disarmament, terrorism, South Africa, the Cuban embargo, and an Israeli-Palestinian political settlement, among other issues, and, since losing effective dominance of the UN in the 1960s, amassing far more Security Council vetoes than any other country.

Reared on *Partisan Review*, the neoconservatives naturally took a keen and pugnacious interest in contemporary culture. But while the intellectuals of the 1930s and 40s were usually concerned to defend avant-garde art and literature against the indifference or hostility of bourgeois society, the neoconservatives were more often concerned to defend bourgeois society against the condescension or contempt of the avant-garde. The root of the problem, as usual for conservatives, was the Enlightenment and the death of God. "The deeper one explores into the self, without any transcendent frame of reference," Kristol wrote, "the clearer it becomes that nothing is there." Hence "utopian rationalism"—in the form of socialism—and "utopian romanticism"—the counterculture, including feminism, gay liberation, drugs, loud music, and other perverse forms of self-expression—"have, between them, established their hegemony as adversary cultures over the modern consciousness and the modern sensibility." If everything is permitted, nihilism ensues. Recoiling from this prospect, neoconservatives have discovered the "paradoxical truth that otherworldly religions are more capable of providing authoritative guidance for life in this world than are secular religions." Are any of these very convenient "otherworldly religions" true? Kristol did not say.

Unbelieving conservatives from Plato to Kristol have lamented the political consequences of other people's unbelief. It's an old number, now played out. It is possible to respect those who doggedly defend one or another traditional, supernatural religion, in all its theological rigor. Likewise those who bravely attempt to stammer out the first terms of a new (or recover the lost fragments of an old) non-supernatural religion, well aware that they will probably sound foolish. But those who merely want the rest of us to accept discipline and obey authority, whatever we believe (they don't really care), deserve no respect. For all his hand-wringing about the dwindling of "the accumulated moral capital of traditional religion," Kristol never gave any indication of what he thought the truth about ultimate matters might really be. He cared about order, not truth.

Kristol was not wrong about everything. In "What Is a 'Neoconservative'?" (1976), he allowed that "neoconservatism is not at all hostile to the idea of a welfare state," including "some form of national health insurance," and that freedom requires only the "right to become unequal (within limits) in wealth ... and influence." A "ruthless dismantling of the welfare state," he wrote in another essay the following year, is "unthinkable." Who knows why he never repeated these concessions to decency in subsequent decades, when his allies were in power and proceeded to ignore them? Perhaps he forgot he'd made them.

He also, on rare occasions, hit the polemical bull's-eye, wittily skewering left-liberal confusions, as in this 1980 speech to foundation executives:

> Everyone is concerned about youth unemployment in the ghetto, as I am, and I have been involved with various foundations and government as well, over the years, in trying to do something about it. It is astonishing how little has been accomplished. The reason so little has been accomplished is that no one was satisfied with doing a little; everyone wanted to do a lot. For instance, it is a scandal in this country that vocational education is in the condition it's in. It is absolutely absurd. Can you imagine a United States of America where there is a shortage of automobile mechanics, and yet there are "unemployable" kids in the ghetto who can strip an automobile in four minutes flat? But when you try to get a program of vocational education going—and I've tried very hard with various foundations—they say "No! No! We don't want to train these kids to be automobile mechanics. We want to train them to be doctors, to be surgeons."
>
> Let's be reasonable. Not everyone can be a doctor or a surgeon. Some people are going to end up as automobile mechanics. Automobile mechanics have a pretty good life. They make a great deal of money, most of it honestly. But the fact is that it has been impossible to get the resources for so limited a goal.

If this is true, it is a far more valuable criticism of political correctness than all of Hilton Kramer's and Roger Kimball's endless fulminations on the subject.

But Kristol was wrong about most things. He was wrong about the Cold War, civil liberties, the "new class," the counter-culture, foreign policy, supply-side economics, religion, and civic virtue. And yet he was perhaps the most politically influential intellectual of his generation. How could that be? Well, as the Old Testament might have said about a false prophet: "He pleaseth the rich exceedingly, and them that have deep pockets he maketh right glad." Sincerely, eloquently, and with an aplomb unruffled by a whisper of self-doubt, Kristol told the rich and powerful exactly what they wanted to hear. They rewarded him in overflowing measure, supporting his ideas, projects, and protégés on a scale unprecedented in American intellectual history.

Kristol thought he had left Marxism behind with his youth. But his subsequent career perfectly illustrates Marx's apothegm: "In every era, the ideas of the rulers are the ruling ideas."

The Zealot

One of the many unfortunate consequences of Stalinism, Maoism, and Third World totalitarianism is to have made life difficult for critics of the status quo in the West. Of course this is a less important matter than those regimes' other sins: the murder, imprisonment, and deportation of scores of millions of innocent people, the impoverishment and oppression of hundreds of millions more, the wholesale poisoning of the environment, the degradation of politics, morals, and the arts. Anyone who doesn't know about these things has a lot of catching up to do; and anyone who knows but still advocates a one-party dictatorship with exclusive state control of the economy—i.e., Marxism-Leninism, the forerunner of Stalinism and Maoism—has a lot of explaining to do. Fortunately, for several decades there have been very few such people in the United States, at least among critics of the status quo with an audience above the low three figures. Nevertheless, so prominent were Stalinists in the American left of the 1930s and 40s, so loud were the tiny fringe of Maoists and Third Worldists in the 1960s, and so attractive has the delusive rhetoric of "revolution" proved throughout modern history, that anyone urging radical changes in the American economy and polity has an obligation to show that these changes are fully compatible with democracy.

If this is anti-Communism, count me in. As we all know, however, anti-Communism has sometimes been more than this. It is a useful standard of intellectual and moral seriousness, but like any other standard, it can be applied crudely, mechanically, or in bad faith; in this case, to discredit criticism from the left without engaging it. Undiscriminating anti-Communism is less common and less damaging now than when there were Communists around, but in concentrated doses it can still be harmful. *The Twilight of the Intellectuals** is a very concentrated dose.

Hilton Kramer is one of America's leading art critics and editor of *The New Criterion*, one of our best and most influential literary-intellectual journals. *Twilight* is a portrait gallery of (mostly) American intellectuals of the Thirties through the Sixties, from Edmund Wilson through *Partisan Review* and the Congress of Cultural Freedom to Susan Sontag. Although Kramer's range is broad, his purpose is narrow. In his "Introduction" he writes: "[I]t was not the Western defenders of Communist tyranny who suffered so conspicuously from censure and opprobrium in the Cold War period but those who took up the anti-Communist cause." Kramer has set out in this book to right the balance single-handedly. *Twilight* is a continuous, controlled discharge of censure and opprobrium. Though elegantly written, it seethes. But ideological animus has its pitfalls. Genuine "Western defenders of Communist tyranny" were usually obscure and obtuse, so Kramer has had to find more interesting, even if less appropriate, objects for his retaliatory indignation. Hence anyone with doubts about the fundamental fairness of capitalism or the wisdom and benevolence of American foreign policy is liable to be excoriated as unpatriotic ("anti-American") or mindless ("incapable of serious thought about politics"). This habit, virtually a reflex, of denunciation extends to many people no less intelligent and honorable—or, for that matter, anti-Communist—than Kramer himself.

For example, Edmund Wilson's "political thought—if it can be called that" is derided in these terms: "no talent for politics … pacifist cliches … an embarrassment … fairly primitive … historical simplifications and moral insensibility … abiding incomprehension of the political life of his time." In other words, he was more skeptical than Kramer about the professed goals of America's military intervention in the Philippines, Cuba, and elsewhere. Dwight Macdonald was a fool, a fantast, a jester, a dandy, a snob, and a lightweight; also a cad who left

The Twilight of the Intellectuals: Politics and Culture in the Era of the Cold War by Hilton Kramer. Ivan R. Dee, 1999

his first wife. He changed his mind a lot, so he was essentially unserious. Curiously, perhaps, other anti-Communists saw him differently, like Czeslaw Milosz, who described himself as an "assiduous reader" of Macdonald's and praised him as a successor to "Thoreau, Whitman, and Melville ... a specific American type—the completely free man, capable of making decisions at all times and about all things strictly according to his personal moral judgments." (Macdonald's rebuke to his overzealous student hosts at Columbia's "counter-commencement" in 1968 was probably, by the way, a more effective blow in defense of Western civilization than all of Kramer's thunderbolts.) Irving Howe's politics amounted to nothing but sentimental piety and ideological opportunism; they were an "utter failure" except as "a ticket to the establishment in a period when his sort of Left-liberal values presided over, and continue to preside over, the precincts of cultural power." *The New Criterion*, incidentally, received more foundation support in its first year than Howe's *Dissent* did in its first thirty years.

Kramer's unquenchable vindictiveness generates endless unfairness and misjudgment. George Steiner's "blistering attack" on Solzhenitsyn and Mary McCarthy's "furious attack" on Orwell were nothing of the sort, as I read them—certainly they were puff pieces compared with Kramer's blistering and furious attacks on just about everyone. Susan Sontag's allegedly "adoring" essay, "Trip to Hanoi," intended to "deify" the North Vietnamese regime, contains this passage: "Having stated my admiration for the Vietnamese (people, society) as bluntly and vulnerably as I can, I should emphasize that none of this amounts to a claim that North Vietnam is a model of a just state. One has only to recall the more notorious crimes committed by the present government: for example, the persecution of the Trotskyist faction and the execution of its leaders in 1946, and the forcible collectivization of agriculture in 1956, the brutalities and injustices of which high officials have recently admitted." Not *completely* "adoring," then. Kramer savages

Diana Trilling's exquisite memoir, *The Beginning of the Journey*, which I (and most reviewers) found to be full of tact and moral delicacy, as cruelly tactless and "utterly indifferent to questions of moral delicacy"; and he blasted Mrs. Trilling (eighty-eight, blind, and failing when his essay appeared) for her "harsh verdicts," "ungenerous characterizations," and "lack of magnanimity." If he does say so himself. He professes disgust with Irving Howe's famous essay, "This Age of Conformity," for being "so abusive, so hypocritical, and so unforthcoming about himself at the very moment he was heaping his anathemas upon so many of his contemporaries, some of whom were in fact attempting to deal with the cultural and political situation ... more honestly and intelligently than he was." That is just what Howe never did, and just what Kramer regularly does.

About the New Left, in Kramer's opinion, there is nothing good to be said. It was in every way a disgrace, simply Stalinism in a new guise. The New Left indulged in a "vociferous revival of the totalitarian ideal," in "the glorification of totalitarian systems," in "an adamant refusal to acknowledge the moral superiority of American democracy over Soviet tyranny," and much more in the same vein. No evidence is offered, though doubtless some could be found. But it would need to be set against this passage from the 1962 Port Huron Statement, the founding document of Students for a Democratic Society and by far the most influential text within the New Left:

> As democrats we are in basic opposition to the communist system. The Soviet Union, as a system, rests on the total suppression of organized opposition, as well as a vision of the future in the name of which much human life has been sacrificed, and numerous small and large denials of human dignity rationalized.... Communist parties throughout the rest of the world are generally undemocratic in internal structure and mode of action. Moreover, in most cases they have subordinated radical programs to the requirements of Soviet foreign policy. The communist movement has failed, in every sense, to achieve its stated intention of leading a worldwide movement for human emancipation.

Anyone who offers unqualified pronouncements about the totalitarian sympathies of the New Left ought not to have been ignorant of this basic text.

This raises the question: what is Kramer's intellectual authority for calling so many people so many names? How persuasive is his own view of how the world outside Manhattan actually works? *The Twilight of the Intellectuals* contains exactly one sentence of geopolitical analysis: "What, after all, was the Cold War about if not the conflict between American (and Western) democracy and Soviet tyranny?" This is by no means an idiotic position. It is hardly, however, the last word. It does not rule out of court, as Kramer seems to believe, every other conceivable interpretation of twentieth-century American foreign policy. The left-wing interpretation, that this policy has been "guided by a primary commitment to improving the climate for business operations in a global system that is open to exploitation of human and material resources by those who dominate the domestic economy" (Noam Chomsky), is debatable, of course. But nothing in *The Twilight of the Intellectuals* suggests that Kramer knows enough about history or political economy to make his contemptuous dismissal of all such views anything but bluster and impertinence.

Kramer does have something good to say about a few people: Matthew Arnold, George Orwell, Lionel Trilling. But I doubt they would have had much good to say about Kramer, at least in his rancorous moments (i.e., most of the time). Arnold, most obviously; in the first place, because Arnold invariably began by putting his opponent's case as fully, generously, and dispassionately as possible—a procedure of which Kramer seems constitutionally incapable. And in the second place, because Arnold subscribed to one or two of the "radical pieties" that Kramer is continually jeering at. Arnold advocated democratic state action to lessen economic and social inequality. Only then, he believed, could the masses be brought to Culture. He would have been aghast at Reaganomics, the largest transfer of wealth from the non-rich to the rich in all of history. Half a trillion dollars could, after all, have brought the masses a lot closer to Culture. Kramer has no objection to Reaganomics.

Orwell, too, was an egalitarian and a democratic socialist. Kramer acknowledges this and makes absolutely nothing of it. His only interest is in arguing that the left has disingenuously sought to "re-interpret the meaning of [Orwell's] work in order to blunt its effect". Once again, the shoe appears to be on the other foot. I think Orwell would have reminded Kramer, as he reminded his readers in 1938: "It is an unfortunate fact that any hostile criticism of the present Russian regime is liable to be taken as propaganda *against Socialism*; all Socialists are aware of this, and it does not make for honest discussion." (Italics in original.)

Lionel Trilling is, quite appropriately, Kramer's lodestar. Kramer too is multifariously erudite, and his prose does occasionally approach the grace and polish of Trilling's—no small achievement. But the unfailingly courteous Trilling would have been appalled by Kramer's unrelenting harshness. More important, the unfailingly subtle Trilling would have been dismayed by Kramer's relentless simplifications. In *New York Jew*, Alfred Kazin made some shrewd observations about Trilling that may also help to place Kramer. "Trilling wrote as if the only problem of society was the thinking of the 'advanced intellectuals.'... In his America there were no workers, nobody suffering from a lack of cash; no capitalists, no corporations, no Indians, no blacks.... Like many less gifted and interesting ex-radicals, he was limited to New York, to his intellectual class, to friends who could never forgive themselves or anyone else for having in misguided youth trafficked in Socialism. But what raised Trilling above the dull zealots, informants, and false patriots of this agonizing period was the critic's gift for dramatizing his mind on paper. A writer of tremulous carefulness and deliberation, he nevertheless became the master of a dialectical style that expressed his underlying argument with himself. There was an intellectual tension in his essays...."

In Kramer's essays, there is no drama, no intellectual tension, because there is no underlying argument with himself. There is only assurance: ungracious, self-righteous, one-dimensional. Kramer is hardly dull; on the contrary, he is as sharp as a wasp's stinger. But he is, alas, a zealot.

The Fastidious Citizen

Gore Vidal has known, or at any rate met, nearly everyone of literary, political, or cinematic note during his lifetime. A great many of his essays feature anecdotes, always charming and often revealing, about his personal encounters with his subjects: for example, Tennessee Williams, Dawn Powell, Christopher Isherwood, Norman Mailer, Paul Bowles, Anthony Burgess, Italo Calvino, Amelia Earhart, Orson Welles, Frank Sinatra, the Roosevelts, Luces, Kennedys, Reagans, Gores.

I have never met Gore Vidal. But that seems a paltry reason for not beginning this *hommage* in the proper Vidalian manner. All right, then ...

One night in the winter of 1970, I was driving a taxicab in New York City. Outside a posh club, I was hailed by a tall, handsome gent in evening dress. "Old bores," he muttered as he climbed in. "Money and brains; never the twain shall meet without giving rise to truly lethal tedium."

"Where to?" I piped up.

"Wherever I can find some intelligent company," he sighed.

From a certain lyrical eloquence in the sigh, I guessed he meant literary company. "How about Elaine's?" I suggested, glancing at him in the rear-view mirror.

He winced. "No-o-o, thank you. Norman is probably presiding tonight. I'm not feeling sufficiently ... existential."

"The Gotham Book Mart is probably still open. Lots of writers hang out there, I think."

The handsome face wrinkled in distaste. "Also a few literary parasites, I'm afraid. I doubt I could control myself if I spotted Truman's malicious mug leering in my direction."

"Well, maybe the White Horse Tavern?"

He blanched. "Good God, no. Anais sometimes holds court there, fabulating reminiscences and emanating her legendary Life Force. Of course, she's the source of that legend."

I looked more closely in the rear-view, and this time I recognized him. "You're Gore Vidal, aren't you?"

Wary, noncommittal, slightly amused, he murmured: "Possibly."

I was inspired. "Well, why don't I just drive you home? Then you can have a nightcap alone, in the company of the most extraordinary assemblage of wit and talent since JFK invited all those intellectuals to dinner at the White House."

He snorted appreciatively, reached over and patted my head, and when I let him off at his hotel, gave me the biggest tip of my short cab-driving career.

Eugene Luther Gore Vidal Jr. has always enjoyed a healthy appreciation of his own, indeed remarkable, wit and talent. So have most other people, though approbation of his moral character has perhaps been less close to universal. His successes—best-selling novels, Broadway plays, screenplays, an enchanting memoir, and five decades of scintillating literary and political criticism—would be tedious to chronicle. (And superfluous, in the Age of Wikigooglepedia.) But what do they add up to? Is he famous for some more enduring reason than ... being famous?

He grew up in the penumbra of fame. His maternal grandfather, T.P. Gore, was more or less heroic: blind, Oklahoma's first senator, and a friend of Bryan and Darrow, Theodore Roosevelt and Woodrow Wilson. His father, Gene Vidal, was an All-American football player, World War I aviator, friend of Lindbergh and Earhart, and founder of TWA. His mother later married socialite par excellence Hugh Auchincloss, who would later become Jacqueline Bouvier Kennedy's stepfather as well.

In the vast attic of his grandparents' house in Rock Creek Park were thousands of books. Up there and downstairs, reading to his grandfather, he acquired an education. At school—St. Alban's, like his younger cousin Al Gore—he picked up Latin and fell in love with a godlike fellow student, who died a few years later, young and still perfect, on Iwo Jima. As told in Vidal's memoir, *Palimpsest*, it is one of the most stirring love stories in recent literature.

Back from the war himself, he published one of the first war novels, *Williwaw*. Public service in the family tradition was one possible future. Instead he wrote *The City and the Pillar*, a novel about a youthful homosexual affair that one of the boys, but not the other, leaves behind. So much for his political career, at least as of 1948.

Vidal spent the 1950s in the trenches, writing for money in television, Hollywood, and Broadway. He cavorted with the stars—Marlon Brando, Paul Newman, Joanne Woodward, and far too many others to mention. More perilously for his soul's health, he also cavorted with the Kennedys. But by the end of 1961, the moral and intellectual hollowness of Camelot was plain to him. With his nest egg, he left for Italy and novel-writing. In that place and that activity he has spent what he would doubtless call, with self-delighting *double entendre*, the better part of his life ever since.

It would be hard—and is, of course, unnecessary—to decide whether Vidal's novels or his essays are his greatest achievement. Certainly the seven-volume "American Chronicles" series is in the front rank of historical fiction; and at least two volumes, *Burr* and *Lincoln*, are indisputably masterpieces. *Julian*, it seems safe to predict, will long remain the only novel set in the fourth century, with a protagonist dedicated to turning back the fateful onrush of Christian fanaticism, ever to ascend to the top of the *New York Times* bestseller list. *Myra Breckinridge* was a minor milestone in the sexual revolution— perhaps not so minor.

Essay-writing was an afterthought. Edmund Wilson too would have preferred writing novels and plays to literary journalism—who wouldn't?—but he was never as successful as Vidal. As a result, Vidal tells us in *Palimpsest*,

> "I never wrote a proper essay until 1954, when I read a new translation of Suetonius' *Twelve Caesars*. Suddenly, I had so many thoughts on the subject of sex and power that I was obliged to write an essay... not for publication but just to clear my own mind. Eventually, it was published ... and that is how I became an essayist. I wrote first for myself; then for those few readers who might be interested in the resulting *essai*.

It was, he acknowledged, "not exactly novel writing, which I missed, but it was prose and kept me thinking" while he was churning out those scripts, earning that nest egg.

The fruits of those fifty-plus years of thinking on paper are harvested in *Selected Essays*.* The first thing to say is that this new collection does not replace *United States: Essays 1952–1992* and *The Last Empire: Essays 1992–2000*. Nothing could. The former, in particular, is the best collection in recent decades of essays by any American writer, except perhaps for last year's two-volume Library of America edition of Edmund Wilson. At 1300 pages, *United States* is, however, a little bulky. So there is every reason to cheer Vidal on his way to Valhalla with the publication of this compact yet comprehensive and very well-chosen volume, a kind of *crème de la crème* with strawberries.

More than strawberries, Vidal is perhaps best known for his raspberries, which are well represented here by "American Plastic," "The Hacks of Academe," and "The Top Ten Best-Sellers According to the New York Times as of January 7, 1973." The first of these, though by no means a hatchet job, does make one grateful not to have read much of John Barth or Donald Barthelme. It also expresses a far more discriminating admiration for William Gass than is usual among reviewers of that over-admired writer. But nothing in "Plastic" equals the joyous havoc wrought on the bestsellers, whose roots, structural and thematic, in bad Hollywood movies Vidal convincingly demonstrates. Poor Herman Wouk (*Winds of War*) and Frederick Forsyth (*The Odessa File*) receive a brisk version of the treatment meted out to James Gould Cozzens by Dwight Macdonald and to Judith Krantz by Clive James. Even "the noble engineer Solzhenitzyn" (*August 1914*), though an exemplar of "man's indomitable spirit in tyrannous society," is chiefly talented at "describing how things work, and it is plain that nature destined him to write manuals of artillery or instructions on how to take apart a threshing machine."

The Selected Essays of Gore Vidal, edited by Jay Parini. Doubleday, 2008.

But though he can be devastatingly snide ("Rabbit's Own Burrow" makes John Updike pay very dearly for a few censorious remarks about our hero and other "frivolous" opponents of the Vietnam War), Vidal's generosity is more characteristic and even more satisfying. Some of his subjects in *Selected Essays*, like Tennessee Williams and Edmund Wilson, may not have needed critical rehabilitation, but William Dean Howells and Dawn Powell did. Twenty-five years ago, Howells was frequently dismissed as dry and lifeless, the faded flower of a genteel tradition. Explicating *Indian Summer, A Modern Instance,* and *Silas Lapham*, Vidal reconstructs Howells' "subtle and wise reading of the world," which "opened the way to Dreiser and to all those other realists who were to see the United States plain." And the first half-dozen pages of the Howells essay contain a surprising revelation. As the judicial murder of the Haymarket Square defendants unfolded in 1886, "of the Republic's major literary and intellectual figures ... only one"—Howells—"took a public stand."

Dawn Powell's novels were all out of print in 1987 when Vidal's long appreciation in the *New York Review* pronounced her "our best comic novelist." Her studies of genuine Midwestern dullness and ersatz New York City gaiety, rendered with fearless, pungent wit and entirely without sentimentality or euphemism, may have been, as Vidal claimed, "Balzacian" and as good a portrait as we have of mid-twentieth-century America. But in this they were fatally unlike the top ten bestsellers of 1973 or any other year. She died more or less obscure in 1965, and Vidal's influential revaluation doubtless brought a smile to her long-suffering shade.

Around half the essays here are broadly political. The hacks of academe (new generation) have put it about that everything is political, especially textual analyses of great literature that reveal, through the application of emancipatory ideology and subversive wordplay, that the past was even less enlightened than the present. Besides allowing critical minnows to patronize artistic whales, this approach frees academic literary intellectuals from having to learn much about history, economics, politics, or how to compose English prose.

Without ever saying so, Vidal also manages to suggest that everything is political, though in a very different, non-postmodern sense. To a sufficiently sensitive and knowledgeable critic, everything will appear intelligent or unintelligent, skillful or shoddy, graceful or graceless, truthful or mendacious. In each of these pairs, the latter is—not immediately, perhaps, but ultimately, in some measure—a threat to our common life, our *res publica*. Intellectual virtues are civic virtues; intellectual vices leave the citizens vulnerable to superstition and demagoguery. There is, of course, no more sense in trying to legislate the intellectual virtues than the moral ones. But one can *propagate* intellectual virtue, first of all by example. This is Vidal's abiding contribution to American politics.

The prevailing American superstitions are: 1) there is a Supreme Being, omnipotent and benevolent; 2) some sexual predilections are more natural than others; and 3) there is no class system in the United States. No one who denies any of these things can be elected to high office. As a patriot, Vidal naturally has no patience with this affront to our civic intelligence. Some of his most memorable onslaughts on our national delusions are included in *Selected Essays*.

"Monotheism and Its Discontents" is forthright. "The great unmentionable evil at the center of our culture … the greatest disaster ever to befall the human race … is monotheism." Vidal's dislike is ecumenical; Judaism, Christianity, and Islam are all "sky-god religions." The sky-god is, alas, a jealous god, whose intolerance and bloodlust have set a very bad example for his more devoted followers, whose unyielding irrationality managed in only a few decades, Vidal laments, to pervert the Founders' entirely secular purposes. "Monotheism" was written in 1992; sixteen years later, the danger is much more widely recognized. I suspect Vidal's puckish but prescient call for "an all-out war on the monotheists" had some effect in stimulating the salutary secularist counteroffensive.

In (possibly premature) retrospect, it appears that the historical function of neoconservatism was to supply an intellectual rationale for the worst impulses of traditional conservatism. The attack on the welfare state rationalized—in effect if not intention—greed and class privilege. With the same qualification, the attack on affirmative action rationalized racial hostility. The attack on multilateralism and international law has, less ambiguously, rationalized national chauvinism and aggressive tribalism. Midge Decter's "The Boys on the Beach," a vaguely Freudian analysis of homosexuality as pathology, was a not at all ambiguous effort to rationalize sexual bigotry. But thanks to Vidal, this was the least successful of all the neoconservative ideological operations. "Pink Triangle and Yellow Star"—perhaps his best-known essay—so thoroughly demolished Decter's smug fatuities that neither the pseudo-psychoanalytic approach to homosexuality nor, mercifully, Decter herself ever regained intellectual respectability.

My favorites among Vidal's essays, both included in this volume, are "Homage to Daniel Shays" and "The Second American Revolution." Soon after the Revolutionary War, the eternal tension between lenders and borrowers, the rich and everyone else, came to a crisis in New England. Daniel Shays led thousands of small farmers, many of them former soldiers in the Revolutionary army who stood to lose their land to creditors, in search of debt relief and tax relief. The rich fought back, first militarily and then by writing a constitution that imposed a strong central government disproportionately weighted in favor of the propertied.

That Constitution has become the American Scripture, our political Holy Writ, and a chronic obstacle to popular initiative. Dissolving the mystique of the Constitution and those who framed it, as well as that of the revered *Federalist Papers*—whose "general tone," Vidal accurately observes, "is that of a meeting of the trust department of Sullivan and Cromwell"—is essential to our civic health. These two essays, along with Vidal's historical fiction, are powerful dissolving agents.

Disillusioning Americans about their government's international behavior is equally essential. After a PEN benefit one night in the mid-1980s, Arthur Schlesinger Jr. confided to his diary: "Gore gave a (relatively) polished talk about the American empire, banal in content, cheap in tone, and delivered to the accompaniment of smiles of vast self-satisfaction." Presumably it was the tone Schlesinger objected to; his own self-satisfied banalities about the American empire were always pronounced with reverence and *gravitas*.

Vidal's *bête noire* (and unsurprisingly, Schlesinger's hero) was Harry Truman. The National Security Act of 1947; the creation of the CIA, with its unconstitutional exemption from Congressional scrutiny; the containment doctrine, supposedly for defense against Soviet expansionism but promptly invoked to justify the rearming of Germany and interventions in Greece, Guatemala, Iran, and elsewhere; the paranoid secret blueprint for the Cold War, NSC-68—all these Truman-era setbacks for democracy are described in "The National Security State," along with a modest and sensible five-point program that, decades later, still sounds like a very good way to begin reclaiming the country.

It's not clear, though, to me and I suspect to Vidal, that American democracy *can* be reclaimed, at least in the form of vigorous, Jeffersonian self-government. (As Vidal points out with his customary sardonic relish, Jefferson himself began selling out Jeffersonianism during his second term.) The reasons are both structural—mass production simply may not leave enough room for individual autonomy—and clinical—like muscles, intellectual and civic virtues may atrophy beyond repair. No matter who is elected President this fall, the country may become an ever more dispiriting place for a conservative-radical aristocratic republican of Vidal's stamp.

If so, he has much to teach us about grace in an era of decline. Twice before, he has lived, in imagination, through the death of a cherished ideal. The first was paganism, splendidly memorialized in *Julian*. In that novel's climactic scene, the eponymous emperor appeals to the assembled Christian bishops, who are bent on destroying traditional religion, "never to forget that the greatness of our world was the gift of other gods and a different, more subtle philosophy, reflecting the variety in nature." Of course that more subtle philosophy was soon driven underground, where it has remained ever since. But things can live a long time underground, especially when nourished by occasional infusions like *Julian*.

"French Letters: Theories of the New Novel," another well-known essay reprinted here, reported on the programmatic writings of Nathalie Sarraute, Alain Robbe-Grillet, Roland Barthes, and their American enthusiasts, none of whom saw much of a future for the traditional novel. Vidal agreed, not because the traditional novel is exhausted but because its traditional audience has been captured by electronic distractions. A melancholy prospect, which he greeted with barbed but eloquent stoicism:

> The portentous theorizings of the New Novelists are of no more use to us than the self-conscious avant-gardism of those who are forever trying to figure out what the next "really serious" thing will be when it is plain that there is not going to be a next serious thing in the novel. Our lovely vulgar and most human art is at an end, if not the end. Yet that is no reason not to want to practice it, or even to read it. In any case, rather like priests who have forgotten the meaning of the prayers they chant, we shall go on for quite a long time talking of books and writing books, pretending all the while not to notice that the church is empty and the parishioners have gone elsewhere to attend other gods, perhaps in silence or with new words.

Whatever dreariness lies ahead for our endlessly benighted and bamboozled republic, Gore Vidal's mocking, disenchanted patriotism will always be a resource for its well-wishers.

Vanity and Spleen

It has always been with me a test of the sense and candor of anyone belonging to the opposite party, whether he allowed Christopher Hitchens to be an ornament of Anglo-American literary journalism. Hundreds of novelists, historians, memoirists, and politicians have undergone Hitchens' critical attentions, to the frequent edification and unfailing entertainment of his readers. Few present-day journalists have a detectable, much less unmistakable, prose style; the suavity and piquancy of Hitchens' prose are unmatched among his critical peers.

Equally admirable is his breadth of reading; he has made an art of casual allusion. "Erudition" is not quite right; it suggests labor, and what is most impressive about the way Hitchens liberally sprinkles unfailingly apposite quotes from Auden and Larkin, Waugh and Wodehouse, Jefferson and Churchill throughout his essays is his apparent effortlessness. He always seems to have been reading just the right book at just the right moment—though at a certain point it dawns on you that it can't be an accident; he really must be intimate with an extraordinary expanse of modern European history and literature.

The essays collected in *Prepared for the Worst* (1988), *For the Sake of Argument* (1991), *Unacknowledged Legislation* (2000), *Love, Poverty, and War* (2004), and now *Arguably**, range almost inconceivably widely. A short gallery of personal favorites would begin with his portrait of Thomas Paine, whom he praises in terms that strikingly parallel Lionel Trilling on Orwell:

> Everything he wrote was plain, obvious, and within the mental compass of the average. In that lay his genius. And, harnessed to his courage (which *was* exceptional) and his pen (which was at

**Arguably: Essays* by Christopher Hitchens. Twelve Books, 2011.

any rate out of the common), this faculty of the ordinary made him outstanding.

It would include his portrait of Conor Cruise O'Brien, to whose variegated political and intellectual career Hitchens renders difficult and delicate justice. His first embattled defense of Orwell (several others would follow) remarks penetratingly that "the essence of Orwell's work is a sustained criticism of servility. It is not *what* you think but *how* you think that matters." There are blistering takedowns of English politicians Reginald Maudling and Michael Foot and American neoconservatives Norman Podhoretz and Charles Krauthammer, which, brief though they are, deserve to outlive their subjects. There is a harrowing report from El Salvador under the death squads, with a muted and diffident (but all the more affecting) tribute to the Catholic resistance.

A brief, tossed-off column from 25 years ago is virtually Hitchens' sole effort to formulate a political philosophy. It is so good that one is furious with him for never returning to the subject:

> I bought an armful of socialist magazines in London recently, and was impressed by their dogged iteration of the new rage for free-market, individualist formulae.... Once the intoxication of this "new thinking" has worn off, it will again become boringly clear that all macro questions are questions that confront society rather than the individual.... This is true of the imperiled web of nature and climate, which when messed around with can lead to dustbowls in one province and floods in the neighboring one. It is true of the water that can bring lead into the blood and bone of children. There is no "minimal government" solution to any of these pressing matters.
>
> One doesn't want or need to argue this with any relish. The idea of the individual should not be glibly counterposed to the idea of society. After all, what is society made up of, if not individuals? But there are two ways of facing collective responsibilities. One is to ignore them until it is too late, at which point things like rationing, conscription, and regimentation become the options, irrespective of whether the system is capitalist or socialist. The other is to recognize them in time and take the necessary measures freely and by consent. But there is no evading these responsibilities altogether, or of dismissing them as "One World sentimentality."

   ... The family, so often piously invoked by Tories, is in fact an elementary form of socialism. It operates, without undue repression, on the principle of "from each according to his/her ability and to each according to his/her need." ... The family core is the recognition that an injury to one is an injury to all—a precept that many people can recognize only when it is put to them in a self-interested way.

   ... there is an amazing persistence to the notion that everybody can, by his or her own efforts, become an autonomous proprietor. Surely this, rather than the socialist vision, is the real utopianism? At the moment, Wall Street is operating on the false promise, not of the usual well-worn casino metaphor, but of a casino *where nobody loses.*... Increasingly, it is the partisans of the unfettered enterprise culture who have to answer that old trick question—who's going to do the hard work?

   ... So certain truisms are beginning to resound again. If we don't hang together, we *will* hang separately. The bell *does* toll for us all. It will not do to listen to the cheerleader business-politicians whose motto is "Only disconnect." The values of solidarity, collectivism, and internationalism are not so much desirable as they are actually mandated by nature and reality itself.

Alas, these examples have only gotten us through Hitchens's first collection, *Prepared for the Worst.* There is no space left to mention his authoritative pieces on the New York intellectuals and Noel Annan's portrait of the British Establishment, or "Booze and Fags," a jolly paean to alcohol and tobacco, or an illuminating essay on *Daniel Deronda* (all in *For the Sake of Argument*); the pair of exquisite tributes to Oscar Wilde, the discerning essays on Conan Doyle, Kipling, and Anthony Powell, or the full-on considerations of Isaiah Berlin and Whittaker Chambers, Gore Vidal and Andy Warhol (in *Unacknowledged Legislation*); the magisterial assessments of Trotsky and Churchill, the wonderfully perceptive, V. S. Pritchett-like essays on Byron, Huxley, Waugh, Joyce, Proust, Borges, and Bellow, or the simultaneously rollicking and haunting record of a trip the length of Route 66 in a rented red Corvette (in *Love, Poverty, and War*).

And even this leaves out his books: *No One Left to Lie To,* a definitive account (or as near as possible) of Bill Clinton's mendacity; *The Trial of Henry Kissinger*, which has convinced hundreds of thousands of readers (some of them sitting magistrates in foreign countries) that President Obama's fellow Nobel laureate should be behind bars; and *God Is Not Great*, the first *New York Times* number one bestseller to advance that claim. It's clear, I'm afraid, that within the confines of a mere book review, any short gallery of personal favorites will be frustratingly incomplete. There's simply too much very good Hitchens.

Of course, not all of Hitchens was very good, even before 9/11 drove him mad. He was always too ready with abuse ("stupid" and "tenth-rate" were particular weaknesses). He is a compulsive name-dropper: in his very short *Letters to a Young Contrarian*, for example, the words "my friend," followed by a distinguished name, appear dozens of times, giving the reader's eyebrows a considerable workout. Some of the aforementioned allusions flow a little too readily: there is a subtle difference between relishing a fine phrase and relishing hearing oneself quote a fine phrase. And in recent years, he has occasionally fallen into what might be called the knightly style, where mellifluousness modulates into orotundity. "The disagreeable and surreptitious element of this story cannot indefinitely remain unexamined." "The masochistic British attitude to inevitable decline seems to have reversed itself, at least to some extent." All too many occurrences of "I think I may venture to say," "if I may make so bold as to observe," "I hope I may be forgiven for pointing out," and the like. Fortunately, Hitchens the staunch republican has so frequently and zestfully insulted the British monarchy that he is in no danger of becoming Sir Christopher.

More damagingly, his politics have always been a little too first-person. Some memorable portraits and descriptions have resulted from his many extensively reported trips to the world's trouble spots, but not much valuable insight. The tendency of one's first-hand experience—the testimony one has heard, the suffering one has witnessed, the bonds one has formed—to crowd other people's arguments to the margins of judgment is hard to resist. To hope for drama and analysis, passion and wisdom, from the same writer, at any rate on the same occasion, is usually vain. Hitchens' genuine, generous, longstanding hatred of oppression—a rare quantity among proponents of America's wars on Serbia, Afghanistan, and Iraq—has nevertheless had disastrous results over the last dozen years.

I began this review by paraphrasing Hazlitt on Burke. When he passed from praising Burke to chastising him, Hazlitt observed sternly that "the poison of high example has by far the widest range of destruction." Hitchens' single-minded advocacy of unilateral American military intervention has been as destructive as any mere scribbler's efforts could be. "The very subtlety of his reasoning," Hazlitt wrote of Burke, "became a dangerous engine in the hands of power, which is always eager to make use of the most plausible pretexts to cover the most fatal designs." Hitchens' reasoning has been anything but subtle, but he has more than made up for the poverty of his arguments with rich stores of invective, anecdote, and—as a last refuge—rhetorical patriotism.

What changed Hitchens' mind about American foreign policy? Three things, it seems. The first was a growing identification, the longer he resided here, with American society and culture, a romance affectingly described in his autobiography, *Hitch-22*. The second was his increasingly militant anticlericalism, fed especially by the Ayatollah Khomeini's *fatwa* against Hitchens' friend Salman Rushdie. The third was a long-gathering disaffection with the Anglo-American left, which he saw as frozen in postures of multiculturalism and anti-Americanism. He refers in the introduction to *Arguably* to an "ongoing polemic … between the anti-imperialist left and the anti-totalitarian left"; announcing his accession to the latter in *Hitch-22*, he described the former as those who "in the final instance believe that if the United States is doing something, then that thing cannot *by definition* be a moral or ethical action." Perhaps because of chronic deadline pressure, Hitchens has never plumbed this important question any deeper than that facile opposition and glib taunt.

Rumbling around inside Hitchens, these ingredients produced dyspepsia in the 1990s, when he eventually accepted
NATO's rationale for its "humanitarian" bombing of Serbia and
berated his comrades for insufficient hostility to the repellent
Clinton (though not because Clinton had destroyed American
manufacturing with his "free trade" agreements and acceler-
ated the financialization of the economy, matters about which
Hitchens had nothing to say). 9/11 churned his feelings to the
point of nausea, and he vomited (or as he would say, spewed).
This reaction did his insides much good—he proclaimed the
relief "unbelievable." But as with most such eructations, the
results were indiscriminate.

His reports from Kurdistan, southern Iraq, and Afghanistan
were vivid and moving. His account in *Hitch-22* of his ideological evolution was admirably honest, even if a little long on anecdote and short on analysis. But his arguments—collected in *A
Long Short War* (2003)—were as feeble as they were smug. A
convenient, though very partial, catalogue of Hitchens' sophist-
ries was assembled by Norman Finkelstein:

> To prove that, after supporting dictatorial regimes in the Middle
> East for 70 years, the US has abruptly reversed itself and now wants
> to bring democracy there, he cites "conversations I have had on this
> subject in Washington." To demonstrate the "glaringly apparent"
> fact that Saddam "infiltrated, or suborned, or both" the UN inspec-
> tion teams in Iraq, he adduces the "incontrovertible case" of an
> inspector offered a bribe by an Iraqi official: "the man in question
> refused the money, but perhaps not everybody did." . . .
>
> Hitchens maintains that that "there is a close . . . fit between the
> democratically minded and the pro-American" in the Middle East—
> like "President for Life" Hosni Mubarak. . ; that the US's rejoining
> of UNESCO during the Iraq debate proved its commitment to the
> UN; that "empirical proofs have been unearthed" showing that
> Iraq didn't comply with UN resolutions to disarm; that since the
> UN solicits US support for multilateral missions, it's "idle chatter"
> to accuse the US of acting unilaterally in Iraq; that the likely kill-
> ing of innocent civilians in "hospitals, schools, mosques and pri-
> vate homes" shouldn't deter the US from attacking Iraq because
> it is proof of Saddam's iniquity that he put civilians in harm's way;

that those questioning billions of dollars in postwar contracts going to Bush administration cronies must prefer them going to "some windmill-power concern run by Naomi Klein."

Hitchens' response to these and all other criticisms—including the fundamental one, that preventive war is a step toward international anarchy—has been sheer bluster, an entirely unconvincing insistence that he has been right all along, in every particular, with 20/20 foresight. Everything that has happened since the invasion—half a million deaths and several million refugees, not to mention the half-million deaths from sanctions that preceded it, and the wholesale and unnecessary aerial devastation of Iraqi infrastructure both in 1991 and 2003, in addition to deep inroads on civil liberties and constitutional government at home—is not our fault. But everything good that has happened is our doing—notably the Arab Spring, whose participants in fact repeatedly tell pollsters of their fear and mistrust of the United States, stemming largely from past and present American military interventions in the region. Although this is not a grown-up position, Hitchens has maintained it unflappably, and his reputation has not suffered. But then, no one has ever suffered much for flattering the prejudices of the American foreign policy elite. Willingness to affirm the unique moral status and prerogatives of the United States has always been the chief prerequisite of political or journalistic Very Serious Personhood.

Arguably is much the longest of Hitchens' collections (and perhaps his last—he has advanced esophageal cancer). It is very rewarding, with book-length (or very nearly) sections on American writers, English writers, writers under totalitarian regimes, and "Offshore Accounts"—reports/profiles/capsule histories of two dozen countries or international episodes. The choicest delicacies on this groaning board are a dozen or so exquisite appreciations: of Rebecca West, Evelyn Waugh, P. G. Wodehouse, Anthony Powell, John Buchan, Saki, Philip Larkin,

Victor Serge, Victor Klemperer, W. G. Sebald, the novels of Fleet Street, the *Flashman* novels, and Hilary Mantel's *Wolf Hall*. Two charming throwaways, one on "like," the other on the (soon-to-be-obsolete?) problem of not enough bookshelves, make one wish Hitchens had not given up to mankind what was meant for a few discriminating readers. But there is fine, mellow writing in each of the book's 107 pieces.

Arguably is low on provocations: most of Hitchens' worst writing appears in his *Slate* column, "Fighting Words," which is mercifully underrepresented here. But slender threads of belligerence and chauvinism run through the book. Some are comparatively inconsequential. An essay on "Jefferson and the Muslim Pirates" offers these reflections:

> [T]he Barbary Wars gave Americans an inkling of the fact that they were, and always would be, bound up with global affairs. Providence might have seemed to grant them a haven guarded by two oceans, but if they wanted to be anything more than the Chile of North America—a long littoral ribbon caught between the mountains and the sea—they would have to prepare for a maritime struggle as well as a campaign to redeem the unexplored landmass to their west. The US Navy's Mediterranean squadron has, in one form of another, been on patrol ever since.

Besides managing to suggest that an American global military presence, particularly in the Middle East, is simply an expression of our national destiny, this passage also nicely elides a century of hideous cruelty and greed. In the phrase, "redeem the unexplored landmass to their west," it is hard to decide which word is more offensive: "redeem" or "unexplored." "Conquer the rest of the continent," though perhaps less sonorous, would have been infinitely less objectionable. It is difficult to imagine the pre-9/11 Hitchens forgetting himself to such an extent; and, to be fair, even Hitchens post-9/11 rarely sounds so Blimpish.

But other, more characteristic remarks are less forgivable. In "The Anglosphere Future," Hitchens again employs ideologically polarized lenses. This time he looks ahead, toward a worldwide commonwealth of English-speaking nations, based on America's indestructible prosperity (the essay was published a few months before the Great Recession began), on the solidarity of America's English-speaking allies against Islamic radicalism ("a barbarism that is no less menacing than its predecessors ... the Nazi-Fascist Axis ... and international Communism"), and on the English language itself ("uniquely hostile to euphemisms for tyranny").

> The shape of the world since September 11 has, in fact, shown the outline of such an alliance in practice. Everybody knows of Tony Blair's solidarity with the United States, but when the chips were down, Australian forces also went to Iraq. Attacked domestically for being "all the way with the USA," Australian prime minister John Howard made the imperishable observation that in times of crisis, there wasn't much point in being 75 percent a friend.

Leaving aside whether an Anglosphere is feasible or desirable, Hitchens here falls into the propagandist's habit of saying "the United States" when he means "the government of the United States." In this case, actually, even "the government of the United States" would have been misleading. The rush to war with Iraq was led, in the words of the appalled chief of staff to the Secretary of State, by "a cabal between the Vice President of the United States and the Secretary of Defense on critical issues, which made decisions that the bureaucracy did not even know were being made." This cabal was the object of Tony Blair's solidarity, not "the United States." Blair might, moreover, have shown a little more solidarity with the British public, which opposed the intervention even in the teeth of drumbeating by the Murdoch press, and indeed with his own government, whose attorney general warned him that the invasion was illegal and whose intelligence service warned him that the American cabal's arguments were dishonest. As for Australia's doughty prime minister, who also disdained solidarity with his own public, he might have been a better friend to the United States by admonishing its government (or governing cabal) to obey international law and cease lying to the American people and the rest of the world. The United States badly needed such admonitions from its foreign friends, since the American media and most intellectuals, with Hitchens in the vanguard, shirked that responsibility.

In his great essay, Hazlitt summed up:

> Burke was an acute and accomplished man of letters—an ingenious political essayist … He had the power of throwing true or false weights into the scales of political casuistry, but not firmness of mind enough (or shall we say, honesty enough) to hold the balance. When he took a side, his vanity or his spleen more frequently gave the casting vote than his judgment; and the fieriness of his zeal was in exact proportion to the levity of his understanding, and the want of conscious sincerity.

Whether or not one finds this true of Burke, it is Hitchens to the life.

Human Scale

In 1994 Christopher Lasch died at the age of 61, an inestimable loss to all those interested in American politics and culture. The same year an even more calamitous loss occurred: the death—or at least a critical stage in the decline—of New Deal liberalism. The newly elected Republican Congress commenced, with ferocious energy and thoroughness, to dismantle or undermine the institutions that had produced, in the decades following World War II, the appearance of a permanent liberal ascendancy. From 1994 through 2008, the "wrecking crew" (Thomas Frank's apt phrase) and the army of corporate lobbyists it invited into government at all levels accomplished a work of sustained demolition, with feeble and intermittent opposition (and sometimes enthusiastic assistance) from Democrats.

The waning of New Deal liberalism has reduced the immediacy of Lasch's critique, which was directed principally at the mid-20th-century liberal consensus. The liberal complacency against which Lasch continually warned has been replaced by liberal demoralization; the optimistic expectations of unlimited progress he deprecated have given way to anxieties about governmental stasis, economic collapse, and environmental catastrophe. No doubt most epochs seem like emergencies to their beleaguered contemporaries. But compared with the decades in which Lasch wrote, the ugliness of American politics in the early 21st century seems almost to justify a neglect of long-term perspectives and wide-ranging theories.

Almost but of course not quite. We may not need Lasch's historical erudition or analytical subtlety to recognize the worst of the present dangers: the corruption of Congress by a flood of money from corporate and ultra-rich donors; the colossal squandering of resources on "defense" spending in all its varieties; the fanatical obstructionism of the Republican Party. But even if our current plutocracy is not succeeded by a restored New Deal liberalism, it will be succeeded by something. The degradation of American politics will eventually bottom out, and reconstruction will begin. Americans then will need to understand the weaknesses of the society that preceded the debacle, and of its prevailing self-justifications. To these weaknesses Lasch was an incomparable guide. Eric Miller's fine intellectual biography will help keep Lasch's thought available as a resource against that (hopefully not too distant) day.*

About Lasch's life, Miller is discreet. There is little about Lasch's wife and children, though a great deal about his warm lifelong relationship with his parents. Robert and Zora Lasch were Midwestern populists and religious skeptics, he a journalist, she a philosopher turned social worker. Their steady encouragement was important to their son, and Miller quotes frequently from their sensible, affectionate, often witty letters. The only other personal relationship that features much in the book is with Eugene Genovese, the noted Marxist historian, who brought Lasch to the University of Rochester with ambitious talk about department-building and founding new journals, but who proved impossible to work with. John Updike, Lasch's first-year roommate at Harvard, also puts in a couple of appearances. Miller's extensive and skillful use of Lasch's letters conveys an appealing impression of him as a generous, cordial, unguarded correspondent. Still, the biography's focus is overwhelmingly on Lasch's writings and the critical reaction to them.

Lasch's books (except for his first, *The American Liberals and the Russian Revolution*, 1962, based on his dissertation) fall into three broad, overlapping categories: essays on American politics and history, with particular attention to the role of intellectuals (*The New Radicalism in America*, 1965; *The Agony of the American Left*, 1969; *The World of Nations*, 1973; *The Revolt of*

*Hope in a Scattering Time: A Life of Christopher Lasch by Eric Miller. Eerdmans, 2010.

the Elites, 1995; and the posthumously assembled *Women and the Common Life*, 1997); psychoanalytically grounded studies of American culture and social thought (*Haven in a Heartless World*, 1977; *The Culture of Narcissism*, 1979; *The Minimal Self*, 1984); and prophecy (*The True and Only Heaven*, 1991).

Lasch's most enduring contributions, in all these phases, had to do with the relationship between modernity and democracy. But his more topical writings also deserve to be remembered. Though he frequently and fiercely criticized the American left, there were few differences among Lasch and his New Left comrades about Vietnam, the Cold War, and foreign policy generally. He unambiguously rejected American exceptionalism, that apparently unkillable delusion among both liberals and conservatives that idealism and "good intentions" have—in reality, and not merely in rhetoric—featured prominently in America foreign policy. His judgment of "Wilsonian idealism"—regularly praised or deplored by contemporary commentators, though largely fictitious—was unsparing:

> The trouble with Wilson was not that he went off crusading for high ideals and ignored American self-interest. The trouble was that, like most statesmen, he found it so easy unconsciously to translate the self-interest of his own community into the language of high idealism. The most striking fact about the twentieth-century dream of world peace and order, of which Wilson was to become the prophet, was not that it was utopian but that it was a one-sided Utopia, a world made safe not for democracy but for ourselves.... From the point of view of three-fourths of the world, Wilson's famous quarrel with Clemenceau, which appeared so momentous to the new "realists" (as to all Western scholars), was less important than their shared determination to keep that same three-fourths in its place.

The Vietnam War appeared to Lasch an illegitimate and undemocratic exercise of executive power, in which "pluralism and countervailing power were nonexistent" and "the public was without effective representation of any kind"—a clear refutation of the "genial theory" of the "consensus school." The "main lines of American foreign policy have remained consistent": above all, "opposition to social revolution" and the "gradual displacement of the old European empires and maintenance of these empires under American auspices or client regimes." Liberal intellectuals have obligingly "supplied a 'tragic' view of the world, stressing the inconclusiveness of diplomacy and the impossibility of quick solutions, that made more palatable the assumption of commitments the consequences of which were impossible to predict."

The irresponsibility of intellectuals was a leitmotif of Lasch's writings. It was their contributions to the evolution of work, education, and the family that occupied him most, but he also had something important to say about intellectuals and Leviathan in such essays as *"The New Republic* and the War" (ie, World War I), "The Cultural Cold War," "'Realism' as a Critique of American Diplomacy," and "The Foreign Policy Elite and the War in Vietnam." Intellectuals' repeated seduction into "associating themselves with the war-making and propaganda machinery in the hope of influencing it" betrayed a loss of faith in democracy, indeed in intellect itself, a "haunting suspicion that history belongs to men of action and that men of ideas are powerless in a world that has no use for philosophy." Time after time in the 20th century, he admonished, "it has been shown that the dream of influencing the war machine is a delusion. Instead the war machine corrupts the intellectuals."

It was not these moral failings that interested Lasch, however, so much as the changing role of intellectuals, and in particular their increasing function as agents of social control in corporate management and in the medical, welfare, and educational bureaucracies. In the new industrial state, intellectuals were indispensable not merely for rationalizing wars but also for supplying technological innovation, directing production, guiding consumer demand, performing psychological maintenance, and socializing the young. The evolution of this "new paternalism"—and more generally, the transformation of knowledge from a means of emancipation to a means of domination—was Lasch's constant theme, especially in the first half of his career.

Lasch's account of this evolution began with the democratic revolution of the 18th and early 19th centuries in the United States, which successively undermined monarchy, established religion, landed elites, and Southern slavery. The protagonists of this movement were artisans, small farmers, and independent entrepreneurs, in alliance with an emerging propertied class of bankers and industrialists. But their goals differed: the former, according to Lasch, sought "the freedom to control the terms of their work, not merely to sell their labor at ruinous prices" in the new, large-scale enterprises, while the latter merely wanted "to free property from its feudal and mercantile restrictions." After the Civil War, faced with "unrest at home and the spectacle of the Paris Commune abroad," the propertied classes drew back. At first they offered top-down reforms, meant to "professionalize the civil service, break the power of the urban machine, and put the 'best men' into office." But these measures could not satisfy credit-starved farmers or harshly exploited factory workers. Agrarian radicalism and labor militancy drove far-sighted capitalists and liberal reformers toward a more thorough rationalization of the industrial system:

> They brought forward their own version of the "cooperative commonwealth" in the name of progressivism: universal education, welfare capitalism, scientific management of industry and government. The New Deal completed what progressivism had begun, solidifying the foundations of the welfare state and adding much of the superstructure as well. In industry, scientific management gave way to the school of human relations, which tried to substitute cooperation for authoritarian control. But this cooperation rested on management's monopoly of technology and the reduction of work to routines imperfectly understood by the worker and controlled by the capitalist. Similarly the expansion of welfare services presupposed the reduction of the citizen to a consumer of expertise.

The mechanisms of this far-reaching rationalization and its effects on the characters and intimate relations of those subject to it are analyzed in the books of Lasch's middle period. At the center of his analysis is the loss of autonomy entailed by mass production and the division of labor. "Before the Civil War," he points out, "it was generally agreed, across a broad spectrum of political opinion, that democracy had no future in a nation of hirelings." Self-reliance was obviously the foundation of such civic virtues as courage, honesty, ingenuity, and self-sacrifice, and no one imagined that any democracy worthy of the name could flourish without such virtues. But the factory system and the new corporate form of business organization rendered the very notion of self-reliance obsolete. The obvious, political consequences—the eclipse of popular sovereignty—were bad enough. It was the less obvious, psychosocial consequences, however, that Lasch attempted to describe with his theory of a "culture of narcissism."

The popular understanding of "narcissism"—excessive self-love, à la Donald Trump or Bernard-Henri Lévy—has little to do with the psychoanalytic conception. Freudian narcissism denotes not overweening self-assertion but desperate self-protection. How, according to psychoanalytic theory, does a secure self come to be? The human infant, born with a brain uniquely undeveloped in comparison with those of other newborn animals, at first can recognize no distinctions or limits. Gradually, the inevitable occurrence of frustration forces on it a recognition of its separateness from, and dependence on, the rest of the world. It reacts against the source of this frustration—its parents—with a rage which, because its parents are also its sole source of nurture, it cannot comprehend or tolerate. So it represses this intolerable rage—which, like all repressed emotion, returns in the form of distorted and outsized fantasies, in this case of idealized or demonized parents.

Fantasies are a kind of psychic specter, which must be vanquished or maturity will be inhibited—they will, after a fashion, imprison the self. In premodern times, what vanquished the child's fantasies—gradually wore them down to manageable dimensions—was everyday contact of a certain sort with its parents. The regular experience of love and discipline from the same source; the gradual lessening of the mother's attention, compensated by "transitional objects" that allowed the child a modest but growing sense of mastery over its environment; and perhaps most important, daily observation of the father at work, which conveyed a realistic sense of both his potency and limitations, freeing the child from hatred and terror of this early rival for its mother's affections—all these made it possible to scale down, and finally lay to rest, the child's potentially imprisoning primal fantasies.

In industrial society, by contrast, with the father stripped of his skills and removed from the home, and with various agencies of socialization supplanting parental authority from an early age, there are fewer opportunities for daily familiarity to reduce the young child's confusing and threatening notions about authority to proper, human scale. The result is a sea change in the characteristic personality type, both normal and neurotic, of our time: from the self-denying, self-controlled petty bourgeois, prone to outbursts of hysteria or obsession but capable of discipline and commitment, to a more fluid, ingratiating, manipulative type, perpetually in quest of fulfillment and self-expression, well adapted to bureaucratic authority and consumer culture.

> In its pathological form, narcissism originates as a defense against feelings of helpless dependency in early life, which it tries to counter with "blind optimism" and grandiose illusions of personal self-sufficiency. Since modern society prolongs the experience of dependence into adult life, it encourages milder forms of narcissism in people who might otherwise come to terms with the inescapable limits on their personal freedom and power—limits inherent in the human condition—by developing competence as workers and parents. But at the same time that our society makes it more and more difficult to find satisfaction in love and work, it surrounds the individual with manufactured fantasies of total gratification. The new paternalism preaches not self-denial but self-fulfillment. It sides with the narcissistic impulses and discourages their modification by the pleasure of becoming self-reliant, even in a limited domain, which under favorable conditions accompanies maturity. While it

encourages grandiose dreams of omnipotence, moreover, the new paternalism undermines more modest fantasies, erodes the capacity to suspend disbelief, and thus makes less and less accessible the harmless substitute gratifications, notably art and play, that help to mitigate the sense of powerlessness and the fear of dependence that otherwise express themselves in narcissistic traits.

So say Lasch and Freud, at any rate. In recent decades, the prestige of psychoanalytic theory has sharply declined. In view of this, how plausible is Lasch's "culture of narcissism"? Those of us unfamiliar with the clinical literature and the theoretical debates must, to some extent, reserve judgment. Lasch's account may sometimes sound like a "just-so" story. But sometimes "just-so" stories are true. The internal coherence, complex articulation, and comprehensive scope of Lasch's analyses, across many books and several decades, are more than impressive; they are astonishing, even epic. Whatever one's final verdict, there is, I would say, more to be learned from grappling with Lasch's efforts than with those of any other contemporary social critic.

Lasch's career was, in one sense, a running argument with the Enlightenment and its modern representatives: "progressive" intellectuals. It was—let there be no mistake—a family quarrel. The authoritarian conservatism of, say, T. S. Eliot or Russell Kirk, who rejected the Enlightenment root and branch, held no appeal for Lasch. No theological dogma or aristocratic hierarchy ever won from him an expression of sympathy, or even a wistful glance. He was a skeptic and a democrat, first and last. Nevertheless, he set his face against what most of the Enlightenment's heirs have called, usually in reverential tones, Progress. *The True and Only Heaven: Progress and Its Critics* was a monumental challenge to modern orthodoxy and a mighty *summa* of a neglected tradition: "producerist" populism.

From Condorcet through Marx and the Fabian socialists to contemporary liberals and social democrats, a certain form of social evolution has been understood as inevitable and desirable. Mass production, economies of scale, and large, centrally controlled organizations have superseded handicraft production, small proprietorship, and face-to-face self-government. Geographical, professional, and interpersonal mobility are the rule; local identification, neighborhood stability, and close-knit, long-term group relationships among kin, family, or friends are the exception. Marriage, child-rearing, and personal relations are no longer governed by instinct or traditional lore but by expert knowledge deployed in schools, courts, welfare agencies, and psychotherapists' offices. Economic output is to be maximized; consumption democratized; work specialized; education standardized; and the whole society mediated impersonally and efficiently by the market and administered transparently and accountably by the state.

This is not a wholly unattractive vision; and in any case, isn't it simply the way things must be? Of course we often chafe under these arrangements, but surely our discontents are over matters of detail—fairness, accountability, and so on—or the inevitable stresses and frictions of change? Given the size and scale of our society, our ever-growing needs and appetites, the sheer, unstoppable momentum of advancing technology, and the tendency of everything to become more complex and connected, what other form of life is possible to us? Even if industrialism is as productive of individual and social pathology as Lasch claims, is there any alternative?

In answer to this apparently irrefutable self-justification, Lasch called up in *True and Only Heaven* a long succession of prophets, some forgotten, others well-known but newly reinterpreted as opponents of the allegedly pre-ordained course of modernity: Jonathan Edwards, Adam Smith, Paine, Cobbett, Emerson, Orestes Brownson, Carlyle, Morris, Henry George, Sorel, Mumford, Niebuhr, King, and the members of what Lasch regarded as the most promising and radical movement in American history, 19th-century Populism. Some of these thinkers preached virtue, some deplored ugliness, some sought after justice. But most of them were agreed, according to Lasch, in "defense of endangered handicrafts (including the craft of farming); opposition to the new class of public creditors and to the whole machinery of modern finance; opposition to wage labor" and support "of the principle, inherited from earlier political traditions, liberal as well as republican, that property ownership and the personal independence it confers are absolutely essential preconditions of citizenship." They mistrusted large accumulations of wealth and insisted, along with Ruskin, that "the reward of labor is not what one gets by it but what one becomes by it." They affirmed human and natural limits and were deeply skeptical of the modern religion of unlimited economic and personal growth.

It sounds hopeless, of course, if indeed it even sounds intelligible to many in our time. Perhaps Lasch will seem merely quaint some day, as the Sermon on the Mount would have seemed to Augustus, or William Morris's *News from Nowhere* to Margaret Thatcher. Eric Miller's intelligent and sympathetic biography is honest enough to settle for wistfulness in assessing Lasch's legacy. Miller succeeds, at any rate, in persuading us to join him in saluting Lasch's "unyielding attempt to force us to revisit our confident conclusions about our world and seize our one moment of responsibility for it."

III. Rant

Plutocratic Vistas

The crash of 2007–8 hit Harvard University especially hard. Thanks to the overweeningly brilliant, unflappably self-confident financial guidance of ex-president Lawrence Summers ("As a former Secretary of the Treasury, I assure you that interest rates will not fall below X," he is rumored to have told the governing board, who were anxious about a particularly daring credit-default swap he was proposing), Harvard lost nearly a third of its $36 billion endowment in one year. Every department's belt was tightened several notches, and widespread layoffs were anticipated (though eventually averted by offering early retirement to older employees, hundreds of whom accepted).

The talk was grim around my office, the building-services center of a large research complex at Harvard. Contractors came by frequently for keys and instructions, and the more gregarious ones often stayed to schmooze. Sports and celebrities, our usual topics, were replaced that year by political griping. As the details of the bank bailout emerged, imprecations were fervently heaped on both bankers and politicians; a respectful hearing was even accorded the office radical (me), usually humored or ignored. But these conversations always ended the same way. One or another of those tough, no-bullshit, can-do guys would shrug: "Hey, what can *we* do about it? Nothin'." And the rest would chorus: "Yeah, what can ya do?" It was an epitome of 21st-century American democracy: people used to coping with dauntingly complex mechanical systems simply took their political impotence for granted.

Their fatalism was entirely appropriate. As we sat around the office grumbling, Congress began responding to nationwide calls for financial reform. The two-year process that resulted in the Wall Street Reform and Consumer Protection Act of 2010, known as "Dodd-Frank," bestowed on the still-battered nation what the (as ever) smilingly earnest President Obama called "the strongest consumer financial protections in history." He paused for emphasis and repeated to his enthusiastic audience, "in *history*."

Another two years on, the invaluable investigative reporter Matt Taibbi has written a lengthy obsequy for Dodd-Frank.

> Dodd-Frank is groaning on its deathbed. The giant reform bill turned out to be like the fish reeled in by Hemingway's Old Man— no sooner caught than set upon by sharks that strip it to nothing long before it ever reaches the shore. In a furious below-the-radar effort at gutting the law … a troop of water-carrying Eric Cantor Republicans are speeding nine separate bills through the House, all designed to roll back the few genuinely toothy portions left in Dodd-Frank. With the covert assistance of quisling Democrats, both in Congress and in the White House, those bills could pass through the House and Senate with little or no debate, with simple floor votes.…
>
> The fate of Dodd-Frank over the past two years is an object lesson in the government's inability to institute even the simplest and most obvious reforms.… From the moment it was signed into law, lobbyists and lawyers have fought regulators over every line in the rulemaking process. Congressmen and presidents may be able to get a law passed once in a while—but they can no longer make sure it *stays* passed. You win the modern financial-regulation game by filing the most motions, attending the most hearings, giving the most money to the most politicians, and above all, by keeping at it, day after day, year after fiscal year, until stealing is legal again. "It's like a scorched-earth policy," says a former regulator who was heavily involved with the drafting of Dodd-Frank. "It requires constant combat. And it never ends."

The final words of Taibbi's article toll the death knell of contemporary American democracy:

> You can't buy votes in a democracy, at least not directly. But our democracy is run through a bureaucracy. Human beings can cast a vote, or rally together during protests and elections, but real people—even committed professionals—get tired of running through mazes of motions and countermotions, or reading thousands of pages about swaps-execution facilities and NRSROs. They will fight through it for five days, or maybe even six, but on the seventh

they will watch a baseball game, or *Tanked*, instead of diving into that morass of hellish acronyms one more time.

But money never gets tired. It never gets frustrated. And it thinks that drilling holes in Dodd-Frank is every bit as interesting as *The Book of Mormon* or Kate Upton naked. The system has become too complex for flesh-and-blood people, who make the mistake of thinking that passing a new law means the end of the discussion, when it's really just the beginning of a war.

It goes without saying that in this regard, the financial industry is no worse than the energy, defense, chemical, pharmaceutical, insurance, entertainment, food-processing, or any other large industry. America is a plutocracy. Freedom House has long published a comprehensive international index of formal democracy, which the US State Department found extremely convenient during the Cold War. If anyone today published a similarly careful and thorough index of effective democracy— a measure of the degree to which governments solicited and responded to public sentiment rather than money in the formation of law and policy—the United States would surely rank as low as many Communist tyrannies ranked on the Freedom House index.

In truth, American democracy has been a long time dying. *Equality* (1897), Edward Bellamy's sequel to the fabulously popular *Looking Backward* (1888), opens with a conversation between the reawakened 19th-century hero Julian West and his generously indignant, increasingly incredulous 20th-going-on-21st-century fiancée Edith Leete:

> "If the people all had an equal voice in the government ... why did they not without a moment's delay put an end to the inequalities from which they suffered?" ...
>
> "The capitalists advanced the money necessary to procure the election of the office-seekers on the understanding that when elected the latter should do what the capitalists wanted. But I ought not to give you the impression that the bulk of the votes were bought outright. That would have been too open a confession of the sham of popular government as well as too expensive. The money contributed by the capitalists to procure the election of the office seekers-was mainly expended to influence the people by indirect

means. Immense sums under the name of campaign funds were raised for this purpose and used in innumerable devices … the object of which was to galvanize the people to a sufficient degree of interest in the election to go through the motion of voting." …

"But why did not the people elect officials and representatives of their own class, who would look out for the interests of the masses?" …

"The people who voted had little choice for whom they should vote. That question was determined by the political party organizations, which were beggars to the capitalists for pecuniary support. No man who was opposed to capitalist interests was permitted the opportunity as a candidate to appeal to the people. For a public official to support the people's interest as against that of the capitalists would be a sure way of sacrificing his career…. His public position he held only from election to election, and rarely long. His permanent, lifelong, and all-controlling interest, like that of us all, was his livelihood, and that was dependent not on the applause of the people but on the favor and patronage of capital, and this he could not afford to imperil in the pursuit of the bubbles of popularity. These circumstances, even if there had been no instances of direct bribery, sufficiently explained why our politicians and officeholders with few exceptions were vassals and tools of the capitalists."

This was not merely a reaction to Gilded Age excess. Twenty years earlier, in *Democratic Vistas* (1867), before canvassing the magnificent possibilities of American democracy, Walt Whitman paused to acknowledge the ghastly actuality:

An acute and candid person, in the revenue department in Washington, who is led by the course of his employment to regularly visit the cities, north, south and west, to investigate frauds, has talk'd much with me about his discoveries. The depravity of the business classes of our country is not less than has been supposed, but infinitely greater. The official services of America, national, state, and municipal, in all their branches and departments, except the judiciary, are saturated in corruption, bribery, falsehood, maladministration; and the judiciary is tainted. The great cities reek with respectable as much as non-respectable robbery and scoundrelism…. The magician's serpent in the fable ate up all the other serpents; and money-making is our magician's serpent, remaining today sole master of the field.

Ten years before that, Emerson growled in his journal:

Is there no check to this class of privileged thieves that infest our politics? We mark & lock up the petty thief or we raise the hue & cry in the street, and do not hesitate to draw our revolvers out of the box, when one is in the house. But here are certain well dressed well-bred fellows, infinitely more mischievous, who get into the government & rob without stint, & without disgrace. They do it with a high hand, & by the device of having a party to whitewash them, to abet the act, & lie, & vote for them. And often each of the larger rogues has his newspaper, called "his organ," to say that it was not stealing, this which he did; that if there was stealing, it was you who stole, & not he …

(It should be noted that there are two sides to this question. Tocqueville, with his usual quasi-Martian apriorism, confidently declared that plutocracy in America was an impossibility:

As the great majority of those who create the laws have no taxable property, all the money that is spent for the community appears to be spent to their advantage, at no cost of their own, and those who have some little property readily find means of so regulating the taxes that they weigh upon the wealthy and profit the poor, although the rich cannot take the same advantage when they are in possession of the government....

Again, it may be objected that the poor never have the sole power of making the laws; but I reply that wherever universal suffrage has been established, the majority unquestionably exercises the legislative authority; and if it be proved that the poor always constitute the majority, may it not be added with perfect truth that in the countries in which they possess the elective franchise they possess the sole power of making the laws? It is certain that in all the nations of the world the greater number has always consisted of those persons who hold no property, or of those whose property is insufficient to exempt them from the necessity of working in order to procure a comfortable subsistence. Universal suffrage, therefore, in point of fact does invest the poor with the government of society.

Justice Anthony Kennedy, speaking for the Supreme Court majority in *Citizens United*, displayed a similarly breezy indifference to fact, though with two centuries' less excuse than Tocqueville: "We now conclude that independent expenditures, including those made by corporations, do not give rise to corruption or the appearance of corruption.")

Is it otiose, in the absence of democracy, to reflect on what democracy might and should be, or at any rate might have been? Possibly, but one must pass the time. In any case, the money power may be overthrown someday—Marx's theory, never yet put to the test, may well be true. Marx predicted that globalization, financialization, the concentration of ownership, and the proletarianization of nearly everyone would result in either socialism or barbarism. Stable barbarism—the unsleeping plutocracy Taibbi describes—seems most likely in the near and medium term. But the world revolves, *et omnia mutantur*. The citizens of a post-capitalist world, if it arrives, will need to maintain a society-wide conversation, consisting of millions of smaller local ones, about how to govern themselves. Perhaps we can help by keeping the subject alive even in the dark times.

The first illusion to kill on the way to self-government is professionalism. Currently, the profession of legislators is getting re-elected. Estimates I have seen of the amount of time legislators spend raising money seem to average around 50 percent. I don't know what percentage of time they spend traveling to and from the district, giving boilerplate speeches, and frequenting prostitutes or otherwise cavorting, but it can hardly be less than 10 or 20 percent. The time they spend studying legislative questions—reading through policy proposals and discussing them with colleagues, staff, and constituents, and acquiring sufficient background knowledge to make those discussions fruitful—must be minimal. (Though plenty of time doubtless goes to taking instructions from lobbyists.) Even an intelligent and conscientious legislator—not likely, in any case, to have survived either major party's candidate-selection process—would scarcely be able to acquire anything resembling expertise, much less wisdom, under these conditions, which may well be inescapable in any system of electoral competition.

Shouldn't I have said "in any system of *privately financed* electoral competition"? Wouldn't public financing of campaigns change everything? No, it would not. Thanks to the ingenuity of the public-relations industry and the complaisance of the Supreme Court's conservative majority, most of the expenses of political competition are or soon will be incurred not by candidates but by supporters—usually very rich—operating, often anonymously, through ad hoc committees. Political money, it has been often and wisely observed, is a hydraulic system; if you stop a leak in one place, it breaks out somewhere else.

Perhaps we should replace competition with sortition, i.e., drawing lots. What is the purpose of political competition, anyway? According to the founders of the republic, it is to produce a legislative body that represents—i.e., speaks with the same mind as—the populace. According to Madison: "The government ought to possess not only, first, the force, but secondly, the mind or sense of the people at large. The legislature ought to be the most exact transcript of the whole society." John Adams seconded this: the legislature "should be an exact portrait, in miniature, of the people at large, as it should think, feel, reason, and act like them." Even that arch-plutocrat William F. Buckley Jr, posing as a democrat, famously proclaimed that he would rather be governed by the first two hundred people listed in any big-city telephone directory than by the Harvard faculty. (Though his antipathy to Harvard was undoubtedly genuine, whether he would have countenanced the rule of ordinary citizens who had not bent the knee to wealthy donors is highly doubtful. After all, he strongly supported his brother's baneful lawsuit, *Buckley v. Valeo*, which aimed at preventing precisely that.)

Is the present American national legislature an "exact transcript of the whole society"? The question invites ridicule. Racially, sexually, economically, and ideologically, the members of Congress more closely resemble the executive ranks of most large corporations, or the membership of most large country clubs, than they do the society as a whole. Polls consistently reveal a sharp variance between the views of the citizenry and those of the political class, which it is the job of political consultants and communications specialists to finesse during election season. Popular approval of Congress, never robust in recent years, has lately been plunging toward the single digits—one of the few hopeful signs in contemporary American political culture.

We can scarcely do worse than what we have; on this the country seems agreed. How would sortition work? Fortunately, there is a blueprint to hand: a short book called *A Citizen Legislature* by Ernest Callenbach (author of *Ecotopia*, one of the finest utopian novels ever written) and Michael Phillips.* The process is not complicated. Every county in America maintains a list of prospective jurors. Combine these lists in one national master list, and a computer may easily be programmed to choose a random sample of 435 (the size of the present House of Representatives). The same categories of people would be excluded from the selection pool: felons, non-citizens, the institutionalized. The resulting Representative House would (unlike the House of Representatives) be an exact, or near-exact, transcript of the society: roughly the same proportion of women, minorities, academics, professionals, blue-and-white-collar workers, homemakers, millionaires, and unemployed persons as in the general population. The representatives would train intensively for three months, would serve three years, and would then return to their communities (or stay in Washington as lobbyists, though perhaps less as a matter of course than at present). One-third of the House would be replaced each year. The Senate and the Executive Branch would, for the time being, remain unchanged.

Would sortition rule out government by the "best"? This question, too, can scarcely be considered with a straight face. We all know what Mark Twain said about Congressmen, and matters have not notably improved since. Besides, as Callenbach

*First published in 1985 and recently reissued together with *A People's Parliament: A (Revised) Blueprint for a Very English Revolution* by Keith Sutherland. Imprint Academic, 2008.

and Phillips write, "pure intelligence—if there is such a thing—is certainly not directly related to political wisdom. The only reasonable assumption is that both are broadly distributed through the population."

This was apparently the Athenians' assumption as well. The Assembly, the city's governing body, was chosen by lot. And Athens was not, as the popular conception has it, a "democracy of orators," of citizens speaking and listening by turns, and then, having said their piece, voting. It was much more like Callenbach and Phillips's Representative House of ordinary shlubs. Political theorist Daniela Cammack has carefully analyzed virtually all uses of the three Greek terms for "to deliberate." Two of them involve speaking; the other—the only one nearly always applied to the membership of the Assembly as a whole—means "reflection" and has an exclusively internal reference. There were orators and advocates, of course, but their function was advisory. There was, Cammack writes,

> a greater cleavage between speakers and listeners in the assembly than is usually imagined…. The [language] suggests that a small number of citizens were conceived as "advisors" to the group, who by the very act of speaking cast themselves outside of the deliberating unit…. Speakers did not cease to be voters, of course, when they came forward to speak; in that sense, they remained part of the decision-making unit…. [But] the key tasks of ordinary citizens did not include speaking. Listening, thinking, judging, voting, and finally holding speakers to account were all far more important.*

The Athenians, that is, entrusted their civic destiny not to experts or professionals (though they made use of them) but to ordinary citizens, selected at random in order to produce a faithful representation of the society as a whole. There is no reason why the United States should not do the same. The only alternative

---

*That last phrase refers to an aspect of Athenian democracy perhaps worth reviving: speakers who were later judged to have given foolish or dishonest advice could be impeached and fined. President Obama has shown no interest in calling to account those who lied their country into war, but the Athenians did.

is elections, and the American electoral process is fundamentally, irredeemably corrupt. Elections cost money, vast and increasing amounts. As long as economic resources are distributed as unequally as they are at present, elections cannot be fair.

Would random selection of legislators produce a less lively political culture? This is yet another question that answers itself. Contemporary American political culture is comatose, kept alive only by such artificial life supports as televised debates between candidates, radio and TV talk shows, and the protracted electoral news cycle, reporting on polls, trends, gaffes, and gossip for 18–24 months before each presidential election and 9–12 months before each Congressional election. The degree to which this panoply of triviality is initiated or controlled by ordinary Americans is zero. Political messaging in our society is, like commercial messaging, wholly unidirectional. Voters, like consumers, exercise only an unavoidable and irreducible minimum of choice at the very end of a process from which their self-organized and unmanipulated input is entirely absent.

What might a live political culture look like? It would no doubt feature some version of the "committees of correspondence" that flourished in the American colonial period, only more permanent and less ad hoc. There would be continuous discussion, in small groups, in living rooms, church halls, school buildings, workplace lounges, libraries, municipal buildings, and other venues, of political issues, organized by ordinary citizens, employees, neighbors, etc. These groups would make use of information about these issues collected by public agencies and made available on the Web, information equal in quality and depth to the information available to policymakers and industry lobbyists. The meetings of these groups would be regularly attended by public officials, who would have plenty to time to do so once they were released from the time-consuming obligations of fund-raising and electioneering.

The local discussion groups would communicate regularly with one another, sharing information and conclusions, and would join in formulating questions and instructions for local officials and legislators. They would also send delegates to state and regional citizens' groups, which would conduct discussions with other such groups and then, jointly or separately, with state and national legislators and policymakers. (Unions would have a parallel structure of member involvement, unlike today.) These delegates would be in continual contact with the smaller bodies that sent them, and would be readily recallable.

Such groups at all levels, particularly the higher-level ones, would also monitor and criticize media coverage of issues that interest them, exactly as industry and other (e.g., religious) interest groups do today. They would commission, and in some cases, write articles for the media—articles which, unlike the continuous stream of corporate propaganda that largely constitutes present-day "reporting" in many local and regional newspapers, would be openly acknowledged—and would propose guests on radio and television discussions of contentious issues. And just as advertisers boycott publications or media programs considered ideologically unsound, the citizen/worker groups would orchestrate pressure, including boycotts, of chronically biased outlets. This is not a complete remedy for the extreme concentration of ownership in newspapers, radio, and television at present, with all the possibilities—fully realized—for censorship and ideological homogenization that implies. But it's a step.

Something like this scheme might help restore some substance to this society's hollow democratic pretensions. Of course, genuine democracy in any form depends on broad economic equality. The preconditions of democracy are that: 1) minimum economic security is universal, so that no one's economic welfare can be jeopardized by political activism that may be anathema to his/her economic or political superiors; 2) gross inequality of resources does not give some political opinions vastly greater possibilities of publicity or promotion (ie, lobbying) than others, as at present; and 3) the material prerequisites of political activity—leisure, education, at least modest disposable income—are universally available. Even this bare preliminary statement suggests how many light-years the United States is from anything worthy to be called democracy, and also makes clear how rapidly we're traveling away from, rather than toward, the ideal.

Granted, no one can be forced to be free or self-governing. Those who are addicted to television, or allergic to meetings, or simply don't give a damn about other people, are perfectly free to blow the whole democracy thing off, though their neighbors will be equally free to call them what the Greeks did: *idiotes.*

Will all—or any—of the above happen? Over Money's dead body. Far more likely is a continued bread-and-circuses electoral oligarchy, with increased surveillance and repression as the allotment of grub and gadgets to the lower orders has to be parceled out among a growing global army of proletarians. Technology without democracy: a *Blade Runner* world.

The American empire has already found its Gibbon, at least in rough draft. The medieval intellectual historian turned social critic Morris Berman has produced a trilogy of works— *The Twilight of American Culture* (2000); *Dark Ages America* (2006); *Why America Failed* (2011)—that diagnose and forecast the country's decline in real time with an imaginative freedom and an unyielding pessimism that no conventional academic historian would permit him- or herself. He has naturally been ignored when not (as, for example, by that bellwether of middlebrow, Michiko Kakutani, in the *New York Times*) ridiculed.

Unfortunately for his trilogy's commercial and critical prospects, Berman has no last-minute proposals to save us from the long descent he foresees into soft authoritarianism and cultural debasement. Possessive individualism has thoroughly routed civic republicanism; hucksterism has vanquished virtue; a mindless commitment to economic growth has rendered the ideals of simplicity, balance, and voluntary renunciation all but unintelligible as guides to public policy rather than merely to individual salvation. It is too late for a happy ending.

It is indeed late, as anyone who reads Berman without extraordinary mental inertness will find herself forced to acknowledge. And yet, *omnia mutantur.* The Dark Ages, if they arrive, will—may—eventually be followed by another Enlightenment, which our present efforts may assist, even though we go under. We may as well give Money a good fight. Hey, what else can ya do?

IV. First-Person

Message from Room 101

After reading George Orwell's *1984* in high school, I would sometimes wonder what was in Room 101. For each person, remember, it was whatever unhinged you, whatever you shuddered at most uncontrollably. "Everyone knows what is in Room 101," Winston Smith is told. "It is the worst thing in the world."

I was a fairly squeamish adolescent, so a good many possibilities suggested themselves, most of them with more than four legs. But I was also devoutly religious, and the hope of Heaven was of infinite comfort, limiting the horror of even the most lurid death. Now I no longer have that faith or that hope, and the question about Room 101 again seems a live one. I think I know the answer. The pain of a severe clinical depression is the worst thing in the world. To escape it, I would do anything. Like Winston, I would—at least I might—wish it on those I love, however dearly. But that's not feasible. The only way to escape it is to inflict my death on them. That is a grievous prospect, and I hope avoidable. But I know that those who do not avoid it cannot help themselves, any more than Winston could help betraying Julia.

Why? What is so unbearable about *this* pain? The primary sources are William Styron's *Darkness Visible*, Kay Jameson's *Unquiet Mind*, the "New York" section of Kate Millett's *The Loony-Bin Trip*, and the chapter on "The Sick Soul" in William James's *Varieties of Religious Experience*. Others will someday improve on these accounts; I cannot. The most useful formulation is James's. Depression is "a positive and active anguish, a form of psychical neuralgia wholly unknown to normal life." Every word tells. "Positive and active": acute depression does not feel like falling ill, it feels like being tortured. "Psychical neuralgia": the pain is not localized; it runs along every nerve, an unconsuming fire. In an agitated depression, like mine, it burns fiercely in the solar plexus and flares elsewhere, fueled by obsessive fears, regrets, self-loathing. "Unknown to normal life": because it feels unlimited in both intensity and duration, it really is like no other pain. Even though one knows better, one cannot believe that it will ever end or that anyone else has ever felt anything like it.

Confidence that an acute episode will last only a week, a month, even a year, would change everything. It would still be a ghastly ordeal, but the worst thing about it—the incessant yearning for death, the compulsion toward suicide—would drop away. But no, a limited depression, a depression with hope, is a contradiction. The experience of convulsive pain, along with the conviction that it will never end except in death—that is the definition of a severe depression. O'Brien tells Winston that the latter's dream of proletarian deliverance is a delusion, that his image of the future should instead be "a boot stamping on a human face—forever." The depressive's image of the future is "me, writhing in agony—forever." Flesh on an electrified grid; a dentist's drill tearing at an exposed nerve; a raging migraine; an implacable metastasis. But never ending.

How does this nightmare happen? Through an unlucky ratio of stress to strength, circumstance to constitution. The weaker one's nerves, the less it takes to inflame them. The more fragile one's neurochemical equilibria, the less it takes to disrupt them. How much you feel the daily slings and arrows depends on how thick your skin is.

Nature cuts most of us plenty of slack. "Most people," as Styron observes, "quietly endure the equivalent of injuries, declining careers, nasty book reviews, family illnesses. A vast majority of the survivors of Auschwitz have borne up fairly well. Bloody and bowed by the outrages of life, most human beings still stagger on down the road, unscathed by real depression." We are all issued neurological shock absorbers, usually good for a lifetime of emotional wear and tear. But if you're equipped with a flimsy one, or travel an especially rough road, the ride becomes very uncomfortable.

My shock absorber seems to be exceptionally flimsy. Both my parents were depressive: constantly worried, easily discouraged, with little capacity for enjoyment and no appetite for change. Except for a brief trip over the border of the next state to visit relatives, neither of them ever travelled more than fifty miles from where they were born. They were children during the Great Depression of the 30s, so during the Great Boom of the 50s and 60s and the Great Bubble of the 80s and 90s, they left their money—not that there was much of it; they were working-class people, conscientious but uneducated and unambitious—under the mattress or rolled up in the hollow legs of metal chairs. "Chronic severe dysthymia in a severely obsessional character" is my diagnosis and would have been theirs. It simply means "born to suffer."

Still, even with worn-out shock absorbers, life in a rich country is, at least some of the time, like a ride on a freshly paved road. Thanks to undemanding day jobs and a trickle of freelance income, I've lived through the worst without institutionalization or destitution. So far. But old age looks grim. Chronic depression is very hard on lifetime earnings; and like many other people's, my retirement account is in trauma. In youth and middle age, one is supposed to store up material and psychic comfort against the years of decline. We all try to, but few people, healthy or ill, can fall back on resources like Styron's, Jameson's, or Millett's. Certainly, all three deserve their eminence, their affluence, their sympathetic friends and supportive families, their happy memories. All, as their accounts make clear, would have died without those things. There is no doubt that good fortune is the best antidepressant.

But what about the undistinguished, unloved, low-income depressed? We must suffer, and why shouldn't we? Life is unfair, after all. No talent, no distinction; no charms, no love. Reasonable enough: how else could admiration and affection, and the comforts they entail, possibly be distributed? Even to save a depressed person's life, you cannot admire or love him at will.

Money is different, though. It is simply a claim on whatever is for sale. There is no natural way to apportion it. Perfect markets don't, cannot, and should not exist. How we produce and distribute is a political question—economics is politics all the way down. Whether our current drastic inequality is fairer and more productive than our former moderate inequality depends entirely on what we're aiming to produce—and become.

People fall ill emotionally for any number of reasons, of course. As Robert Lowell remarked, if we all had a little button on our forearm that we could press for a painless and instantaneous death, very few of us would reach old age. In some cases of severe depression, like mine, financial insecurity is central; in others, less so or not at all. There is always some way to help, and though nearly every way costs money, some would cost very little. Exercise, for example, is highly therapeutic for depression, but it is just what you cannot force yourself to do. Young people doing a year of national service could drag severely depressed people out for a vigorous walk each day, or do an hour of yoga with them. Or call them a few times a day to remind them to drink water—depressed persons nearly always dehydrate. Or drive them to a therapist—climbing the Himalayas is easier in some states of mind than getting out the front door is in others. The quantity of suffering diminished per dollar expended in these ways would be impressive.

Or you could give them money. As I slid into my most recent episode, wrung by money worries, I saw an article by Robert Reich in *The American Prospect*. He proposed exempting the first $20000 of income from the payroll tax, the most regressive of all taxes. This would save 130 million American households an average of $5000 per year. You could pay for this fully, he pointed out, by retaining the estate tax, the most progressive of all taxes, which affects only 2% of American households. Five thousand dollars a year would save a lot of ordinary people a lot of grief, and incidentally fix the economy. And it might save some lives.

Suicide, Camus wrote, is the sole philosophical problem. Perhaps; but it is also, from the depressive's point of view, a political problem. The official figure for suicides in the United States is 30,000, generally thought to be an understatement. Call it 40,000. I've read that two-thirds of these were severely depressed—say 25,000. Ten to fifteen percent of severely depressed people, it seems to be agreed, will eventually kill themselves. So—very, very approximately—each year 250,000 of your fellow citizens, one in twelve hundred Americans, will be at risk of death from the protracted indescribable pain of severe depression.

Reich's article mentions that half of the estate tax, or around $350 billion, is paid by only 3300 families. That's roughly one in 40,000 American households. If that money were simply handed over to the severely depressed, they would receive $1 million each. That would definitely save my life, and doubtless quite a few others.

In the same issue of the same magazine, another writer cites now commonplace figures on President Bush's income tax cut: $1.5 trillion over ten years, forty percent of it, or $600 billion, going to the richest one percent of taxpayers. Six hundred billion dollars over ten years works out to a little more than $200,000 for each suicidally depressed person. Once again, many lives saved, much extreme anguish averted or diminished.

Also around this time, the philosopher John Rawls died. Everything is grist for one's obsessions, it's true; but the connection with Rawls is not really so far-fetched. Standing behind Rawls's famous veil of ignorance, you face a choice. You can accept one chance in 1200 of being locked screaming in Room 101 and, at the same time, one chance in 40,000 of leaving a huge estate tax-free. Or you can escape Room 101, and perhaps help many others to escape it, by giving up a miniscule chance of leaving your heirs not colossal riches (that would still be permitted) but super-colossal riches. Rawls would have thought the right choice obvious, and I suspect most Americans would agree with him, even if Congress doesn't.

Admittedly, there are other, perhaps worthier candidates

for relief. Severe depression almost always ends, usually non-fatally. For many other people—a billion or so—illiteracy, malnutrition, diarrhea, infection, and other conditions far more easily preventable or curable than depression do not end. Even if these people's nerves are not on fire, Rawls might have judged theirs the more pressing claim. I think I could accept that judgment, even if for me it meant ... Room 101.

Why, you may be wondering, was this long whine ever written down? It's not a memoir, not an argument—what is it anyway? The first draft—very much shorter and even more purple—was a suicide note, to be left behind on the riverbank or rooftop or night table. Emotional blackmail in a good cause, I told myself; though perhaps it was only spite, the feeble revenge of the ill on the well. In any case, I dithered. Like many other acutely depressed people I was, fortunately, too exhausted and disorganized to plan a suicide, much less compose an eloquent rebuke to an uncaring world. And then, very slowly, the fire died down. My viscera gradually unknotted, my energy seeped back, speech became less effortful, the world regained three dimensions. Blessedly, miraculously, everyday unhappiness returned.

Then why persist with the fantasied blackmail? Why risk bathos rather than keep a stoical and dignified silence? This was my third devastating depression, and probably not my last. I hope and intend to survive the coming ones, but already it seems urgent to try to salvage something from these ordeals. The conjunction of my pecuniary panic with a large-scale transfer of our national wealth to the already rich seemed to make an occasion. The vast popularity of depression memoirs and manuals in recent years suggests that there must be tens or hundreds of thousands of others whose sufferings, as intense as mine, would also have been lessened by crumbs of that wealth. And behind them, endless legions of the merely miserable. Perhaps they would want someone to say all this, however ineptly and futilely. If so, I won't have come back from hell empty-handed.

Progress and Prejudice

I.

Nietzsche taught us that our loftiest pronouncements on the most abstract, universal subjects are just as idiosyncratic, just as much the product of our individual temperament, metabolism, and earliest influences, as our most peculiar predilections, our most eccentric crotchets. So let me declare a prejudice.

Of my great-grandfather I know only that he was recruited from rural Sicily to work on constructing the Panama Canal, and died there of yellow fever. My grandfather was illiterate and worked as a laborer in a factory of the Hood Rubber Company. A few months before he was eligible to retire with a pension, he was fired for no reason; speaking no English, he had no recourse. My father had a high-school education, but because his childhood was shadowed by the Great Depression, he held on to a safe, undemanding civil service job for fifty years and saved every penny, much of it under his mattress. He lived on the same street throughout his adult life and never travelled outside New England. My mother's background, opportunities, and outlook were equally restricted, in some ways more so.

In *Notes Toward the Definition of Culture*, T. S. Eliot wrote: "The primary channel of culture is the family; no man wholly escapes from the kind, or surpasses the degree, of culture which he has acquired from his early environment." As far as I know, neither of my parents ever read a novel, saw a play, or heard a concert. Nevertheless, their son has two Ivy League degrees, has written books, and has seen the world, in person and at the movies. I spend hundreds of blissful hours each year listening, on splendid but inexpensive equipment, to splendid but inexpensive recordings of the complete works of Bach and Mozart. Durable, inexpensive paperbacks furnish my rooms and my life. Even across one generation, this seems like progress. When I imagine my great-grandfather's great-grandfather, sunk in the immemorial poverty, ignorance, and humiliation of the Sicilian peasantry, the conclusion feels irresistible: I, at least, am the lucky beneficiary of two or three centuries of progress. And since the carbon footprint of classical music, great novels, independent film, and most of my other chief pleasures is fairly low, it seems like sustainable, universalizable progress.

Do I embody moral progress as well? That's a harder case to make, but not impossible. Some astute and astringent judgments have been passed on the traditional morality of southern Italians. In *The Golden Bowl*, Prince Amerigo implores Fanny Assingham, who has brought him together with his rich but inexperienced fiancée Maggie Verver, to "keep him straight." She replies:

> "Oh, you deep old Italians!"
> "There you are," he returned.... "That's the responsible note."
> "What on earth are you talking about?"
> "Of my real, honest fear of being 'off' some day, of being wrong, without knowing it. That's what I shall always trust you for—to tell me when I am. No—with you people it's a sense. We haven't got it—not as you have."
> "I should be interested," she presently remarked, "to see some sense *you* don't possess."
> Well, he produced one on the spot. "The moral, dear Mrs. Assingham. I mean, always, as you others consider it. I've of course something that in our poor dear backward old Rome sufficiently passes for it. But it's no more like yours than the tortuous stone staircase—half-ruined into the bargain!—in some castle of our *quattrocento* is like the 'lightning elevator' in one of Mr. Verver's fifteen-storey buildings. Your moral sense works by steam—it sends you up like a rocket. Ours is slow and steep and unlighted, with so many of the steps missing that—well, that it's as short, in almost any case, to turn around and come down again."
> Trusting," Mrs. Assingham smiled, "to get up some other way?"
> "Yes—or not to have to get up at all."

Later in the twentieth century, in the sociological classic *The Moral Basis of a Backward Society*, Edward Banfield theorized the southern Italian ethos as "amoral familism." This unhappy moral culture was defined by a narrow dedication to the interests of oneself and one's immediate family and a thoroughgoing absence of intellectual or political integrity, disinterestedness, trust, solidarity, generosity, civic virtue, or professional pride, along with equal measures of cynicism about and servility toward all forms of authority. Robert Putnam also found amoral familism flourishing—if that's the word—among southern Italians in his seminal *Making Democracy Work*.

Amoral familism was certainly the prevailing ethos in my largely second-generation inner-city neighborhood. At college, ivied brick walls, timbered dining halls, and portraits of Puritan college fathers prepared me for a change; and in my sophomore year enlightenment arrived, full blast and double-barrelled: *On Liberty* and *Middlemarch*, between them a complete moral education. Mill's noble purity and Eliot's wise magnanimity had their inevitable effect. I will never be, like them, incapable of a pettiness, but I am a little less of an amoral familist than I would otherwise have been. Hardly perfection, but for one whose not very distant ancestor was very likely, in the words of another Henry James character, "a squalid, savage-looking peasant, a tattered ruffian of orthodox Italian aspect," undoubtedly progress. And again, in principle at least (notwithstanding the ivied walls), universally achievable.

This two-century trajectory, from squalor to modest comfort, from ruffian to harmless schlub, doubtless predisposes me to see the slope of history tending upward. So does another accident of biography: deliverance from *l'infame*. I grew up devout and was recruited as a high-school student into Opus Dei, a Catholic lay order of the strictest Counter-Reformation traditionalism and authoritarianism. Majoring in modern European intellectual history was awkward, since much of modern European literature and philosophy was on the Index of Forbidden Books and therefore proscribed. Unwisely, however, the Church failed to forbid everything. Even more unwisely, the order tried to teach its members the elements of Scholastic philosophy, which I found extremely unconvincing. I suppressed my doubts for a long while, out of conscience and natural timidity. I confided them to my confessor, of course, who at first urged prayer and mortification of the flesh. Eventually, after consulting his superiors, he ordered a *sacrificium intellectus*: I must leave intellectual history alone, on peril of sin and perhaps damnation. This was a serious matter: I was terrified of Hell, and moreover, my confessor very much resembled my mental image of Dostoevsky's Grand Inquisitor. But it was too late: I felt the Enlightenment at my back. Emulating the *philosophes'* great refusal, I lodged my little one, enrolling timorously but proudly in what I had learned from Peter Gay to call the Party of Humanity—of freedom, science, and progress. Because this mini-heroic auto-emancipation has been the supreme drama—to tell the truth, the only drama—in my life, I am perhaps understandably inclined to see all of history as this drama writ large: "humankind's emergence from its self-imposed minority," as Kant defined "enlightenment." Certainly I am reluctant to consider that my tiny but arduous affirmation has no resonance beyond my own life, no part in furthering a grander scheme of liberation and collective advance. But that's just a prejudice, I know.

II.

Some part of our perplexity about human progress is surely a result of the size of our sample. If we knew the histories of even a few more intelligent species, it would be much easier to extrapolate our future. All we have are imagined histories; that is, science fiction. Some of its guesses seem truly inspired, though; none more so than *Childhood's End* by Arthur C. Clarke. The fundamental intuition underlying all visions of perfection through cosmic evolution may be summed up as "matter into mind." It is an ubiquitous trope in intellectual history, from the Middle Ages through Teilhard de Chardin, and in futuristic fiction since Wells and Stapledon, if not before. Matter is limitation, disorganization, inertia. Mind gradually, inexorably rationalizes not only our material and social relations, but eventually even our organismic form, our species being. We become gods.

In Clarke's version, the path to godhead is not exactly rationalization. A race of super-intelligent, super-powerful beings arrives on earth to midwife humankind's passage across a cosmic evolutionary barrier. The midwives, or Overlords, have reached a cul de sac of scientific rationality. Their civilization is immeasurably superior, but humans have something they lack: imagination. Most races with this psychic endowment have destroyed themselves, and sometimes others, the Overlords explain. The few that have flourished have fused into an entity that its servants, the Overlords, call the Overmind: a being in which (or whom) beauty, truth, power, and love are indistinguishable and are present in a degree that is, for practical purposes, infinite. Like the Christian God (Clarke must have known some theology), the Overmind seeks to draw up into itself those species capable of sharing in—participating, as Thomistic theologians would say—its beatitude. The Overlords and other apostles are sent to harvest them.

This is not exactly what Condorcet or Spencer or Teilhard, or Joachim da Fiore for that matter, had in mind. Some critics (and some characters in *Childhood's End*), find Clarke's vision objectionable, because humankind does not decide its own fate. Of course this objection only has force if humankind is grown-up enough to comprehend its choices and discipline its lethal (potentially on an interstellar scale, the Overlords warn) energies. Clarke's answer, implicit in his title and indicated, though not fully developed, in the novel, is persuasive to me. More important, *Childhood's End* is at once the most extreme and the most plausible futuristic fantasy I know of. It answers to my (admittedly crude) intuition that fourteen billion years is enough time, and trillions of light years enough space, for a great many things to have happened that have so far eluded most terrestrial imaginations; and also to my (equally crude) sense that at least a few of humankind's innumerable mystics have glimpsed something ineffable. Those are two very disparate intuitions; I don't know of any other story that accommodates both.

III.

Other stories or (what amounts to the same thing) historical interpretations answer to different, sometimes opposite intuitions. "Matter into mind" is a formula for limitless transcendence. Intuitions of immanence, of the necessity and wisdom of limits, produce visions of stasis or decline and hopes for, at best, a steady state.

The two most persuasive 20th-century anti-progressives I've encountered could hardly be more different: D. H. Lawrence and Christopher Lasch. Lawrence championed matter against mind. He despised "thin-minded" rationalists like Shaw and Wells; he scoffed at labor-saving technology; and he believed in natural hierarchies and charismatic leaders. Yet he was hardly a friend of any status quo, past or present. From an unpublished manuscript:

> I know that we could, if we would, establish little by little a true democracy in England: we could nationalize the land and industries and means of transport, and make the whole thing work infinitely better than at present, *if we would*. It all depends on the spirit in which the thing is done.
>
> I know we are on the brink of a class war.
>
> I know we had all better hang ourselves at once, than enter on a struggle which shall be a fight for the ownership or non-ownership of property, pure and simple, and nothing beyond.
>
> I know the ownership of property is a problem that may have to be fought out. But beyond the fight must lie a new hope, a new beginning....
>
> I know we must take up the responsibility for the future, now. A great change is coming, and must come. What we need is some glimmer of a vision of a world that shall be, beyond the change. Otherwise we shall be in for a great debacle.

Lawrence's "glimmer of a vision" flickers throughout the two volumes of *Phoenix: The Posthumous Papers*, especially in the "Study of Thomas Hardy," "Reflections on the Death of a Porcupine," and "Education of the People." It involves a far more direct connection with the sun and the solar plexus, with cosmic mysteries and instinctual rhythms, than he observed in his contemporaries. Against the prevailing rationalism, he defined reason as "the glitter of the sun on the surface of the waters" and conceived "man's body as a kind of flame ... and the intellect is just the light that is shed on the things around."

What kind of future follows from that image of humanity? Lawrence never explained in detail. His vision found its strangest and most lyrical expression in another unpublished fragment, a utopian fantasy in the form (and something like the spirit) of William Morris's *News from Nowhere*. The speaker has woken up in his native place after sleeping a thousand years. The new humans are "flower-like" and "comely as berries"—not at all disembodied Mind. He watches them at sunset:

> When the ball of fire touched the tree-tops, there was a queer squeal of bagpipes, and the square suddenly started into life. The men were stamping softly, like bulls, the women were softly swaying, and softly clapping their hands, with a strange noise, like leaves. And under the vaulted porticoes, at opposite ends of the egg-shaped oval, came the soft booming and trilling of women and men singing against one another in the strangest pattern of sound.
>
> It was all kept very soft, soft-breathing. Yet the dance swept into swifter and swifter rhythm, with the most extraordinary incalculable unison. I do not believe there was any outside control of the dance. The thing happened by instinct, like the wheeling and flashing of a shoal of fish or of a flock of birds dipping and spreading in the sky. Suddenly, in one amazing wing-movement, the arms of all the men would flash up into the air, naked and glowing, and with the soft rushing sound of pigeons alighting the men ebbed in a spiral, grey and sparkled with scarlet, bright arms slowly leaning, upon the women, who rustled all crocus-blue, rustled like an aspen, then in one movement scattered like sparks, in every direction from under the enclosing, sinking arms of the men, and suddenly formed slender rays of lilac branching out from the red and grey knot of the men.
>
> All the time the sun was slowly sinking, shadow was falling, and the dance was moving slower, the women wheeling blue around

the obliterated sun. They were dancing the sun down, and dancing as birds wheel and dance, and fishes in shoals, controlled by some strange unanimous instinct. It was at once terrifying and magnificent, I wanted to die, so as not to see it, and I wanted to rush down, to be one of them. To be a drop in that wave of life.

This was Lawrence's answer to Wells's *Men Like Gods* and Shaw's *Back to Methuselah*: a vision of human perfection achieved by going not onward and upward but inward and downward. Whether it means going forward or backward depends on whether one believes—and is glad—that organic, embodied human nature has unalterable limits.

Christopher Lasch believed that and preached it eloquently in *The True and Only Heaven*, his masterpiece of social criticism and intellectual history. That book, like Lasch's entire career, is an extended quarrel with modernity, defined as the advance of an overlapping, mutually reinforcing phalanx of political centralization, mass production, expanded consumption, automation, geographical mobility, the bureaucratization of education, medicine, and family life, moral cosmopolitanism, and legal universalism. Against this march of abstractions, Lasch insisted on the fact of human scale. The human creature has a specific evolutionary endowment and gestational history; as a result it has a specific infantile fantasy life, which it can only outgrow gradually, through a range of close-up interactions, involving both authority and love, with the same caregivers over many years. The bureaucratic rationalization of work and intimate life plays havoc with this scheme of development, producing a weak self, stripped of traditional skills, tools, and autonomy, entirely dependent on large forces beyond its comprehension, much less control, and crippled by ambivalence toward remote, impersonal authority. What sustained the strong premodern self was the virtue of hope; what sustains the weak modern self is the ideology of progress.

I have learned, with some reluctance, from Lawrence and Lasch how readily things go wrong, how ingeniously progress can be faked. The division of labor, advances in industrial and information technology, the growth of medical knowledge, even the emancipation of women: every liberation can be captured and exploited. We had better stay inside our own skins—and even, perhaps, within traditional social forms—until we are sure that it's safe to discard them. And as long as modernization is involuntary—imposed within a class system, for profit or social control—it's difficult to know that.

Two other, minor masterpieces teach similar lessons about false promises. Whether or not (as Nicholas Carr argues in *The Shallows*) the Internet makes us stupid, it undeniably makes us different, especially as readers. In *The Gutenberg Elegies*, Sven Birkerts masterfully elaborates a phenomenology of "deep reading": the heightened focus, the inner stillness, the imaginative motility, the immersion in a linguistic matrix. It is a habitus that, like the attention of a meditator, strengthens gradually, as a muscle does. It requires verticality and temporary isolation. The capacity for such concentration must erode and eventually dissipate in a horizontal, hyperlinked, continuously connected world. The alteration in our psychic metabolism that Birkerts foresees seems to me no less probable and fateful because his is a qualitative, literary description, without benefit of neurobiology or social science.

The alteration Bill McKibben discusses in *Enough* (and, not quite so sensitively and eloquently, Francis Fukuyama in *Our Posthuman Future*) is even more radical. Not all scientists agree that germ-line genetic engineering will be feasible within the next hundred years, but most do. The elimination of genetic diseases will be a blessing, of course, but a market in "designer children," programmed for outstanding cognitive, athletic, and other abilities, may transform present economic inequalities into irreversible caste distinctions—eventually even species distinctions. No doubt the free market knows best, and if it decrees that the master class should become a master race, who is wise enough to interfere? "There is no alternative," Mrs. Thatcher instructed us; in which case, Jefferson's ringing declaration that "the mass of mankind has not been born with saddles on their backs, nor a favored few booted and spurred, ready to ride them legitimately, by the grace of God," is only sentimental egalitarian rhetoric.

IV.

Perhaps the problem of progress is a pseudo-problem. Coleridge observed that every great and original poet creates the taste by which he is judged. But tastes, criteria, perspectives can also be destroyed or wither away. Print-based civilization, for example, has not answered the earliest objections to the eclipse of oral literacy; it has merely ignored them. No doubt the inhabitants of the Electronic Hive that Birkerts foresees will miss deep reading about as much as most of us miss having vast quantities of verse committed to memory, as many educated people did in the age of oral literacy. And a population that has exchanged its skills, tools, and independence for SUVs and consumer electronics may be perfectly happy, or at least comfortable, with saddles on their backs. To measure progress, one needs a standard; and if standards alter drastically, what are measurements worth?

George Orwell had a view of the question. Though best known for his dystopias, he did write one—characteristically skeptical and downbeat—piece about Utopia, a Christmas 1943 *Tribune* essay entitled "Can Socialists Be Happy?" "All efforts to describe *permanent* happiness … have been failures, from earliest history onwards," he began cheerfully. Utopias "seem to be alike in postulating perfection while being unable to suggest happiness." Even *News from Nowhere* induced in him "only a sort of watery melancholy." Orwell was never a blithe spirit, and in London in December 1943 it was probably hard to conceive even temporary happiness.

Anyway, he continues, happiness is not the point.

Men use up their lives in heart-breaking political struggles, or get themselves killed in civil wars, or tortured in the secret prisons of the Gestapo, not in order to establish some central-heated, air-conditioned, strip-lighted Paradise, but because they want a world in which human beings love one another instead of swindling and murdering one another. And they want that world as a first step. Where they go from there is not so certain, and the attempt to foresee it in detail merely confuses the issue....

Nearly all creators of Utopia have resembled the man who has toothache, and therefore thinks that happiness consists in not having toothache. They wanted to produce a perfect society by an endless continuation of something that had only been valuable because it was temporary. The wiser course would be to say that there are certain lines along which humanity must move, the grand strategy is mapped out, but detailed prophecy is not our business.

This seems reasonable to me, and I suspect it would have seemed reasonable to Condorcet, who ended the penultimate section of his great *An Outline of Human Progress* with a passage of near-Orwellian sobriety:

The labours of recent ages have done much for the progress of the human mind, but little for the perfection of the human race; much for the honour of man, something for his liberty, but so far almost nothing for his happiness. At a few points our eyes are dazzled with a brilliant light; but thick darkness still covers an immense stretch of the horizon. There are a few circumstances from which the philosopher can take consolation; but he is still afflicted by the spectacle of the stupidity, slavery, barbarism, and extravagance of mankind; and the friend of humanity can find unmixed pleasure only in tasting the sweet delights of hope.

That sounds as much like 2013 as 1794 (except that recent ages haven't done as much for "the honour of man"). "Thick darkness" accurately describes the American economic and political outlook; and toothache is the only possible response to either Democratic or Republican politicians or pundits. Occupy and Wikileaks and 350.org, Krugman and Greenwald and Chomsky, seem to me a "few points" of "brilliant light," from which I "take consolation." Are they, along with the last three centuries or so, enough to furnish the "sweet delights of hope"? I suppose so—but that's just a prejudice, I know.

Publication History

The foregoing pieces were published in the following places:

AGNI
Message from Room 101

BARNES &NOBLE REVIEW
Do the Right Thing
Notice Thy Neighbor
Illfare
Socialist Without a Party,
    Christian Without a Church

BOSTON GLOBE
No Respect

BOSTON REVIEW
Afterthoughts of a Nader Voter
Reasons and Passions
The Zealot

COMMONWEAL
Camping
The Common Fate

COMMON WEALTH
In Literacy We Trust

DISSENT
Outgrowing All That
Human Scale
Republic or Empire?

L.A. REVIEW OF BOOKS
Plutocratic Vistas

NATION
Zippie World
Just a Journalist
The Fastidious Citizen
The Impresario

RARITAN
What Would Orwell Say?
An Enemy of the State

SALMAGUNDI
Progress and Prejudice

THE AMERICAN CONSERVATIVE
The Workingman's Friend
Vanity and Spleen

THE AMERICAN PROSPECT
Only Fair
Minimal Democracy
Copywrongs

VILLAGE VOICE
Starting Over

George Scialabba is a contributing editor of *The Baffler* and the author of *What Are Intellectuals Good For?* (2009) and *The Modern Predicament* (2011). He lives in Cambridge, Massachusetts, and his work is archived at www.georgescialabba.net.